A
HISTORY OF
TRANSPORTATION
IN CANADA

VOLUME II

National Economy, 1867-1936

G. P. deT. GLAZEBROOK

A HISTORY OF Transportation IN CANADA

VOLUME II
NATIONAL ECONOMY
1867-1936

The Carleton Library No. 12

McClelland and Stewart Limited

By permission of the Ryerson Press and
the Carnegie Endowment for International Peace

A History of Transportation in Canada
was first published in 1938
by the Ryerson Press, Toronto;
one of the series
The Relations of Canada and the United States,
prepared under the direction of the
Carnegie Endowment for International Peace,
New York.

0-7710-9712-3

The Canadian Publishers
McClelland and Stewart Limited
25 Hollinger Road, Toronto 374

PRINTED AND BOUND IN CANADA

Contents

PREFACE TO VOLUME TWO
OF THE CARLETON LIBRARY EDITION

This study of transportation was first published in 1938 in the series The Relations of Canada and the United States prepared under the direction of the Carnegie Endowment for International Peace. This second edition will again make available a book which has been out of print for many years. Essentially the text is the same as that of the first edition, although a few minor errors which came to light have been corrected, and the table and accompanying map on the railways of Canada in 1886 which appeared in Chapter IX of the original edition have been omitted.

It has been thought best to use two volumes for this edition, which has been made practical by the fact that the book was in any case divided into two parts, with the break coming approximately at the time of Confederation. The Preface to the original edition, explaining the scope and purpose of the book, and an Introduction specially written by Professor Glazebrook for this Carleton Library edition, will be found in Volume One.

This volume also contains the Bibliographical Note prepared for the original edition, as well as a new list of Suggestions for Further Reading.

CHAPTER 6

From Continental to National Economy

1. CONFEDERATION AND RAILWAYS

The decade of the sixties marks a turning-point in the history of Canadian railways, as, indeed, it does in the whole political and economic position of the provinces. The evident failure of the Canadian trunk lines to secure such a portion of American business as would repay their generous expenditure led to a major change of policy; and the circumstances and atmosphere of the day suggested as an alternative the exploitation of national territory. Perhaps the balance sheets of the railway companies would in themselves have pointed to such a recourse, but undoubtedly the political and other economic features of the time were additional and powerful factors tending to the same end. Long before Canada became British her people had carried on a struggle for the control of the west and south-west of the continent; and so it had gone through phase after phase, by land and water. Both success and failure had attended their efforts, but in the end the attempt had evidently to be abandoned. Thus the movement toward a single British country in North America, as approached from the political point of view, coincided in time with the recognition, from the economic point of view, of the end of the continental projects. The two are in operation almost inseparable, and yet they sprang in part from different causes. It was, however, the combination of these two groups of motives that gave enough strength to the union movement to carry it to completion.

If the leaders of commerce and transportation had, perforce, to turn their eyes from the mirage of a promised land, what picture was presented by that more modest portion, the northern half of the continent? In the province of Canada nothing more encouraging could be seen than a steady increase of population with a corresponding growth of business for shippers: little here to take the place of the dreams of the Montreal merchants. To the east lay the British provinces on the sea, with their winter ports. To the merchants and producers of Canada the maritime ports would afford that outlet to foreign markets which they lacked, and for the sake of which they had entertained in the early fifties the plan of an intercolonial railway; to the people of the Maritime Provinces a political and economic union with Canada spelt a new volume of business for their ports and an uninterrupted contact with the interior of the continent. Both attitudes assumed the construction of a railway, which became an integral part of the union scheme.

For a volume of business sufficient to justify the link between central and eastern provinces, the eyes of the people of Canada and the Maritime Provinces alike were increasingly turning to the west. For the people of the St. Lawrence valley the receding west had ever been the goal. For more than two centuries that vast land had had but shadowy political boundaries, and even in the nineteenth century the American west seemed open in an economic sense to the enterprise of Canadians. By the middle of the century the situation had materially changed. The disillusioned shareholders of the Great Western and the Grand Trunk knew to their sorrow the difference between a prospectus and a dividend. At the same time, urged on by the slogan of Horace Greeley, the people of the eastern states were hurrying to take possession of their heritage, reinforced by immigrants from abroad, many of whom spent their first years in America working on the construction gangs which were pushing the railways across the land of the Indian and the buffalo. In 1854 the steel reached the Mississippi, and in the late sixties the first transcontinental railway (Union Pacific–Central Pacific) was approaching completion. Apparently the people of the United States intended to develop their own country and to transport their own goods without the aid of Canadians. But would the westward flood stop at the international boundary? The close contact which had been established between the Red River settlement and St. Paul to its south worried those Canadians who were beginning to think of the future of the British territory in the west. It must not be allowed to fall into American hands, and yet for the province of Canada alone to assimilate such a great area was virtually impossible. Again the situation of the time pointed to political union.

No group of men were more vitally concerned with the future of British North America than those who guided the destinies of the Grand Trunk Railway. Having weathered the storms of the early sixties, secured a more favourable position in regard to their obligations, and improved their personnel, the directors were looking for that increased volume of business which alone could give them any permanent relief, and, having failed in their original design of taking traffic from the American west, they turned to the alternative of a through route on British territory. In general their plan is described by E. W. Watkin in his reminiscences:

The result of mature consideration, reasoning carefully upon all the facts I had collected, was, that, at that time, 1863, the best route for a Railway to the Pacific was, to commence at Halifax, to strike across to the Grand Trunk Railway at Rivière du Loup, 106 miles east of Quebec, then to follow the Grand Trunk system to Sarnia; to extend that system to Chicago; to use, under a treaty of neutralization, the United States lines from Chicago to St. Paul; to build a line from St. Paul to Fort Garry (Winnipeg) by English and American capital, and then to extend the line to the Tête Jaune Pass, there to meet a Railway through British Columbia starting from the Pacific.[1]

To Watkin the plan hung together as a whole – both the east and west links must be forged. "Intercolonial is . . . absolutely essential to Grand Trunk and Intercolonial is, under present circumstances in Canada, dependent upon this other movement [control of the west and communication with the Pacific]."[2] To carry it out involved a formidable series of achievements: union of the provinces, control of the Hudson's Bay Company, settlement of the north-west, and the building of the railways. All these were, in fact, accomplished. For his part in bringing about the union Watkin was knighted by the king, and thanked by Cartier "for all the *political services* you have rendered to 'Canada' in having so *efficiently helped* the carrying of the *great confederation measure.*"[3] And it may be taken that Cartier, who was both the solicitor to the Grand Trunk and a member of the coalition government, knew of what he wrote. The Grand Trunk group bought the control of the Hudson's Bay Company and publicly declared their purposes of colonizing the western plains and establishing communication between the Atlantic and the Pacific.[4] But it was the misfortune of the Grand Trunk Railway on more than one occasion that others reaped where it had sowed. Neither of the railways connected with confederation was built or controlled by it: indeed, the Pacific link in Watkin's transcontinental railway proved in operation to be the great rival of the Grand Trunk. The story of the Grand Trunk interest in the Hudson's Bay Company and the rejection of the proposed line south of Lake Superior belong to the next chapter: it is only necessary here to notice that the company which operated what was by far the most important transportation agency in Canada was working with all its energy toward a political and economic union based on a transcontinental railway. A. A. Dorion, who so often enlivened the confederation debates in the Canadian assembly, had strong views on the relation of the Grand Trunk to confederation.

This project [the Intercolonial, in 1862] *having failed, some other scheme had to be concocted for bringing aid and relief to the unfortunate Grand Trunk – and the Confederation of all the British North American Provinces naturally suggested itself to the Grand Trunk officials as the surest means of bringing with it the construction of the Intercolonial Railway. Such was the origin of this Confederation scheme.*[5]

Later in the debate, when Cartier referred to the Interoceanic Railway, Dorion broke in with the comment: "Yes, I suppose that is another necessity of Confederation. . . . Some western extension of the Grand Trunk scheme for the benefit of Messrs. Watkin and Company of the new Hudson's Bay Company."

The question was asked then, and has been repeatedly asked since, whether the Dominion of Canada was, economically, an artificial creation, built on ephemeral political considerations made palatable by a coating of sentiment. To such a far-reaching question there can be no simple answer, but some evidence may be adduced from the situation in the pre-confederation period. Annexation of the provinces to the United States might – though it is a moot point – have provided an acceptable economic future; but annexation was undesirable on other grounds to the people of the provinces, and probably to the people of the United States. What, then, was the alternative? The St. Lawrence entry to the continent had seemed to dominate a vast territory, but years of painful experience had proven beyond all reasonable question that the draw of the Hudson and Mississippi valleys was too strong. Yet the commercial community of Canada, as typified by Montreal its centre, was not content to rest on the local needs of a sparsely peopled province. Rupert's Land – British, if not Canadian – had been won and lost through the fur trade, and might be reconquered for peopling and agriculture. The Maritime Provinces would form an integral part of a national economy because of their ports, while other doors to the new country were open on the Pacific and Hudson Bay.

The mutual interdependence of railways and general economic development is a theme which runs through the history of the Dominion, and one which played no small part in its creation. To make possible a stable economic structure a sufficiency of natural resources was required, and was found in the wheat and grazing lands of the west, the lumber of British Columbia and the central and eastern provinces, the fisheries of the Maritime Provinces and British Columbia, and the rich mineral deposits of the Canadian shield and the mountains of British Columbia. These, with the mixed agriculture of the east and centre, formed a basis of staples on which a superstructure of financial institutions, industrial concerns, and transportation facilities could be built. It is possible, then, to argue that confederation was not an illogical step taken by embarrassed politicians, but the fulfilment of an old dream, made possible by the linking of economically complementary areas by railways.

A number of factors combined in the sixties to make a federation both desirable and politically possible. The American Civil War led to friction between the North and Great Britain and emphasized the lack of unity in defence. The American objections to the addition of free soil, which would destroy the nice balance between North and South, were automatically removed by the Northern victory; and in the British provinces the fear of the force of "manifest destiny" was revived. The failure of the marriage of French and English

Canada led to suggestions of a general union as a solution of political deadlock; while at the same time the Maritime Provinces were earnestly discussing a union either of themselves only or of all British North America. A few of the far-sighted saw need of action in regard to Rupert's Land lest it fall into the hands of the United States, and argued that it could be taken over only by a larger unit than the province of Canada. The British government, at first luke-warm toward the project, threw its powerful influence in favour of union, influenced in great part by the problem of defence.

In addition to this array of causes, may be added some others that have a more direct bearing on the present study. In 1849 an influential body of Canadians professed to be in favour of annexation to the United States. In so far as this was the expression of an economic grievance it was met by the Reciprocity Treaty of 1854, which established free trade in agricultural and forest products, minerals, and fish, and gave to American citizens the right to fish in the waters of Canada, Nova Scotia, New Brunswick and Prince Edward Island, and to navigate the St. Lawrence. On the whole the treaty seems to have been advantageous to both parties, but especially to the British provinces, whose exports to the United States rose steeply, especially when the Civil War created an abnormal demand in the States. Before the treaty had been in force for many years, however, it began to be attacked in the United States as a one-sided bargain, the particular complaint being that it did not cover manufactured articles. Such objections were felt more strongly when Canada began to adopt a protective tariff; and the whole arrangement was further compromised by the irritation arising out of the war. Throughout 1862 and 1863 the treaty was discussed in congress, its critics dwelling chiefly on the iniquity of the Galt tariff. At the end of 1864 it was sent to the senate's committee on foreign relations, which reported in favour of abrogation. In spite of the efforts of the friends of the treaty, the senate voted against it, and in 1865 official notification was given to the British government that it was no longer in the interests of the United States to continue the arrangement.

Neither in the United States nor the British provinces did the belief in a reciprocal trade agreement die in 1865, but for the time being reciprocity had been abolished; and the favourable conditions which had been created for colonial producers disappeared. When it was apparent that the treaty was likely to be abrogated, it became necessary to find alternative avenues of trade, the most obvious of which was that between the provinces themselves. For some years previously, and especially since 1849, arrangements had been made between the provinces providing either for mutual free trade or for free exchange in specified goods. Little had come out of this, largely owing to the lack of adequate transportation facilities, and it was hoped that a political union, together with an intercolonial railway, would compensate for the closing of the American market. A large free-trade area would thus be created, which might bring advantages similar to those in the German *Zollverein* or the American union. To tear down the tariff walls, however, without at the same time providing for adequate communications between the provinces would be manifestly ineffective; and thus the establishment of an intercolonial railway was closely associated with the plan for political and economic union. Thomas Scatcherd, indeed, went so far as to say in the Canadian assembly that "this Confederation scheme is nothing more or less than a scheme to construct the Intercolonial Railway." This may be an exaggeration, but it is evidence of strong demand for the Intercolonial by the Maritime Provinces. Prince Edward Island was an exception, and one of her delegates at the Quebec conference, A. A. MacDonald, stated that "it is a matter of indifference to our people whether the Intercolonial Railroad is built at all or not." The island was safe from invasion, and, as no plan was included for a local railway, it simply meant assuming a part of the railway debt of the other provinces.[6] Opinion in New Brunswick and Nova Scotia, however, was set on the Intercolonial. "They [the delegates from Nova Scotia and New Brunswick] will not leave the construction of the Intercolonial to the legislation of the new Assembly — They say that the construction of this Line is the great inducement to them to go into the compact, and that its construction must be a condition precedent, or rather a base of the operation itself. . . ."[7]

Two resolutions on the improvement of communications were passed at the conference. The first concerns the Intercolonial Railway.

The General Government shall secure, without delay, the completion of the Intercolonial Railway from Rivière-du-Loup through New Brunswick to Truro, in Nova Scotia.

It will be observed that this is a definite commitment without any conditions as to cost or route. The second is less definite.

The communications with the North-West Territory, and the improvements required for the development of the Trade of the Great West with the Seaboard, are regarded by this Conference as subjects of the highest importance to the Federated Provinces, and shall be prosecuted at the earliest possible period that the state of the Finances will permit.

The west was not immediately to be a part of the Dominion; but the Intercolonial was a *sine qua non* to the people of the Maritime Provinces. No railway, no federation was in effect the attitude of their delegates, an attitude which was clearly appreciated by the Canadians. The Intercolonial had to be promised, and promised definitely, if the negotiations were to have any hope of success. On the other hand, the far west was remote from the Maritime Provinces, and, while the second resolution was phrased so as to suggest an increased use of their ports, it would not have been acceptable in the form of a binding agreement. Nor was the pressure of opinion in Canada such as to make a guarantee of western communications politically necessary.

The situation was threshed out again and again in both branches of the Canadian legislature when the Quebec resolutions were brought down in February 1865. The view of the government was ably put to the legislative council by Sir Etienne Taché on the first day of the debate. "If the opportunity which now presented itself were allowed to pass by unimproved," he told the council, "whether we would or would not, we would be forced into the American Union by violence, and if not by violence, would be placed upon an inclined plane which would carry us there insensibly." This note of the pressure from without was struck over and over again on the government side. There was little attempt to conceal the argument that the Intercolonial was necessary because federation was necessary – because the alternative was annexation. The political necessity of the railway was acceptable, whatever might be its intrinsic merits. George Brown admitted that, "as a commercial enterprise, the Intercolonial Railway has not . . . any considerable merit," but Taché went on to find economic reasons in its favour. Canada, he said, had fine railways and canals but no seaport. She was "shut up in a prison, as it were, for five months of the year in fields of ice." The St. Lawrence and Atlantic Railway had been a boon; but now that there were threats both of the abolition of the bonding system and of the abrogation of the Reciprocity Treaty, the escape from this dangerous situation was to build a railway to the ports of New Brunswick and Nova Scotia. Much the same line of argument was taken by Cartier in the assembly. Canada had territory and population, but not a seaboard, while the Maritime Provinces lacked a hinterland and a large population.

Members of the opposition then began some well-directed sniping at the highly vulnerable position occupied by the government. How much was the railway going to cost? No amount had been given except an unofficial estimate of $15,000,000, and no maximum was indicated in the resolutions. Moreover, the burden would now be chiefly shouldered by Canada. By the arrangement of 1862 Canada was to find five-twelfths of the cost, but her proportion under confederation would be about nine-twelfths. What was to be the route of the railway? This again was not settled. How could anyone vote for a railway when neither the cost nor route were known? To these criticisms no adequate answers could be given because no definite information existed. More telling blows were struck at the probable usefulness of the Intercolonial. One point made in favour of the line was that it was needed for purposes of military defence, the general problems of which were much to the fore in the debates. It would be placed well away from the American border and could transport (from the Atlantic ports) troops and supplies that could hardly be moved by road. After some rather amateurish discussions of the use of railways in warfare, a member of the opposition pointed out that the Inter-colonial would link up with the Grand Trunk, and that the line of the latter was at some points only twenty-six miles from the boundary of Maine. Here, he said, the whole communication could be cut by a hostile force.

Turning to the peace-time use of the railway, members of the opposition expressed everything from scepticism to scorn of its economic value. Members of the council and assembly on the government side had defended the Intercolonial on the grounds that it would carry grain and other goods to tidewater, especially in the winter, and in general would develop interprovincial trade, but William McMaster (Midland) threw cold water on the idea that grain would move over the Intercolonial.

We are told by honourable gentlemen that the abrogation of the Reciprocity Treaty renders this road an indispensable necessity in order to secure an independent outlet to the sea-board; but, if this view of the case be correct, why do not our merchants and millers forward their produce during the winter months to New York, Boston, or Portland, by our or any of the other different railway lines which have long been open to these points? The reason is obvious. The freight by railway is so expensive that they find it to be for their advantage to pay interest, storage, and insurance on their wheat and flour until the opening of the navigation. And if they do not now avail themselves of the shipping ports referred to, neither of which are more than six hundred miles from Toronto, will they send their produce double that distance over the Intercolonial road to Halifax?

The member for Trent drove another spike into the government's case by arguing that, assuming (as had been stated) that two cents per ton-mile was a reasonable charge for freight, it would cost $2.08 to ship a barrel of flour from Toronto to seaboard – a cost which he held was prohibitive. Others in the council and assembly made similar comments: in fact the legislature was fully warned that either the Intercolonial would have to be subsidized to allow artificially low rates, or else it would not be used sufficiently to make it pay. The critics of the railway had, in fact, touched one of the fundamental problems of Canadian transportation and uncovered difficulties which were blissfully ignored half a century later.

It need not be assumed that those who voted in favour of the railway were wholly unconscious of economic arguments. The Intercolonial was not, directly, a sound financial proposition; it never was really thought to be so; and never became so. It was, however, an integral part of the federation scheme. It may not unreasonably be held that without such a communication political union would be absurd; and at least it was clear that, without the railway, no union would be accepted by the Maritime Provinces. The length of the line was dictated in large part by military considerations which were at that time pressing. In other words, both government and opposition were, from different points of view, presenting unanswerable arguments.

The question of communication with the north-west also received no little attention. George Brown was put up in the assembly to talk to this point and made a spirited and optimistic speech on what had become his favourite topic on the platform and in the *Globe*. He looked forward to the day when the fur trade would again pass through Canada instead of being "smuggled off through the icebound regions of James' Bay, that the pretence of the barrenness of the country and the difficulty of carrying merchandise by the natural route of the St. Lawrence may be kept up a little longer." Passing from this rather shaky argument to "the fertile plains of that great Saskatchewan territory," he looked forward to settlement and cultivation. Unfortunately Brown had little to say of what was going to be done about it – an omission which did not pass unnoticed by his hearers. Member after member commented regretfully, coldly, or bitterly on the fact that the Intercolonial was given precedence over a railway to the west. Some felt that the latter would simply be delayed, and others that the cost of the Intercolonial would prohibit any further expenditure on great public works.

> *We find* [said one] *that the representatives at the Conference from Nova Scotia and New Brunswick made it a point of the proposed Constitution to construct the Intercolonial Railway, also took good care to make the opening of the North-West contingent upon the state of the finances, and the Confederation will commence life with a debt of $150,000,000. It is evident, therefore, that the North-West is hermetically sealed, as far as Canada is concerned.*

Members of both parties called attention time after time to the importance of communications with the west. One member regretted that the Dominion had not immediately stretched to the Pacific, while others more modestly hoped that this would come in time. No definite suggestions were made about a Pacific railway, although the possibility of one was often mentioned.

Many references were made by the members from Canada West to canals, and sometimes with regret that they had not received more consideration at the Quebec conference. Some members thought that public funds should have been spared for the enlargement of the canals generally; others emphasized the Ottawa or Georgian Bay water routes to the west as worthy of special attention. One member harked back to the older ideas. "See the outlet we possess to the ocean," he cried, "look at the magnificent St. Lawrence. . . . Is it not possible to so improve this channel as to bring the produce of the Great Western States to market through our territory?" Presumably this was a rhetorical question, as no one troubled to tell him that the answer was in the negative. Little time need, however, be devoted to the discussion of canals in the legislature, for no plan was then seriously contemplated for enlargement or additions. With the successful conclusion of the federation movement there came as its first fruits in the sphere of public works the construction of the long-talked-of Intercolonial Railway. By section 145 of the British North America Act the construction of a railway connecting the St. Lawrence with Halifax was to be begun within six months after the union.

Prince Edward Island was unfriendly toward the Intercolonial, regarding it only as a cause for additional taxation, while not solving local transportation problems, and rejected the Quebec resolutions. In 1871 the assembly passed an act providing for the construction of a railway through the length of the island, the contractors to accept debentures in payment, and in the following year a further act authorized branch lines to Souris and Tignish, with the same provision for payment. All went well for a while, and then difficulties began to arise. The original act allowed a maximum sum of £5,000 per mile for construction but contained no word as to the number of miles. The contractors extended the line (and hence the cost) unduly for the twin purposes of adding to their receipts and avoiding expensive cuttings and embankments. At the same time they either sold the debentures to the local banks or pledged them against cash advances. Both the government and the financial community (between which there was an overlap) became alarmed, and looked to confederation as the means of easing a financial situation which was becoming threatening. In spite of the remaining opinion to the contrary, therefore, Prince Edward Island joined the confederation in 1873, the Dominion taking over the partially constructed railway, and relieving the minds and pockets of both the debenture-holders and the taxpayers. At the same time the Dominion government promised to establish and maintain steam communication between the island and the mainland, thus linking the former with the Canadian system of railways.

2. THE INTERCOLONIAL RAILWAY

Throughout the fifties and sixties negotiations concerning an intercolonial railway went on between the provinces, and between the provinces and the British government, with the indefatigable Watkin hurrying from one to the other with advice and encouragement. After a series of refusals of loans from the British government, another conference of representatives of the provinces was held in Quebec in the autumn of 1861, the delegates from New Brunswick and Nova Scotia having been transported thither by Watkin over the Grand Trunk. Again deputations went to England, interspersed by further conversations at Quebec. In the end the negotiations broke down once more. The final British terms included the establishment of a sinking fund which Nova Scotia and New Brunswick were willing, but Canada was not willing, to accept. By the end of 1862 a stalemate had been reached.

From 1863 on the situation was a peculiar one. Although the financing of the railway had not been arranged, it was decided to go on with a survey. In the course of the negotiations in London the British government had insisted on a survey being made before parliament should be asked to guarantee a loan. Accordingly the Canadian government proposed that one should be undertaken, and appointed Mr. Sandford Fleming, an engineer with considerable local experience, as the Canadian surveyor. From Nova Scotia, New Brunswick, and Great

Britain came expressions of willingness to accept Fleming as their nominee also, but a series of misunderstandings and bickering between the provincial governments led to the survey being undertaken by Canada alone, with the suggestion that Nova Scotia and New Brunswick should later contribute to the cost if they saw fit. In the spring of 1864 Fleming began his task, and submitted his report in February 1865.

With Fleming and his staff hard at work between Rivière du Loup and Truro, the governments of Nova Scotia and New Brunswick began to attempt construction without waiting for Canada. The section they chose to start on was the hundred miles between Truro (to which a line already ran from Halifax) and a point on the Saint John–Shediac railway. Acting on behalf of the two provinces, Watkin obtained from the British government a promise that the proposed work would be considered to come under the guaranteed loan, if such were raised. Thus encouraged, the two provinces appointed English contractors, but these failed and their successors never turned a sod in Nova Scotia, and little was done in New Brunswick. While attempting to make some progress themselves, the Maritime governments had little hope of help from Canada. The agreement to build the railway, therefore, which formed a part of the Quebec resolutions, may be seen as a means of reaching a goal which had proved unattainable by other paths. After all the years of conferences, agreements, misunderstandings, hopes, and failures, it is not surprising that Maritime opinion insisted on the Intercolonial being explicitly written into the British North America Act.

Would the Intercolonial have been built without confederation? That is a question to which no definite answer can be given. It may be argued that good progress was being made toward an agreement, and that the objection by Canada to the sinking fund would have been overcome by some kind of compromise. The survey would hardly have been undertaken by Canada if the railway project had been regarded as dead, although it must be remembered that by 1864 the close relation between the railway and the union was already recognized. Certainly there could have been in 1867 no confederation without the Intercolonial: there might have been an Intercolonial without confederation. The majority in the Maritime Provinces would probably have preferred railway without union, and the majority in Canada union without railway. Without confederation it would have been difficult, if not impossible, to secure a common tariff policy. Such a policy was held to be a need of the time, and was advanced as an argument in favour of federation. In practice, however, it was tied to the railway between the provinces; for, without adequate transportation, there could be little hope of extensive interprovincial trade, and without the markets and industries that could be built up behind the tariff, the railway would be hard put to find traffic. In deference to the opinion in the Maritime Provinces, the early tariffs of the Dominion were low, but within ten years they had begun to climb steeply.[8] As a source of revenue the tariff helped to finance the railways, as in the old province of Canada; and as a protective measure it contributed to creating and directing traffic.

For the thirty years or so during which a railway between the Maritime Provinces and Canada had been under discussion there had always been disagreement about the port to which it should lead and the route to Quebec. By the confederation agreement the port was to be Halifax – but there remained a choice of routes from Halifax to Rivière du Loup, the terminus of the Grand Trunk. It fell to Fleming's lot to examine the possible routes, and in his book, *The Intercolonial*, he explains the problem at some length. He was deeply impressed by the results of the boundary settlement of 1842. Had the territory in dispute fallen to New Brunswick, an almost direct line could then have been run from Quebec to Fredericton, bringing Halifax within 650 miles of Montreal, Saint John within 415 miles, and leaving St. Andrews only 250 miles from Quebec.

The distance between Montreal and Halifax might thus have been lessened nearly 200 miles. St. Andrews would have taken the place of Portland as the winter terminus of the Grand Trunk Railway, and would have commanded, together with St. John, a traffic now cut off from both places, and centred at a foreign port.

This, indeed, was perhaps the most fundamental problem of the Intercolonial. Not many years later the Canadian Pacific Railway built the "short line" through Maine to avoid the expensive detour, but the Intercolonial had to be built on Canadian soil. Nor was it only the position of the boundary which caused a problem in the location of the line. A hot controversy raged over the location of the line in New Brunswick. Some fifteen separate routes found advocates, but in general they fell into three main divisions: the northern route, by Bay Chaleur; the frontier route by the valley of the St. John River; and a central route in between the two running north from Saint John. Around these a somewhat confusing series of arguments and counter-arguments were built up.

From a military point of view the frontier line seemed to be the least desirable, although its supporters held that any railway would be vulnerable, and that there was no longer reason to fear hostilities. The northern line – which had been chosen by Major Robinson – seemed the safest in case of war, but the central line supporters claimed that it was vulnerable from the sea. On the whole, however, there could be little doubt that the northern line was the most desirable for military purposes. The rival routes were also compared with respect to cost of construction and operation. It was said that the frontier line would have the advantage of taking over fifty-five miles of railway already built; to which the reply was that the railways in question were in bad condition and hopelessly in debt, and further that the frontier line would cost $1,000,000 more than the northern. The central line supporters produced an alternative argument: that their route could make use of existing railways by securing running rights. From a commercial point of view a case could be made out for each. The supporters of the frontier line claimed that the St. John valley was well settled, and that it offered a local lumber trade as well as that from the Aroostook district in Maine. The central route was defended on the ground that through freight could be shipped to the port of Saint John. The advocates of the northern route argued that there was a high population per mile of railway, also lumber establishments, and a potential export of fish to Quebec and Ontario. Moreover, the northern route would be most useful to Prince Edward Island and Newfoundland.

The sharp division of opinion in New Brunswick was an embarrassment to all the governments concerned. "The questions of Confederation," wrote Peter Mitchell, the prime minister of New Brunswick, "are entirely subordinate to the question of *Railroad* in our province and now that the latter has become almost a certainty, the sectional interest has arisen, and a disregard of that, will do much to affect the standing of whatever government may be formed, either on the Northern and Eastern or South and Western sides of our Province for that is the way they now side off."[9] Macdonald was anxious to move cautiously, especially since opinion in New Brunswick was none too friendly toward the federation.

. . . So far as Canada proper is concerned you are aware that we have no sectional interests to serve. We want the shortest and best route. Whichever line will best secure the through traffic, and at the same time serve the purposes of New Brunswick locally, is the line we will go for. As you say, when a railway is first projected every man wants it past his own door. It certainly would appear to me, on the first impression, as the lawyers say, that it would be politic to select a St. John's River man, and a Northern route man for the Cabinet. Both interests would then have advocates at the Council table, and the government as a whole would decide after hearing both, and after considering all the evidence before them.[10]

A few days later Mitchell wrote that his party "was on the eve of disruption" from the strife of sectional interests over railways, but that he had tided over the crisis.[11]

In the end the choice of routes was made on military and commercial rather than political grounds. From a military point of view there had never been much doubt as to which was the best; and, in any case, the correspondence with the British government in the summer of 1868 indicates that financial backing would certainly not have been given to the frontier, and possibly not to the central line. In February 1868 Fleming was asked to express his own opinion as to the best route, and in his reply to Macdonald he definitely advocated the northern. The chief consideration he had in mind was through traffic, for he attached little importance to local traffic on any of the proposed lines. A railway was being built from Saint John to Bangor, Maine, which would be "fatal to the Intercolonial" unless the northern route were chosen; for the latter would make possible a port on the Bay of Chaleur, which would enable the

Intercolonial to secure some through traffic with Europe.[12] It was one of Fleming's favourite beliefs that communication with Europe could begin at such a port, cross Newfoundland and Ireland by rail, and so cut down the sea voyage. Fortunately, however, it was not an integral part of his plan for the Intercolonial.

To avoid charges of political favouritism the construction of the railway was placed under a board of four commissioners, consisting of A. Walsh, the chairman, E. B. Chandler of New Brunswick, who had taken an active part in the earlier attempts to commence the railway, C. J. Brydges, managing director of the Grand Trunk, and W. F. Coffin of Montreal, who resigned and was succeeded by A. W. McLelan of Nova Scotia, a former opponent of confederation. Tupper had first been asked to act as chairman, but had declined on the ground that it would weaken his influence in making federation acceptable in Nova Scotia. The appointment of all officers was vested in the commissioners with the exception of the chief engineer, a position which was well filled by Fleming.

Differences of opinion arose between Fleming and the commissioners, first as to the manner of letting contracts. A number of tenders had been made for the construction and equipment of the whole road, two at the rate of $35,000 a mile (Robinson's estimate), another for $14,600,000 and a fourth for $14,800,000. The government determined, however, to let a series of small contracts by measurement and price. The commissioners concurred in the principle of contracts by sections but favoured letting each section for a bulk sum. To this the engineer objected, but was unable to have the decision of the commissioners overruled. The other subject of dispute was the materials of bridges, the commissioners preferring wood and the engineer iron. The former opinion was, no doubt, due to the influences of Brydges, who, in a private memorandum of October 1868, argued that the original cost of the Intercolonial should be kept low to correspond with the light traffic that was expected. Later, he said, more costly structures might be erected. In particular he advocated wooden bridges, which, he said, were universal in Canada, except on the Grand Trunk.[13] Fleming, however, was a firm believer in a permanent type of construction being used from the start, arguing that it would be cheaper in the end than constant replacement. In general it was a difference of opinion which has been important throughout the history of Canadian railways. In the case of bridges Fleming held that iron was not only safer and more lasting, but cost little more in the first instance. A long argument arose, the two experts – Fleming and Brydges – appealing to the privy council. In this case the engineer was upheld, and all bridges, large and small, except three which were made of wood against his protest, were of iron. It is worth noticing that the actual cost of the iron bridges when built was slightly less than the estimate for either iron or wooden structures. On the whole the Intercolonial from a technical point of view represented the triumph of Fleming's principles. The rails used were all of steel, although iron ones had originally been planned, and the road throughout was of a high standard. The cost of the whole, which both Brydges and Fleming estimated at $20,000,000, turned out to be $34,363,896.

It is a somewhat remarkable fact that it was not until after construction had begun that a decision was reached as to whether the railway should be under public or private management. As late as the end of 1870 Macdonald still apparently contemplated having the Intercolonial operated by the Grand Trunk, as the following exchange of letters suggests.

I think the time is approaching when we must take into consideration the manner of working the Intercolonial Railway when finished. I presume that the G.T.R. looks to running arrangement for the whole line, and my present impression is that that would be the most satisfactory mode, in the Public interest, of working the railway. Still, there will be an attempt made by Brown, McKenzie and Co. to get up a feeling against any such arrangement, and we must take care the terms are such as to disarm criticism.

We may expect great and powerful resistance from the steamboat and shipping interest, who will be afraid that water borne freight to Quebec will not receive fair play, and that it will be made secondary to the through traffic on the G.T.R. It is, of course, the duty of the government to see that no preference of any kind is given, or possible, and that a barrel of flour arriving by water at Quebec will have just as good a chance as if it were sent by railway from Sarnia.

It appears to me, then, that in any arrangement with the G.T.R. that that portion of the line lying between Quebec and Rivière du Loup should be considered as a portion of the Intercolonial Railway, and that the arrangement between Government and the G.T.R. should have effect on all traffic between Quebec and Halifax. The matter is of such great importance that it will require grave consideration, & probably entail a large amount of correspondence; therefore the sooner we address ourselves to it the better. I have not yet brought it up in Council but have had a quiet talk with Cartier on the subject. It is for the interests of the Grand Trunk Ry that arrangements should be made with the present government, which is well inclined to act fairly by your company, rather than leave the matter to the uncertain chances of the future. There is little doubt that we will hear a good deal on railway matters during the next General Election.

When you are in England you had I think better commence discussing the matter with your board. Pray let me have your ideas on the subject, if you have time before you leave

P.S. The Board should give you full powers.[14]

Brydges was apparently pleased with the suggested arrangement.

I received your letter yesterday morning, and have to-day seen Cartier upon other matters, and mentioned the subject to him.

I am glad to find you take the view you do, as to the prospective working of the Intercolonial Line. As you know, I was rather afraid of saying anything about it since my appointment as Commissioner, lest it should be supposed that I was seeking to use my position for the purpose of aiding Grand Trunk interest.

I have tried to do what I considered right for Intercolonial, regardless of any other consideration but its own good.

I do not see well, how, in the interests of the country, any other or better arrangement could be made than Grand Trunk working the Intercolonial; but the terms, I admit, will require very careful consideration, and considerable discussion.

I see no difficulty in accomplishing what you refer to in

regard to water-borne traffic to Quebec seeking transport over the Intercolonial Line.

If you are not prepared, as I suppose is the case to purchase the line from Quebec to Rivière du Loup, on the part of the Government, I think I can suggest, without much difficulty, all the safe-guards that you are likely to require. I do not believe that Quebec will be the point where water-borne traffic for the West will find the best means of reaching the railway. It should be, I think, at Montreal. This, however, is a matter of detail, which it will not be difficult to deal with at the right time.

I should very much like to know, when you speak of the Intercolonial, what your view is in regard to the existing Railways in the Lower Provinces, which of course must be a part, practically of the Intercolonial Line. For instance, you cannot reach the two Ocean termini of Halifax and St. John, without including portions, at any rate, of the existing Government Lines. When, therefore, you talk of an arrangement between Grand Trunk and Intercolonial, I assume that you mean to enable Grand Trunk trains to run both to Halifax and St. John. This is an important question, because the existing lines have a certain traffic, now, the value of which is known, and the incorporation of those Lines into the Intercolonial system, would undoubtedly tend to modify the conditions upon which alone, the other parts of the whole system could be worked. If you have time, on receipt of this letter to drop me a line to say whether or not you contemplate any arrangement in regard to include the working of the existing Roads in the Lower Provinces as well as the Intercolonial, it would enable me to discuss the matter more intelligently when I am on the other side. I will come back with full authority to talk and write definitely upon the subject. . . .[15]

Unfortunately there is no means of knowing whether Macdonald clung to the idea of operation by the Grand Trunk, or whether he changed his mind. One would imagine that the cabinet was divided on the subject, for Howe had been a staunch upholder of public operation of railways, while Cartier had a close association with the Grand Trunk. Whatever may have been the decision of the cabinet, the decisive action was left to the succeeding administration under Alexander Mackenzie.

Since the Liberal government contained influences hostile to the Grand Trunk, it is not surprising that the earlier scheme was abandoned in favour of governmental operation – a policy which was in any case probably more acceptable in the Maritime Provinces. In 1874 the Intercolonial was placed under the direct control of the department of public works, which assumed the powers formerly held by the commission.

The construction of the Intercolonial was principally financed by means of an act of 1867 (31 Vict., c. 13) which empowered the government to raise a loan of four million pounds sterling, the interest on three millions of which was guaranteed, or promised, by the imperial government. The loan proved to be encouragingly popular, being subscribed four times over. The sum provided by the loan was equal to the estimate, but as the cost exceeded the estimate by over $14,000,000 the balance had to be met on general account.

By 1876 the new parts of the railway were finished, and a through line was provided from Halifax to Rivière du Loup. The greater part of this was that built by the Dominion, but use was also made of the sections already completed by the Maritime Provinces. The Nova Scotia Railway, taken over by the Dominion, provided the sixty one miles of rail from Halifax to Truro; while the European and North American contributed the few miles built from Moncton eastward and the Shediac–Saint John line, which made the necessary connection with the chief port of New Brunswick. The first railway to be owned by the Dominion consisted of the "Ocean Mail Line" from Rivière du Loup to Halifax (562 miles), the Prince Edward Island Railway, together with branch lines – of which the principal were those from Truro to Pictou and Moncton to Saint John – and a few side lines to wharves. Although the connection with the Grand Trunk, which had the same gauge (5 feet, 6 inches), gave the Intercolonial entry to the railway systems of central Canada and the United States, this dependent position was not altogether satisfactory. At the same time the Grand Trunk was willing to dispose of its line east of Quebec which had ceased to have any future importance, and in 1879 the line from Rivière du Loup to Hadlow, opposite Quebec, was purchased, with running rights to Point Lévis. According to the report of the department of railways and canals,

The control of the section became indispensable to the successful working of the Intercolonial Railway. The permanent way was in bad condition, and it was not possible to maintain the line established for the through Intercolonial Traffic owing to the detentions which were experienced between River du Loup and Quebec. Indeed the interests of the Intercolonial system were throughout affected by the important link in the connection, being under independent management. The necessity for removing these difficulties was early foreseen, and the fact of such a possible transfer did not encourage the Grand Trunk Railway Company to expend more money on maintenance than could be avoided. It was also held to be of primary importance that access should be had to a landing pier on the River St. Lawrence near Quebec.

In 1898 the Drummond County Railway from Chaudière Junction to Ste. Rosalie Junction was purchased, and this, with running rights over the Grand Trunk Portland line, gave access to the Bonaventure station in Montreal. The Intercolonial was, in fact, steadily fulfilling its purpose of acting as a through line from east to west. To carry the process a step further it had been stipulated at the time of the purchase of 1879 that the sum paid over to the Grand Trunk ($1,500,000) was to be "devoted towards obtaining an independent Railway connection from Sarnia to Chicago," which arrangement "virtually confers the same advantages to the Intercolonial Railway system, owing to its close connection with the Grand Trunk." By 1916 the Intercolonial had 1,450 miles of track, acquired at a cost of $108,131,150.

It remains to consider briefly the success of this first experiment by the Dominion in public ownership of railways. Care must be taken, however, in drawing general conclusions from the bare figures of the financial returns of the Intercolonial. It is doubtful whether even its sponsors expected to see it as a paying proposition, for it was – in no sinister sense – a political railway: that is to say, it was designed to serve the political and economic needs of the state.

Considering the circumstances under which the road was built no amount of statistical analysis of surplus and deficits can prove or disprove its success. A deficit may be an indication of success inasmuch as it results from lower rates and a more satisfactory union between Canada and the Maritime Provinces. If the road must be regarded as an essential part of Confederation, its success is measured in terms of the value of Confederation.[16]

Constructed at a high cost with a view to fast through traffic, the Intercolonial never was able to achieve a sufficient volume of business to carry this capital investment. At the same time it could not, and had not been expected to, secure adequate local traffic. The route which had been chosen carried the line in a sweeping curve through eastern Quebec and northern New Brunswick, through districts where neither people nor industries were plentiful. Even the beauty of the Metapedia valley could not compensate for the scanty population of that forested area. In general, too, it is well to remember that the greater part of the Intercolonial was in the provinces which had the smallest population and the fewest industrial centres. All this had been foreseen by Fleming, who had deliberately planned for through traffic, but that traffic proved hard to procure. Even when the Intercolonial had penetrated to Montreal it was still dependent on competing private companies for access to the long-haul business originating in the west. Then its own territory was invaded by the Canadian Pacific Short Line to Saint John – a line which was able to take advantage of the dissipation of the fears of a war with the United States.

It was to be expected that the Intercolonial would show a deficit in the first years in which it was operated. The incompleteness of the system together with the general depression of business at that time gave little chance of a surplus. Even in better times, although surpluses were shown in some years, they were not consistent. The extension to Quebec, coinciding with one improvement in general business, and the extension to Montreal, coinciding with the long-awaited period of prosperity, brought better times to the Intercolonial, but never made of it a profitable enterprise, if only the balance sheet be considered. In addition to the reasons for this which have already been indicated, were the low rates, designed to satisfy the Maritime Provinces, and to compete with water-borne traffic and with the Short Line. Management was not always efficient, nor was the railways always free from the more prenicious forms of political interference.

The building of the Intercolonial was neither the first nor the last step made by governments – before or after confederation – to meet the peculiar transportation needs of Canada. Like roads, canals, and other railways, it has borne upon the taxpayer, and like them its has had compensating advantages in indirect ways. No balance can really be struck where such diverse factors exist at once. Nor was the Intercolonial the first or last railway to be subsidized by the taxpayers. And while its history throws much light on public ownership, it no more proves that public railways cannot pay than the periodic collapses of the Grand Trunk prove that private railways cannot pay.

CHAPTER 7

The Project of a Pacific Railway

1. WESTERN TRANSPORTATION BEFORE THE RAILWAY

The history of the Canadian west may be divided into three overlapping but distinct periods: that of the Indians, that of the fur traders, and, finally, that of assimilation to modern culture. From the point of view of transportation there is no marked break between the first two; but the change from the second to the third is a radical one. The building of railways from Lake Superior to the Pacific coast revolutionized conditions in that area and led to its exploitation from the eastern centres. To some extent exploitation had long been carried out by the fur traders, but in a form which, while it affected the lives of the natives, did little to introduce settlement, industries, or modern communications. The growing interest in the west, which became effective about the middle of the nineteenth century, was focused on three aims: to preserve it as British (or Canadian) territory; to people and develop it; and to establish overland communication with the far east. The last directly, and the others indirectly, called for improved transportation, which to most men of the day meant railways: railways, because any other form of transport seemed hopelessly inadequate for the purposes mentioned, in view of the size and nature of the western area. The means of travel in the west in the period before 1821 have already been examined in the first three chapters of this book. The changes after that time, however, were of sufficient moment to justify some study of the conditions prevailing in the period between 1821 and the construction of the first railway to the Pacific.

The fusion of the Hudson's Bay and North West companies in 1821 under the name of the former began a new era in the west. The bitter rivalry between the two companies had culminated in a kind of guerilla warfare; high prices and quantities of liquor had debauched the Indians; many regions were drained of furs; and both companies were in financial straits. The end of intense competition brought order into the west, and the Indians, at first suspicious, became reconciled to the new régime. At the same time as the union a grant of exclusive trade in all the territory of the west not in the British provinces or the United States was granted to the company, subject to the rights of American citizens west of the Rockies. The relaxation of the tension which had existed in the previous years and the pooling of personnel and interests enabled the company to set its house in order. Such reorganization as was carried out was due in great part to the genius of Sir George Simpson, who became first governor of the new northern department and a few years later governor in chief in America. Simpson's professional curiosity and energy knew no bounds. He covered his whole district, constantly breaking records for fast travel, and making notes on every person and thing which could possibly concern the company. His reports to London are a mine of information.

Such were the circumstances under which the last chapter of the history of the Hudson's Bay Company as a monopolistic and governing body began. In some ways the power of the company in these fifty years was greater than ever before. From Montreal to Victoria, from the Arctic to the American border, its servants dominated the scene. Just as in later years no adventurous traveller would think of plunging into the untravelled areas away from the railways without seeking the counsel and help of the nearest Hudson's Bay factor, so in the days before railways, transportation in the west on the whole was either conducted by the company or modelled on its methods.

The first major change in method which followed the union of the companies was the eclipse of canoes as the chief craft in the west — a change which coincided with the eclipse of the Montreal "pedlars" who had taken them there.

We are confident [wrote the committee in London to Simpson] *that it will be found cheaper and safer to use boats in preference to canoes and that it will be practicable to do so in every part of the country except in New Caledonia and McKenzie's River. And as Orkneymen are better adapted for the constructing of boats than Canadians, and are generally more careful servants we recommend that all the Canadians, whose contracts expire this year should be discharged, with the exception of such useful men as may be in debt to the concern, or whom it may be desirable from some particular circumstance to retain in the service.*[1]

Simpson agreed about the advantage of boats, but was not so happy about the Orkneymen.

Wherever Boat Navigation is practicable no other Craft I think should be used as it certainly will be found cheaper and better in regard to safety than Canoes and it is ascertained that it can be adopted in all parts of the country except New Caledonia; next season we hope to have a sufficient number for all the Establishments to the Southward of Portage la Loche and thereafter as the people become acquainted with the management of them they will be brought into more general use. Orkneymen from their slow inanimate habits would not I apprehend be found to answer the purpose for long Voyages requiring exertion to get to the Wintering grounds; it moreover takes a length of time after their arrival in the Country to give them a knowledge of Inland Navigation, whereas Canadians with proper management are active and indefatigable; one Voyage in Boats in quite sufficient to make them acquainted with the management of them and their passage into the country gives them a knowledge of the dangers of the navigation and the precautions necessary. Canadians therefore unquestionably have the preference for the Duty. . . .

Light Canoe Travelling is unavoidably attended with a heavy Expense and the Council are of opinion that in the present state of the Country it is quite unnecessary except in regard to the Columbia and Athabasca Departments. . . .[2]

A year later Simpson had begun to substitute boats for canoes and still was of the opinion that the former were better.

The advantage of Boat instead of Canoe transport are so obvious that we mean to adopt it wherever it may be found practicable; the saving in wages alone will materially exceed one-third and the property moreover will not be so liable to damage and injury on the voyage. . . . .[3]

In the Athabasca department the use of boats was not altogether successful, but they were steadily introduced into other departments. When it was decided to supply the Lake Huron district from Moose Factory instead of from Montreal, for example, boats were planned for the transport system. In districts near the bay, such as the Albany River, boats had always been used. In fact the Hudson's Bay Company had always believed in boats, and it was only during the period in which they were most actively competing with the North West Company in the interior that they had used canoes for some of their transport. Now they were free to return to their first love.

Types of boats varied. The best known was the York boat, a keel boat propelled by heavy sweeps or a square sail, developed after 1821 especially for use on the Hayes River between Norway House and York Factory. It was light enough to be pulled over rollers at portages, but seaworthy in the storms of Lake Winnipeg. In length it varied from thirty to forty feet. A forty-foot York boat would carry 110 pieces of 90 pounds each, with a crew of a steersman, a bowsman, and eight middlemen. On shallower waters, such as those of the Saskatchewan, the flat-bottomed bateaux were used. For the Columbia also bateaux were found more suitable, propelled, according to Simpson, by paddles instead of oars. Where canoes were still retained, they were of the same types as formerly.

Throughout the west an elaborate machinery of communications had been built up, with regular routes and time-tables. The hub of the system was Norway House at the head of Lake Winnipeg, a "Store or Warehousing Establishment, kept up for the accommodation of the interior Posts or Districts. . . ."[4] Sir Charles Piers[5] describes four main routes, centring on Norway House. The northern route led, by the Hayes or the Nelson River, to York Factory, which until the day of the American railways was the chief port for Rupert's Land. The southern route was down Lake Winnipeg and up the Red River to Fort Garry. The eastern was the old canoe route to Montreal, or rather to Lachine, which was the depot, but after 1821 this became of secondary importance. Little through traffic went by it on account of the expense, and the trade in the area near Lachine and even near Lake Huron was ruined by competition. "The only object of maintaining the posts is to keep the petty

Traders in play, so as to prevent their pushing further into the interior."⁶

The longest, of course, were the western routes. From Norway House Lake Winnipeg was followed to Grand Rapids, with a portage to Clear Lake and the Saskatchewan River, which took the brigades as far as Fort Edmonton. From there a long portage was made on horseback to Fort Assiniboine on the Athabasca; up the Athabasca by boat or canoe to Henry House; from there on horseback and foot over the summit to Boat Encampment. Here the bateaux could be taken down the Columbia to the Pacific at Fort Vancouver. The brigades to the north-west left this route at Cumberland House and went by a series of small lakes and portages, over Portage la Loche, to the Athabasca River and Lake; to the Slave River, Great Slave Lake, and thence to the Mackenzie River, running down to Fort McPherson on the Peel River. These were the main trunk lines, though there were many other regular routes. The most romantic, perhaps, was the Yukon Packet which travelled 4,500 miles from Fort Yukon to Montreal, summer and winter.

The whole of this elaborate system of communication was designed for an unpeopled country, and for the carriage of standard goods and small numbers of passengers. It was dependent primarily on waterways, the sections travelled by horse or on foot being regarded as portages. It was highly complex, but made possible by the fact that all who were concerned in it were on the business of one company. Finally, it assumed one chief entrance, from Hudson Bay, and two minor entrances, Montreal and the Pacific posts, to the whole area. Two main and interdependent changes followed: the progress of settlement in Red River, and in the American states to the south of it. In Sir George Simpson's régime it became the policy of the company to utilize the Red River settlement for the production of food and whatever other supplies could be produced, to avoid the heavy expense involved in bringing everything from England and re-shipping it from York Factory to the posts. A stronger magnet in the south was in the American railways, the first of which reached the Red River in 1871, after the cession of Rupert's Land but before the Canadian Pacific touched Winnipeg. The development of agriculture and of American railways led the company to abandon the bay posts as the sole entrance to their territory, and to work out land routes to the northern department. About 1829 a "winter road" was begun from York Factory to Norway House, and although at first not successful, the plan was followed up. Rather than risk another failure (a large amount of goods had been lost in 1830) Simpson determined to go slowly.

We are, however, clearing the road, erecting stage houses, and making such other preparations connected with this object as we consider necessary, and the work is in such a forward state that, in the winter of 1834-35, I think we may safely undertake to convey 100 tons up and 100 tons down by that route. . . . This mode of transport, when conducted on a large scale, will, I am satisfied, be less expensive than what anyone, who has not given particular attention to the subject, can have any idea of. The conviction in my own mind is that it will not exceed 2/6 p. cwt. between Norway House and York, and that when large decked vessels [built at Norway House] are in use between Norway House and Red River, the transport between these places will not exceed 1/- p. cwt., making the whole charge for transport between Red River and the coast 3/6 per cwt.[7]

With the building of storehouses and stables a regular post-road was available, by means of which supplies from the Red River could be drawn overland to the northern department.

South of Fort Garry an overland route was established to St. Paul, and by 1858 Simpson was suggesting that an agency be established there. He argued that the posts could no longer be supplied only from York Factory, for the cost was too high: from York to Red River it had increased recently from 12 shillings to 28 shillings sterling per 100 pounds, whereas he calculated that the same amount could be shipped from Liverpool to Red River via New Orleans and St. Paul for about $4.50. In addition there would be a saving of interest because of the shorter period involved between shipment and use. About half the outfit should be sent this way and half by the bay. By keeping a good stock at St. Paul, it might also be possible to sell to the American traders.[8] The land route between St. Paul and Fort Garry had for some years been followed by the Red River carts, high, two-wheeled carts, made entirely of wood and drawn by a single ox or horse. "Brigades" of several hundred carts made the journey each year, carrying goods of all sorts for the merchants of Assiniboia, and taking some twenty to thirty days. The way was made easier with the introduction of steamboats on the Red River in 1859, as Simpson had hoped. In the meantime, however, the Hudson's Bay Company had made an arrangement with the Grand Trunk to ship their goods via Detroit and Milwaukee to St. Paul, from which place they would go on to Fort Garry by cart. This plan was carried into effect, for a time at least.[9] An alternative one was to build a road from Crow Wing (north of St. Paul) to Superior, at the western end of the lake. An officer of the Hudson's Bay Company succeded in stirring up a considerable interest in the scheme in Superior, but his suggestion that the citizens should pay $5,000 in cash and $20,000 in city property if the company built the road was not greeted with enthusiasm.[10] In 1871 the whole problem of communication through the United States was simplified when the Northern Pacific Railway reached the Red River at Brainard and there connected with the steamboats. In the same year a stage line was started between Fort Garry and Abercrombie, Minnesota. At first it gave a tri-weekly service, and in 1877 became daily. The mail was carried in the coaches.

To see the problems of transport between the prairies and British Columbia before the introduction of railways, one may look through the eyes of those who visited the country in the sixties and seventies, men who were particularly concerned with studying the existing means of travel as well as their possible improvement. Two classical accounts of such expeditions may be taken, as illustrating in the one case the approach to the west from Minnesota, and in the other the approach from Ontario. *The North-West Passage by Land*, written by Viscount Milton and W. B. Cheadle, is a restrained but vivid account of an overland journey made from the Atlantic to the Pacific by two Englishmen. Landing at Quebec, they proceeded by train through Detroit and Chicago to La Crosse on the Mississippi, which was then (1862) the nearest point to Fort Garry that the railway touched. At La Crosse their adventures began. An uncomfortable stage took them across to Georgetown on the Red River, but being in doubt whether the steamer that plied between there and Fort Garry would arrive on account of low water they started on the five-hundred-mile journey in two birch-bark canoes. Paddling through uninhabited country, in leaky canoes, they were not sorry to be picked up by the paddle-wheeler which finally turned up near Pembina and landed them at Fort Garry. At the fort they made preparations for their long trek to the Pacific. With half-breeds as guides they set out near the end of August on horseback, the luggage following in Red River carts. Passing through Portage la Prairie and Fort Ellice, they made for the valley of the Saskatchewan and got as far as Carlton House, near which they passed the winter in a home-made cabin.

In the following spring the difficult part of the trip began. Starting early in April, before the ice was out of the rivers, they made for Fort Pitt and Fort Edmonton, and beyond the latter they were in almost trackless country. Their expedition consisted of themselves, two Indian guides, with the wife and son of one, and a timorous schoolmaster who attached himself to the party and who proved a constant encumbrance thereafter. Twelve horses were taken along, six of which were to carry the provisions. Jasper House was reached with some difficulty on June 29, and from there they made for the Yellowhead Pass, minus one Indian who had deserted. The story of the journey across the mountains by the Fraser and Thompson valleys is a saga of continued hardships and daily dangers. The early part was bad enough, but the journey beside the Thompson was a struggle which nearly ended in tragedy. They had constantly risked their lives in swimming rivers, and scaling mountainsides, but now, short of food and with almost no game to be found, they literally had to cut a path through the forest with fading hopes of getting through alive. The last part of the trip was a nightmare in which exhausted men fought with the never-ending trees, staving off starvation by living on the horses they killed. More dead than alive, they staggered into Kamloops at the end of August. While waiting to take the Cariboo Trail for Yale they were regaled with stories of other parties who had attempted to pass by the way they had come and had met death by hunger or drowning.[11]

Ten years later the same trail over the prairies and through the Rockies was taken by Sandford Fleming, but under very different conditions. Fleming, who had to examine the proposed route for the railway, took with him a party, one of whom,

G. M. Grant, left a record of the trip called *Ocean to Ocean*. On July 16, 1872 the party left Toronto by train for Collingwood, where they could catch a steamer for Thunder Bay, and which they reached after a slow but uneventful voyage on July 22. From there they followed the Dawson Trail, which was part road and part water. They took waggons over a fair road to Shebandowan Lake, where canoes with Indian guides were ready for the next stage. From there to the end of the Lake of the Woods they followed the series of lakes and rivers, but even the Indians had an easy time for steam tugs towed them over all the open water. From the Lake of the Woods they drove over the trail to Fort Garry, which they reached on July 31. From Fort Garry they followed the same route as Milton and Cheadle to Edmonton, using Red River carts, buck-boards, and saddle-horses. Taking then to saddle and pack-horses, they reached Jasper House on September 2. Then they began the part of the journey that had all but defeated Milton and Cheadle. Not only was their equipment far better in every way, but in the intervening years a passable trail had been cut, and on several occasions they met parties of surveyors or miners on the trail. Whereas their predecessors had treasured bits of horse-flesh, Fleming and his party never lacked good fare. Near Kamloops, which they reached on September 28, they found settlers where before had been wilderness.

The main change in ten years was in the trail through the Yellowhead Pass. Neither of the two expeditions mentioned had met any insuperable difficulties either in getting to Fort Garry or crossing the prairie, but it can be seen that by 1872 it was possible for a well-equipped party to cross the Rockies without any untoward danger or hardship. But no part of the way from Fort Garry – or even Thunder Bay – to the Pacific slope could be passed by ordinary travellers. The time alone was a barrier, and the expense was very heavy. Even had the authors of these two diaries not expressed themselves so strongly on the subject, it might be deduced by any reader that the moral of their experience was the need of railway communication from the Great Lakes to the Pacific.

2. THE OPENING OF THE WEST

It was in the interest of the Hudson's Bay Company, as it would have been of any fur-trading company, to keep the west as a preserve for fur-bearing animals, and to restrict the population to trappers and those few farmers — retired company's servants — who could raise food for the small population needed for trapping, transportation, and management. Had the company been able to maintain this position it is probable that no number of prophets would have been able to bring within the sphere of practical politics the building of a railway to the Pacific. But, while the central prairie remained almost untouched by the plough of the settler, at each extremity civilization was advancing sufficiently to raise the question of the future of the west; and, since these advances were close to and even overlapping the American border, there loomed the danger of losing what was coming to be regarded as a Canadian heritage.

It was the fate of the Hudson's Bay Company to nurse in infancy the two settlements which were to precipitate the decision on the sovereignty of the west. After the early troubles of petty wars and grasshoppers had been passed, Assiniboia (the Red River colony) began to progress under more peaceful conditions. The population — largely made up of Métis, or French-Indian half-breeds — rose to 3,649 in 1835, and 6,691 in 1856, and then began to show resentment toward the rule of the company and especially toward its efforts to enforce the monopoly in fur-trading. Smuggling became the vogue, and the Métis openly resisted the maintenance of the company's justice. The opposition to the company was mingled with talk of a new régime. Aided by the advocacy of the first newspaper in the west, the *Nor'Wester,* a growing Canadian party preached the necessity of adding the colony to Canada — a sentiment which was warmly reciprocated in Canada itself, where the *Globe* hammered on this note for month after month.

By many such people, both in Assiniboia and Canada, there was felt to be urgent need of action because of the rival pull from the south. Since the virtual abandonment of the Ottawa route by the Hudson's Bay Company no link remained to bridge the gap of the Lake Superior region. On the other hand the development of regular communication with St. Paul by the brigade of carts or the steamers on the Red River made a connection which threatened to grow into a political one. The question came before the government of Canada in relation to postal service to Assiniboia. The extension of the American postal system to the north of Minnesota led residents of Fort Garry to establish a monthly communication with the post office there, which by 1857 had reached Pembina. Such an official link with the United States further stirred opinion in Canada West, and in the same year the Toronto Board of Trade appealed to the government to start a postal and telegraphic communication, over British soil, with British Columbia. The appeal did not fall on deaf ears, for in 1858 a postal service to Fort Garry twice a month in summer and once a month in winter was begun. During the period of navigation the mail was carried to Collingwood by train, to Fort William by steamer, and thence by canoe: in the winter dog-teams had to be substituted. These heroic measures, however, could not compete with the American route and two years later were abandoned.[12] That the residents of Assiniboia were anxious to establish communication with Canada is shown by the calling of a number of public meetings in 1863, where resolutions were passed, and a memorial addressed to the British and Canadian governments praying that a road should be built that would give access to the settlement without dependence on a foreign state.[13]

While this short-lived experiment represented at that time the sole contribution of Canada to the establishment of communications with the west, Americans were adopting more modern weapons for the same struggle. In 1864 the Northern Pacific Railroad Company was chartered by congress and empowered to build from a point on Lake Superior to Portland, Oregon. After some delay the banking firm of Jay Cooke and Company undertook in 1869 to raise the capital and construction began. By 1873, when the firm collapsed in the financial crisis, five hundred miles of the main line had been finished, and a new way was opened to Assiniboia – and a way which struck at its most vulnerable point the plan for linking the colony with Canada. Faced by the wide barrier of the Canadian shield, how could Canada compete with such a connection – unless it were by a railway? Yet if nothing was done to offset the economic and social pull of such a close neighbour as Minnesota, surely Assiniboia – the very gateway to the prairies – must fall into the arms of the republic?

Meanwhile a similar problem had arisen on the Pacific coast. As in the area to the east of the Rockies, the early history of British Columbia centres around the fur trade. The monopoly of trade given to the Hudson's Bay Company in the territory west of the mountains in 1821 was seriously diminished by the settlement of the boundary at the forty-ninth parallel in 1846. In 1849 Vancouver Island was ceded to the company, subject to requirements as to colonization; but on the mainland only the trade monopoly was continued. After a short and unhappy experiment with an independent nominee, the British government appointed James Douglas, a prominent servant of the company, as governor of the island.

Such was the situation when the first gold rush began in 1858. Discovery of gold in the tableland between the Upper Columbia, Thompson, and Fraser rivers, along the Quesnel River, and in the Cariboo district forced the development of a transportation system. A number of roads were cut to the mining districts, the most famous being the Cariboo trail from Yale to Quesnel, which was converted into a waggon road in the sixties. In the south of the province a combination of water and land transport was used as far as possible. An important route in that area was the Dewdney trail built in the sixties, and affording communication with the Kootenay country. A change in the centre of gravity of the transportation system was caused by the increase of shipping on the Pacific. The first of three vessels for the Hudson's Bay Company was built in 1836, and at least by 1847 an annual voyage was made from London. The company also used its smaller vessels for coastal work between their various posts.

The transportation system thus built up was slow and expensive, the high cost being in particular an impediment to the mining industry. Such a weakness in itself was enough to suggest the need of railways. That, however, was as yet a remote hope; while the immediate problem was what was to be the future of this land which had changed almost overnight from a fur-trading area to one rich in minerals and with a rush of population. Canadians began to take stock of this situation, too, to see whether British Columbia would remain a separate colony, enter into union with Canada, or fall to the United States. As the Pacific coast of the northern part of the continent it had a distinct importance for Canada, but, as in the case of Assiniboia, there was a strong pull toward the United States. Canada was far and Oregon near; Canada could be reached only by a harassing land journey, while Seattle was within easy steaming distance of Victoria or New Westminster. To add to this natural link came the invasion or threatened invasion by American communication systems. In 1865 the Western Union Telegraph Company placed several miles of line in British Columbia as part of a project for a cable between Europe and America by way of Alaska and Russia, though the scheme collapsed with the successful laying of the Atlantic cable in 1866. In 1867 the purchase of Alaska brought American soil on two sides of the colony; while the approaching American railways promised to draw British Columbia as well as Assiniboia toward the south.

Much hinged on the position of the Hudson's Bay Company, particularly in its chartered territories of Rupert's Land and Vancouver Island. Since the latest grant of trade monopoly was due to expire in 1859, a select committee of the house of commons was appointed in 1857, "to consider the State of those British Possessions in *North America* which are under the Administration of the Hudson's Bay Company, or over which they possess a License to Trade." To Great Britain, to the company itself, and to Canada the deliberations of the committee were of primary importance. On the invitation of the colonial secretary Canada sent Chief Justice Draper to London to appear before the committee. In his evidence Draper fairly represented the cautious ambitions of Canada in the west. He expressed anxiety that the territory should remain British, disputed the claims of the Hudson's Bay Company, and looked for an opportunity for Canadian expansion. He admitted, however, that Canada was not yet ready to govern the whole area.

I should myself propose . . . that Canada should have in the first place a free right to explore and survey, in order to ascertain the capabilities of the country; in the second place, to open communication roads in the manner pursued in that country, by putting settlers on each side of them with free grants . . .

in the next place I should propose that Canada should be permitted to lay out townships, and that as fast as she did actually lay them out and settle them, those portions of the territory so settled should become incorporated with and form part of the province; I would limit it under all circumstances and at any distant period by the Rocky Mountains; I should never dream of pushing beyond them.

Draper then emphasized the need of communications with Canada since "the natural outlet of the country appears rather to be into the United States," and as Hudson Bay was open for only part of the year, the only outlet on British soil was through Canada. Draper himself did not advocate the expulsion of the company from the whole of Rupert's Land, but rather that their boundary should be pushed farther north – say to Norway House. As to the country west of the Rockies, a different situation would arise if a railway were built. His attitude on this point is rather suggestive:

I hope you will not laugh at me as very visionary, but I hope to see the time, or that my children may live to see the time when there is a railway going all across that country and ending at the Pacific; and so far as individual opinion goes, I entertain no doubt that the time will arrive when that will be accomplished. I should desire, for the sake of Canada, that permission should be reserved to her to that extent only, that if she makes a railway through her own portion of the territory, it shall go to the terminus.

John Ross, then president of the Grand Trunk, was the other Canadian to give evidence. As might be expected, his examination hinged on the possibility of a western railway; and he argued that one could be built north of Lake Superior to the Red River, and so, in time, to the Pacific. As a preliminary stage he suggested a road and a policy of settlement. The scheme involved, of course, displacing the Hudson's Bay Company from at least a portion of their territory.

The evidence showed a clear line of cleavage between the interests of the fur-trading company and those of Canada. Sir George Simpson, in the course of a lengthy examination, was surprisingly outspoken in denying the possibilities of agriculture in any but small sections of the country. The company evidently was anxious to stave off the undesired advance of civilization; and even the report of the committee, which advocated – though in equivocal terms – an agreed cession of such districts as the Red River and Saskatchewan to Canada, led only to a series of diplomatic marches and counter-marches. Vancouver Island, following the advice of the committee, was taken from the jurisdiction of the company, and the charter for trade on the Pacific coast was allowed to lapse in 1859. The appointment of the select committee, then, raised the whole question of the future of the west, and carried it some distance in the direction which Canada wished it to take. Yet the company was able to prevent for some years any decision being reached on the validity of the charter; and it may be, that if it had not been for internal developments within the company, the west might have longer remained the domain of the fur trader.

In the years 1862-1863 a strange play was being performed which involved the west, the Hudson's Bay Company, the Grand Trunk Railway, the province of Canada, and various financial groups. The *dramatis personae were*: E. W. Watkin, who played the leading role, the Duke of Newcastle, the directors of the Hudson's Bay Company and the Grand Trunk, Sir Edmund Head, Baring, Glyn, and a number of Canadian politicians, the last having minor parts. Unfortunately some of the scenes were acted in private, so that the course of the play is partially obscured. The general plot centres around the following circumstances: a telegraph line and a road or railway to the Pacific had been suggested, and the Grand Trunk – which was influential both in England and Canada – was anxious to secure control of any such railway. The Hudson's Bay Company was camped on the ground through which the railway must pass, but might be induced, for a consideration, either to grant a right of way or withdraw from the territory. If it withdrew, it would presumably do so in favour of Canada – or, better, a Canada federated with the Maritime Provinces.

In the fifties the Hudson's Bay Company, reading the signs of the times, saw that the old régime was passing, and that the west would not always remain the preserve of the fur trader; but it held a strong legal position, and while it was not unprepared to sell some of its rights, it did not propose to give them away. "The Hudson's Bay Company," wrote Edward Ellice, "are quite willing to dispose of their territory and their establishments. It is a question of a million of money."[14] Having survived the select committees of 1857 with Rupert's Land still firmly in its grasp, the company proceeded on the one hand to spar with the British and Canadian governments over legal investigation of its charter, and on the other to await offers.

Watkin representing the Grand Trunk group, and the Duke of Newcastle, colonial secretary, began in 1862 to force the pace. Both had, apparently, a genuine interest in the promotion of British imperial power in North America. In addition, Watkin was concerned for the Grand Trunk, which he was trying to put on its feet; and Newcastle, perhaps, was looking for the political stability of a single and united colony, strong enough to act as a barrier against American expansionism. In July 1862 the colonial office forwarded to Berens, governor of the Hudson's Bay Company, a letter from Thomas Baring, K. D. Hodgson, R. W. Crawford, G. C. Glyn and his son G. G. Glyn, and W. Chapman, which the colonial office supported. It proved to be a scheme for "providing a telegraphic service, and of securing the means of travelling with regularity to the British Territory on the Pacific." Would the British government grant a large tract of land in aid of construction?[15] As they held the land in question, the Hudson's Bay Company were asked in turn if they would concede a line of territory: to which Berens replied that they would do so if adequate security were given for the completion of a road and telegraph.[16] A rather fruitless exchange of letters then took place during which the colonial office asked how much the company would grant, and the company asked for further information about the project.

At the beginning of November both G. G. Glyn and Watkin were trying to persuade Baring to sign a letter to Newcastle. "You must really help me in that Pacific matter," wrote Watkin. "If, on conclusion, you prefer not to be on the board of any company formed to *carry out* the scheme . . . I will endeavour to meet your views . . . the Pacific affair is part of our *policy* – the success of which will make – believe me – a vast difference in the value of your Grand Trunk property."[17] In the same letter to Baring Watkin explained that "all I propose to do . . . is to get up a Company, with a capital not exceeding £300,000." It is improbable, however, that Watkin did not then have a more ambitious plan in his mind, for at the end of a fortnight more important negotiations were under way. The following letter from the colonial under-secretary to Berens, dated November 21, 1862, was shown to the committee of the company seven months later.

With reference to your interview with the Duke of Newcastle on the 18th Instant on the subject of a proposed postal and telegraphic route from the Canadian frontier to that of British Columbia, at which His Grace understood you to express the willingness of the Hudson's Bay Company to enter into personal communication with some of the gentlemen who are desirous, under certain conditions, of undertaking the scheme and to confer with them upon the basis of forming a road through the country comprised in the Charter of your Company, or upon that of the purchase of the whole of the Company's rights, I am directed by His Grace to inform you that he has to-day seen a deputation of the gentlemen referred to and they on their part expressed their readiness to attend the proposed meeting.[18]

From that time — the end of November — personal conferences took the place of this rather indirect correspondence. Berens met a deputation and told them that the company would grant a right of passage. Privately he explained to A. G. Dallas, governor of Rupert's Land, that this generosity was to avoid a demand for taking the land from the company.[19] In reality he was not at all happy about the situation.

. . . The Duke of Newcastle [he wrote confidentially to Dugald McTavish] *has . . . far more extended views than prudence and sound judgment can comprehend. We must therefore remain quiet, observing every move and taking care that His Grace does not steal a march upon us which I am persuaded he would do if he could. His object appears to be to favour Canada and almost at every step he takes for this purpose he is thwarted by Canada herself.*[20]

A little later he avowed to Dallas that "there can be no doubt but that the Duke of Newcastle is most anxious to get rid of us, and would I believe, do all he can to further this purpose. He is certainly encouraging other parties to move vigorously in the promotion of his views. . . ."[21]

During the early months of 1863 the two plans – cession of land or sale of the company – were carried forward concurrently, but there seems to have been more reality in the second. It is true that as late as May the colonial office was submitting proposals for a plan involving only a grant of land, but by that time negotiations for a sale were well advanced. The idea of purchasing a controlling interest in the stock originated with Watkin and Richard Potter, the future president of the Grand Trunk, who were supposed to be finding the capital themselves.[22] Only later did the International Financial Society appear on the scene. This society, which had been formed shortly before, came into play after a memorandum had been signed by Watkin and Potter on the one part and by the governor and committee on the other by which the first parties agreed to purchase the whole of the stock of the company at the rate of £300 for every £100, and the purchasers were to be invested with the management and control of the company.[23]

The mantle of Edward Ellice had fallen on Watkin. The sale went through, and the old board was swept away. Only Eden Colvile and George Lyall remained on the committee. Sir Edmund Head was the new governor, and C. M. Lampson (representing United States interests) deputy governor. Potter took a seat at the council table, but Watkin, the king-maker, remained discreetly in the background. With the new men in charge, the attitude of the company took a distinct change. The prospectus of the International Financial Society, in offering shares to the public, spoke of developing the company's territory, encouraging settlement, and establishing communication from the Atlantic to the Pacific. Watkin was despatched to the Red River in July, and although Head said somewhat bitterly that his report might as well have been written in London, he soon had to reprimand him for prematurely ordering telegraph wire.

In the summer of 1864 Dr. John Rae was put in charge of a survey for a telegraph across the company's territory and reported favourably. At the same time he examined the possibilities of travel by road, water, or rail. The only real difficulty he found for the construction of a railway was in the Yellowhead Pass.[24] Attached to the expedition as an assistant was an official of the Gzowski firm, who reported on the possibilities of a railway from St. Cloud (on the Mississippi, and not far from St. Paul) to Fort Garry – a project which seems contradictory to the avowed purpose of establishing communications on British soil.

There the story of the Grand Trunk–Hudson's Bay plan for a Pacific railway ends. It is the paradox of Watkin's career that his long-laid schemes were defeated by a palace revolution in the Grand Trunk itself, which caused him to resign from the presidency in 1869 – just as confederation was to be completed by the addition of Assiniboia and British Columbia. And although Potter, his associate in the purchase of the Hudson's Bay Company, succeeded him as president of the Grand Trunk, that railway was soon to lose command of the western link of the transcontinental line just as it lost the eastern. Whether Watkin could have averted the disaster – for disaster it was to the Grand Trunk – must be left as a subject for speculation.

3. THE RAILWAY PLANNED

Long before the day of Watkin, books, pamphlets, memoranda, letters, and speeches had been written or spoken on the need of a railway from Canada to the Pacific. Probably the most voluble of the advocates of such a railway was Sir John Smyth, who described himself as "Baronet and Royal Engineer, Canadian Poet, LL.D., and Moral Philosopher, etc., etc., etc." In the thirties Smyth was sketching various railway lines in Canada, and in the forties had progressed to one from Halifax to the Pacific by way of Chicago. Steamers on the Atlantic and Pacific were to connect with the railway; and in a burst of generosity he added steamers and railways in Europe and the east to complete the circle of the globe.[25] Four years later his namesake wrote pamphlets that were more imperial and somewhat more specific. His railway was to run across the prairies north of the boundary to the valley of the Columbia.[26] Other writers with imperial considerations in mind carried on the campaign: for example, Wilson and Richards in *Britain Redeemed and Canada Preserved* (1850), and Synge, in *Great Britain one Empire*

(1852). In 1854 Sir Richard Broun produced a prospectus for an "Imperial British American Main Trunk Railway, Ocean Ferry and Freehold Land Company," and invited the Hudson's Bay Company to co-operate in this with the Heirs of the Hereditary Viceroy of New Scotland and the Baronets of Scotland and Nova Scotia. The company, however, "declined to entertain" the project in spite of the illustrious associates. In 1851 Joseph Howe, fresh from his conversations in England about the Intercolonial, told a public meeting in Halifax that "many in this room will live to hear the whistle of the steam-engine in the passes of the Rocky Mountains and to make the journey from Halifax to the Pacific in five or six days."

In the meantime there had been some activity in Canada. A group of men of whom Allan Macdonell was the leading spirit had a bill introduced into the Canadian assembly in 1851 to incorporate the Lake Superior and Pacific Railroad Company. The standing committee on railroads and telegraph lines reported unfavourably on grounds of feasibility, though approving the principle. Again in 1853 and 1855 similar bills were introduced, but all were turned down. Macdonell claimed that the opposition came from the Hudson's Bay Company,[27] but efforts to persuade that company to build the railway itself did not meet with success. Three years later John Young, A. N. Morin, A. T. Galt, and J. A. Poor petitioned for a charter, but failed to get it. At last in 1858 a group which included Macdonell secured a charter for the North-West Transportation Navigation and Railway Company. The new company proposed to build from Lake Superior to Rainy Lake, where steamers would be used to Lake of the Woods, and thence by rail to the Red River. Lake Winnipeg and the Saskatchewan were to be navigated by steamers. The company proposed by this means to revive the Canadian fur trade and to supersede the Pembina outlet; capital, however, was not available and no work was undertaken.

Such schemes have a more than antiquarian interest, for they not only indicate the growth of a belief in the practicability of a Pacific railway, but served at the time to stimulate opinion in Great Britain and Canada in favour of improved communications with the west. The transition of the Pacific railway from the world of dreams to that of reality belongs to, and is intimately connected with, the period of confederation. The "Dominion stretching from sea to sea" that is supposed to have inspired the members of the Quebec conference to choose the curious name for the united provinces was more than a vision of a distant future, for events were rapidly developing in the settled parts of the west that made imperative some adequate communication between them and Canada – unless the hope of absorbing the west was to be abandoned for ever.

Provision having been made in the British North America Act for the admission into the Dominion of Rupert's Land, the north-western territory, and British Columbia, the new government and parliament set about the task. A formidable obstacle to the acquisition of Rupert's Land lay in the fact that it was still held by charter by the Hudson's Bay Company. That the company was willing to sell was further evidenced by its favourable reception of a tentative offer for purchase by a group of Anglo-American capitalists – a move which stimulated the activity of the Canadian government.[28] In the end the old controversy over the legal position of the Hudson's Bay Company in Rupert's Land was tacitly dropped, and both parties accepted the terms drawn up by the imperial government. The deed of surrender, signed on November 19, 1869, called for the payment by Canada of £300,000. The company was to retain all posts actually occupied, and might select blocks of land adjacent to each to a total of 45,160 acres. In addition the company might select within the next fifty years one-twentieth of the land in the fertile belt made available for settlement. Canada was to take over the materials for the telegraph at cost, and the company was to be free to carry on fur-trading.

The prairie was not conquered by legal documents alone. The half-breeds of Assiniboia saw in the invasion of civilization the end of the life of hunting and trapping which they had always known; saw the land over which they had freely roamed taken by the chain of the surveyor and the plough of the settler. They resisted with the same dim consciousness of the future that had moved the Indian tribes under Pontiac to attempt to stem the tide of white invasion just over a century before. The rebellion under Louis Riel in 1869-1870 demonstrated, if indeed any demonstration were needed, the lack of communications between Ontario and the west. The Dawson route from Thunder

Bay to Fort Garry, with 131 miles of waggon road between the portages, was used by immigrants in the early seventies, but it was at best a stop-gap, and the demand became more insistent for a railway to Manitoba and the North West Territories, as the area east of the Rockies was now to be known.

The connection between the entrance of British Columbia into the Dominion and the Pacific railway was even closer. In 1866 the colonies of Vancouver Island and British Columbia were united under the name of the latter, and the new colony showed a close interest in the federation that was about to be consummated in the east. In 1867 a resolution of the legislative council in favour of admission into the Dominion was the first formal step taken by British Columbia. For a time it appeared as if the movement would fail; but the cession of Rupert's Land, the appointment of a pro-confederation governor in Musgrave, the decline of gold-mining, and continued financial difficulties together smoothed the way, and in 1870 delegates were sent to Ottawa to arrange terms. In regard to communications, the representatives of British Columbia asked that a survey for a railway be commenced at once, and that a waggon road be completed within three years after confederation. The Dominion government, however, on its initiative shouldered the much more onerous burden of beginning within two years, and completing within ten, a railway to connect the seaboard of British Columbia with the railway system of Canada.

Why the Canadian government undertook this gratuitous obligation is not altogether clear, but a number of explanations may be offered: that the waggon road was an additional and unnecessary expense; that there was fear of an invasion of American railways; or that it was useful for the Canadian government to bind parliament to a task which perhaps could not have been attempted under any other conditions. The terms were accepted by parliament, but not before Alexander Mackenzie, the leader of the opposition, had moved an amendment that Canada should be pledged only to make surveys and to build the railway as finances might allow. The *Globe*, while reiterating its belief in a Pacific railway, was indignant at the terms: "We utterly scout the notion that a rash and may be disastrous step should be taken at the dictation of a handful of people 2,500 miles away, and to whom we are already making concessions that they may well be satisfied to accept in exchange for union. . . ." This line of argument was continued in several editorials, but a month later the editor was even more indignant with the New York *Albion*, which lectured Canadians on the foolish attempt to build their own railway, when they should use the Northern Pacific. The *Albion*, he said, was probably subsidized by Jay Cooke, and no doubt the Americans wanted to absorb the Canadian west, but Canada would have its own railway. Here the *Globe* was touching an important point, for there can be little doubt that the building of the Northern Pacific was regarded as a real danger to Canadian power in the west, and was stimulating parliament and people to undertake a herculean task.

4. THE STRUGGLE FOR THE CONTRACT

The railway to the Pacific was to be built: the Dominion was committed to it by a solemn agreement with British Columbia. The circumstances were peculiar. In the first place the population of the whole country was small for such a great undertaking – some three and a half million, of whom only 23,000 lived west of Lake Superior. Secondly, no surveys had been made of the route through the mountains of British Columbia. The Yellowhead Pass was thought to be feasible for a railway, but no way had yet been found through the Selkirks. Captain Palliser had even advised against a line to the north of Lake Superior, but in the meanwhile this had been reported as practicable.

Who was to build the railway? From the start it was intended that it should be built and operated by a private company rather than by the government. The act which was passed to implement the agreement with British Columbia (35 Vict., c. 71) stated this explicitly and provided that aid was to be granted in land and subsidies to a maximum of fifty million acres and thirty million dollars. The gauge was set at four feet, eight and one-half inches. No company was named in the Act, the government having power to make arrangements with any one company or group within the terms of the act. This was a new subject of worry for the *Globe* (which may be taken as representing the attitude of the opposition). The government, complained the editor, might by order in council come to terms with "any company who may be disposed in return to give their political support, or may become subservient followers, ready enough to grab the land and money; but in the end quite unable to keep faith with the country. This, of course, opens at once a door for just that political jobbery and corruption which has made the Intercolonial a great national scandal and the Grand Trunk a seething mass of political immorality." Later he saw in such a company "a monstrous and unclean offspring of the secret and immoral intrigues that call it into being." There was to be ample scope for such language before long.

While surveys under government direction were being pushed forward, the cabinet awaited a group of capitalists. For the past three years inquiries had been made by individuals or groups as to the probable terms of the contract. Alfred Waddington of British Columbia, who had shown great energy in promoting the idea of the railway, was well to the fore, but his petition for the incorporation of the Canada Pacific Railway (1871) was not seriously considered: in any case the petition was premature. C. J. Brydges was in touch with Macdonald as well as with other interested capitalists, and was officially empowered to negotiate.[29] Indeed the leaders of the Grand Trunk could hardly have been far from the scene; and, according to the *Globe*, intervened with vigour in the Ontario elections of 1871 on behalf of government candidates. The Grand Trunk, however, seem to have failed to sway the government toward their own plan of a Pacific railway, and, having failed, took no part in the scramble for the charter. Their point of view is clearly expressed in a letter from Brydges, in which he explains his refusal to join Sir Hugh Allan's group. This attitude is no doubt partly based on the strategy of the existing Grand Trunk system.

I have no belief myself in any line of railway running to Fort Garry, for a long time to come through British territory. What I believe in, and what I think must be done in the first instance is to make a connection between Fort Garry and Lake Superior in British territory, a railway west from Fort Garry, built in sections, and not attempted too fast, and a branch down to Pembina to meet the United States system of railways, which will certainly get up to that point during the present year. That would give a rail connection in winter, and by Lake Superior, water connection would be had throughout the summer during the season of navigation, which, for the next 10 to 15 years will be all that can possibly be wanted. I am quite clear that railways from Fort Garry around the north shore of Lake Superior and Lake Nipissing could not be built except at a frightful cost, when built could not be worked successfully in winter, and if it could be worked would have no traffic to carry upon it.[30]

With the Grand Trunk eliminated from the race, there remained two favourites who were to run neck and neck for some months. The origin of these two companies requires some explanation. In the summer of 1871 Alfred Waddington, who was in Ottawa attempting to get a charter himself, met G. W. McMullen of Chicago, who became interested and arranged a meeting in Ottawa on July 14 of a number of Canadians and Americans: McMullen himself, C. M. Smith of Chicago, Mr. Hurlbut of New York, W. Kersteman of Toronto and his son-in-law Wood, James Beaty of Toronto, and Waddington. There were also represented by their signatures: General George W. Cass, W. B. Ogden, M. K. Jesup, T. A. Scott, Winslow, Lanier & Company, S. J. Tilden, and the Honourable G. Jackson. All the latter, except Jackson, were Americans. Three of them were directors of the Northern Pacific, and were deeply interested in the Canadian project as a possible competitor. It is probable that they sought to hinder rather than help, by working from the inside. The government, however, regarded the proposals made by the group as premature.

Subsequently Sir Francis Hincks suggested to Sir Hugh Allan that he should open negotiations with the group of Americans. "In this," commented Macdonald, "Hincks made a mistake and acted without authority, but Allan did not know that."[31] By the beginning of October the new combination was ready to discuss terms with the government, but Macdonald would go no further than to receive a memorandum. In December an agreement was drawn up in New York, and in February Allan submitted their proposal to the government. It provided for a railway from a point near Lake Nipissing to the coast, with branches to Pembina and Sault Ste. Marie, the whole to be completed within twelve years. For this they asked a subsidy of $15,000 and

20,000 acres a mile, to be increased to 25,000 acres in the Lake Superior section. The associates whom he mentions are: Andrew Allan, J. J. C. Abbott of Montreal, Donald Smith of Manitoba, Henry Nathan of British Columbia, A. B. Foster of Ottawa, Thomas McGreevy of Quebec, Donald McInnes of Hamilton, and the Americans – Jay Cooke, T. A. Scott, W. B. Ogden, J. G. Smith, C. M. Smith, and G. W. McMullen. The company was, in fact, to be made up of the directors of the Northern Pacific, allied with a number of Canadians. Allan affected to believe that such a connection would be of advantage to Canada, apart altogether from its value as a source of capital:

From Fort Garry westward to the Pacific it was intended the Road should proceed on the route afterwards determined by the Surveys and it was regarded as a possibility that the Northern Pacific when it got as far west as the Missouri River might be defected [sic. deflected] so as to join the Canadian Pacific, get the advantage of our easier pass through the mountains, and run on its track to some point west of the mountains where they would again separate; the Northern Pacific passing south to New Westminster, and the Canadian Pacific seeking the shore of the Pacific Ocean at such point as determined by the surveys.

I favoured this scheme, because it not only gave us such a Pacific Railroad as we might desire, but also the advantage of a direct connection with the States of Northern Michigan, Wisconsin, Minnesota and Dakotah, the traffic and produce of which would naturally find its way to and from the seaboard through Canada, as being much the shortest, and consequently the cheapest route, even for the traffic of New York and Boston.[32]

The latter part of this argument was not altogether unsound, as the Northern Pacific wished to secure access to Boston via Montreal: on the other hand, some of the Canadians whom Allan approached had not his confidence about the western end. One such was C. J. Brydges, whose refusal to become connected with Allan's company has already been noticed. Brydges's decision was important, because it meant that the Grand Trunk would not be friendly – and in fact proved to be hostile – to the whole plan of a Canadian railway to the Pacific. Another man who was critical of the project was Senator D. L. Macpherson of Toronto, who had been a partner in the Gzowski firm. Allan approached him in February, asking him to be one of the Canadian directors. Macpherson, however, objected to the proposed organization, and "remonstrated against giving our rivals the control and ownership of our Trans-continental Railway."[33] He told Allan that the Northern Pacific would work it for their own purposes. He therefore proceeded to organize a rival company, the Interoceanic. Although, of course, only one company could build the railway, in the meanwhile parliament was neutral and passed charters for both the Interoceanic Railway Company (35 Vict., c. 72) and the Canada Pacific Railway Company (35 Vict., c. 73). They are almost identical, both calling for the construction of a railway from a point at or near Lake Nipissing to a point on the Pacific coast, with branches to the River St. Mary, Thunder Bay, and Pembina. The first act, naming Macpherson, William McMaster, E. W. Cumberland and some fifty other men, emphasized in the preamble that such an enterprise should as far as possible be controlled by British subjects. The other act was, of course, silent on this point. It named Allan, Abbott, Donald Smith, Donald McInnes, and others. The two acts received royal assent. In June both companies were officially organized. Allan was drawn toward the project of a western railway through a desire to feed his steamship line, for which purpose he had already promoted the North Shore Railway on rumours of a Grand Trunk line of steamers from Portland to Europe. The two companies also represented the rival commercial interests of Toronto and Montreal. To placate both, the eastern terminus of the Pacific Railway had been placed at Lake Nipissing, a neutral point.

The government was in an awkward position. The Interoceanic directors made much of Allan's American connections, and while Allan secured a new agreement at the end of March, his company was still tainted with American capital. Nor could an exclusive charter be given to either an Ontario or a Quebec group. An election was coming on (in August), and the "friends" of the party would be friends no longer if they were ignored. Allan had already shown his political power by organizing a campaign against Sir George Cartier that drove that unhappy statesman to capitulate to Allan's request for a charter. Macpherson made it quite clear that Ontario would not support the government if the charter were granted to Quebec. Macdonald, therefore, took the only course possible under the circumstances – an attempt to secure an amalgamation of the two "rings," as they had come to be called. Here again there was a stumbling-block. The rings argued about the number of directors each should have, and – worse still – Allan insisted on being president. This Macpherson would not hear of, arguing that the president would be in virtual control and should be elected by the directors. Moreover it would still leave the danger that the railway would be handed over to the Americans. "His alliance of last winter with Jay Cooke and the directors of the Northern Pacific Ry. is well known, and it is also known that he agreed with them to hand over to them our great Railway and its vast land subsidy. . . . That scheme . . . had to be abandoned and the British flag was ostentatiously hoisted by Sir Hugh and Co. This was done too late, however, to satisfy ordinary mortals that the newly professed loyalty to Canada was sincere. . . ."[34] Allan gradually drew away from his former American associates, explaining to them that Canadian opinion would not tolerate anyone connected with the Northern Pacific being concerned in the Canadian line. Macpherson, however, remained adamant, and early in October the secretary of the Interoceanic Company "declined peremptorily to enter into the scheme of amalgamation."[35] Conference after conference had failed, and finally the idea of an amalgamation had to be abandoned.

The government then approached the question from still another angle. A new charter was drawn up (February 5, 1873) the preamble of which refers to the failure to amalgamate the two companies, holds it inadvisable to agree with either, and therefore incorporates and charters a new company. In reality the change was not radical, for the new company included men from both of the old ones. The subscribers mentioned were: Hugh Allan, A. G. Archibald (Halifax), J. O. Beaubien (Montmagny), J. E. Beaudry (Montreal), E. R. Burpee (Saint John), F. W. Cumberland (Toronto), Sandford Fleming (Ottawa), R. H. Hall (Sherbrooke), J. S. Helmcken (Victoria), Andrew McDermot (Winnipeg), Donald McInnes (Hamilton), Walter Shanly, and John Walker (London, Ont.). The company was named the Canadian Pacific Railway Company, was to have a capital of ten million dollars; and the line had to be begun within two, and – unless an extension were granted by parliament – to be finished within ten years. A railway was to be built from a point on or near Lake Nipissing to some point on the Pacific, with branches to Lake Superior and the American border. The course of the line was to be approved by the government; construction and equipment to be determined by the government and company together. The Union Pacific was to be taken as the general standard. The company was to receive thirty million dollars and a land grant of fifty million acres, with additional land grants for branches. "John A.," said the *Globe*, "has made an Act of Parliament. That which in Great Britain requires the joint action of King, Lords, and Commons, and has hitherto required in Canada the co-operation of Governor-General, Senate, and House of Commons, has been effected with a stroke of the pen by the one-man-power that has taken everything into its own hands at Ottawa. . . ."

It was, however, one thing to grant a charter and another to ensure that the company thus created could raise sufficient capital. After the connection had been severed with the American capitalists, Macdonald also refused the offer of an English group who came late into the game. At the end of November 1872 he received a cable from a certain Kersteman in London asking if he would accept an "English company of peers and commoners prepared to carry out conditions in Cartier's Act ready with one million sterling." Macdonald put him in touch with Sir John Rose, who reported that Kersteman would not disclose the names of the promoters, but was sailing for Canada. The mysterious Kersteman then submitted a memorandum offering to build the railway, but still held back the names. Macdonald's reply was that it was too late to enter into negotiations with another body of capitalists. In March representatives of the new Canadian company set sail for England to raise money, but to the difficulties which they may have anticipated was added a new and unexpected development, known as "the Pacific scandal."

The general election of 1872 resulted in a gain for the Liberal opposition, helped by the passions raised by the Riel rebellion, dissatisfaction with the Washington Treaty, and alarm over the government's railway policy. Shortly after the opening of the session a Liberal member, L. C. Huntington, made general charges of a corrupt relation between the government and the Allan "ring." His resolution was as follows:

That in anticipation of the Legislation of last Session, as to the Pacific Railway, an agreement was made between Sir Hugh Allan, acting for himself, and certain other Canadian promoters, and G. W. McMullen, acting for certain United States Capitalists, whereby the latter agreed to furnish all the funds necessary for the construction of the contemplated Railway, and to give the former a certain percentage of interest, in consideration of their interest and position, the scheme agreed on being ostensibly that of a Canadian Company with Sir Hugh Allan at its head –

That the Government were aware that negotiations were pending between these parties, –

That subsequently, an understanding was come to between the Government and Sir Hugh Allan and Mr. Abbott, M.P., – that Sir Hugh Allan and his friends should advance a large sum of money for the purpose of aiding the Elections of Ministers and their supporters at the ensuing General Election, – and that he and his friends should receive the contract for the construction of the Railway, –

That accordingly Sir Hugh Allan did advance a large sum of money for the purpose mentioned, and at the solicitation, and under the pressing instances of Ministers, –

That part of the monies, expended by Sir Hugh Allan in connection with the obtaining of the Act of incorporation and Charter, were paid to him by the said United States Capitalists under the agreement with him, – it is

Ordered, That a committee of seven Members be appointed to inquire into all the circumstances connected with the negotiations for the construction of the Pacific Railway – with the legislation of last Session on the subject, and with the granting of the Charter to Sir Hugh Allan and others; with power to send for persons, papers and records; and with instructions to report in full the evidence taken before, and all proceedings of said Committee.

The resolution was defeated on a party division, but the charge was too grave to be ignored; and Macdonald shortly afterwards moved for the appointment of a select committee of five, including two prominent Liberals – Blake and Dorion. Since parliamentary committees were not then empowered to take evidence under oath, a bill was passed to remedy this: it was, however, disallowed as *ultra vires*. Macdonald then renewed a suggestion which he had made earlier, that a royal commission should be issued, and offered to the committee to change their status in that way. The Liberals, who had been anxious to keep the inquiry within parliament, resisted the commission. L. H. Holton urged Blake not to accept. He argued that the government had from the first meant to thwart the inquiry, and would be able to do so by adjourning the commission or ruling out evidence.[36] Both Dorion and Blake did refuse: the latter saying bluntly that ministers should not establish a commission to try themselves.[37] The others refused to act without them. Cartwright ventured the suggestion that Allan might be summoned to the bar of the house, but it was not acted on.[38] After this jockeying for position, a royal commission was issued on August 14 to three judges, C. D. Day, Antoine Polette, and J. R. Gowan.

Meanwhile parliament and public were startled by a series of revelations in the Montreal *Herald*. Three of the letters published – between Allan and G. W. McMullen – were presumably contributed by the latter, who had long been indignant over the way in which he and his associates had been thrown over.

. . . I regret to have to communicate [he had written to Macdonald] *that no offer for an arrangement had been made by Sir Hugh and it is becoming evident that he has sacrificed our interests* and acts as if he concluded we should let the matter rest there. . . .

Sir Hugh Allan came to us, *with offers of his services to secure unity of action to two wings of the Syndicate, which had agreed to build the Canada Pacific on the terms of the Government.* We *did not go to him. He stated that he came to us by direction of the ministry. . . .*

The Government alone had the address of our syndicate, and Sir Hugh's approach could not be viewed by us in courtesy or practically, as resting on less than direct authority from the Cabinet, and we accepted him as their representative. The

Government it is understood has agreed to give the contract to another party; with Sir Hugh as the virtual head of the company, and he evidently expects to retain his position of Government contractor after a flagrant breach of faith with us. . . .[39]

It seemed at first as if Allan would be the chief sufferer from these revelations.

Sir Hugh [wrote Macdonald] *as you may fancy, was in considerable distress about the publication of his letters. On the other hand I was exceedingly glad to see them in extenso. They prove Allan to be an exceedingly untruthful man; but what he would feel more they would show even to himself as he re-read them, that he had been a very foolish man. . . . Last night, before the letters came out, I told him that if they were published, as I supposed they would be, I must insist upon his making an affidavit of all the facts as to his relations with the Government, the Railway and the Elections, which he promised to do. I have held him to his promise, and Mr. Abbott, M.P., his Counsel, has prepared an affidavit. . . . This truly states his relations with the Government, so far as I am aware of them. . . . The affidavit is very skilfully drawn by Abbott. He has made the old gentleman acknowledge on oath that his letters were untrue. . . .*[40]

This affidavit was published in the Montreal *Gazette*, denying that any bargain had been made with the government, and it seemed as if the storm might calm down. On July 18, however, a further blast appeared in the *Herald* in the form of a statement by McMullen, together with a number of letters and telegrams written during the election, and showing that ministers had constantly called on Allan for funds. The latter letters were copied from the originals stolen from Abbott's office.

The royal commission sat during September and the early part of October, and parliament reassembled on October 23. Attacked for alleged corruption, the government resigned on November 5. The guilt or innocence of Macdonald's government must remain a matter of opinion. There is no doubt that ministers had requested and accepted large sums of money (totalling $350,000) from Sir Hugh Allan, and that Allan was the head of a "ring" which hoped to get a charter from that government. On the other hand it was argued that subscriptions to election funds were common practice. In his evidence before the commission Macdonald admitted that Allan had a personal interest in the result of the election in that his steamship line and other railway interests called for a Pacific railway, which a new government might drop. But, Macdonald stated, Allan knew that his company could not be left out; and he knew that a purely Quebec group would not get a charter. An understanding had been reached between Allan and Cartier at the end of July 1872 that if the attempt at amalgamation failed, Allan's company should get the charter. This unfortunate step, which Macdonald attributed to the "failing health and waning mental faculties" of Cartier, was immediately repudiated. To be exact, the company which received the charter was an entirely new one, formed after the election. It is not surprising, however, that the opposition were struck by the fact that Allan was still president.

The effects of the "Pacific scandal" on the progress of the Pacific railway project were disastrous. In the first place, the news of the early revelations reached England while the representatives of the new company were engaged in searching for capital. The delegation consisted of Sir Hugh Allan, the president, John Walker, vice-president, with Abbott and A. G. Archibald. The lack of success of earlier Canadian railways had made English investors wary of further schemes; the financial crisis of 1873 made railway securities less attractive; and the opposition of the powerful Grand Trunk group closed the doors of the English banking houses to the Canadian delegation. While, no doubt, the Grand Trunk was in any case none too friendly toward a Pacific railway in other hands, its stern opposition was accentuated or perhaps caused by Allan's personal interests, which he had tacked on to the mission. Macdonald, who was growing less and less confident in Allan ("the worst negotiator I ever saw in my life"), had foreseen some such trouble. "I fear," he wrote to Rose in telling him of the delegation, "that he will be attempting to fasten his North Shore Railway and the Northern Colonisation scheme upon the Pacific, and if he does he will of necessity arouse the opposition of all those interested in the Grand Trunk Railway."[41] In April Allan cabled Macdonald asking him to hold up a bill proposed by the Grand Trunk (the Grand Trunk Arrangements Act) as a means of putting pressure on that company.[42] On their side, the Grand Trunk officials offered to call off their dogs if the Allan lines were dropped. In Ottawa the government put what pressure it could on the Grand Trunk, but by that time the latter's efforts had been only too successful and all the ordinary channels were closed.

The only bite the delegation had in England was from McEwen, Grant and Company, a firm of financiers which had recently proposed to raise a large new issue of stock for the Grand Trunk. Alexander McEwen, who seems to have had a dashing financial career, drew up a memorandum – after discussions with the Canadian Pacific delegation in the middle of June – the purport of which was that he was ready to form a syndicate to purchase immediately $25,000,000 of bonds of the Canadian Pacific at 82½ per cent of par value, to be followed by the purchase of a like amount at the same or a higher price, at the end of three years. As security the syndicate was to hold the government subsidy and land grant.[43] To his proposal the delegation and the directors of the Canadian Pacific agreed;[44] but the government were not satisfied either with the details or the security offered, and refused to sanction the agreement.[45] In the meantime, too, McEwen had found that his side of the bargain could not be maintained, partly, no doubt, owing to the lack of confidence which had arisen out of the revelations in Ottawa.

The decade of the sixties had held many important changes for the provinces of British North America. Confederation had been proposed and carried through, and with it a commitment to a railway connecting the Maritime with the central provinces. In the area to the west of Ontario two colonies which the Hudson's Bay Company had planted were fast growing beyond the stage of the fur trade, and the problem of their future, long of interest to Canada, became a matter of urgent importance. Both were added to the Dominion as the sixties changed to the seventies, but it was a constitutional union which could only be given life by the establishment of adequate communications. The plan of a railway to the Pacific, called logical by its advocates and ruinous by its opponents, for a time fell foul of party politics; but as the rings, the syndicates, the companies, and the charters melted away, a new chapter began in the history of the Pacific railway.

CHAPTER 8

The Building of the Pacific Railway

1. RAILWAY POLICY OF THE LIBERAL GOVERNMENT

The Liberal government which came into office late in 1873 – the first since confederation – was headed by Alexander Mackenzie, who, as well as being premier, assumed the added burden of minister of public works, which department then was responsible for railways. During the previous discussions in parliament of the Pacific railway the Liberals had pictured it as an impossible task for the Dominion to undertake in a short time; had urged that no additional burden be put on the taxpayer; and had encouraged its construction by private enterprise. On taking office they were obliged to pick up the Pacific railway question in the unfortunate state in which it had been left on the fall of the Macdonald government. The new policy was announced in 1874: a subsidy of $10,000 and 20,000 acres of land per mile. In reality, however, there was little hope of enticing private capital into the railway. The beginning of a period of depression made money tight; American capitalists would be unpopular for obvious reasons; and the British money-market had already refused a more tempting bait. In 1876 tenders were solicited in England and the United States for the construction and operation of all or part of the line, but only one offer was made, and that unsatisfactory. The opposition of the Grand Trunk and the suspicion of English investors continued to operate as they had five years earlier. In May 1878 Fleming wrote of a "memo. of information for the parties proposing to tender for the whole Pacific Railway."[1] but it is not clear as to who these were, and in any case nothing came of it. Whatever was done had to be done with the aid of the public exchequer, and $2,500,000 of a loan recently guaranteed by the British government was earmarked for this purpose.

True to their former views, the Liberals were not prepared to plunge into the construction immediately of a railway from central Canada to the Pacific. Indeed, in the previous four or five years, Conservatives as well as Liberals, experts and amateurs, had advocated communication to the Pacific first being established by making use of waterways and American railways. It was a reversion to this plan that the government now proposed. The most easterly link was to be made up of an existing railway, the Canada Central, from Ottawa to Pembroke, and a subsidized extension to Lake Nipissing. The line around Lake Superior was to be left for the time being, and a railway begun from Fort William to Selkirk, north of Winnipeg. A line was then to be built south to the American border, so as to connect with the American railways. Other sections were to be built as finances allowed.

The difference between the Conservative and Liberal policies in regard to a Pacific railway was essentially in the speed at which they were prepared to go ahead: the Conservative government had accepted a time limit for the whole line through Canadian territory; the Liberals were ready to accept such a line as the ultimate goal, but believed that it would have to wait. Their objection to rapid construction was partly on the ground that it entailed great immediate expenditure, and partly that haste would swell the total cost. While later generations may think of the government construction in the seventies as slow, to Mackenzie it seemed that the "enormous expenditure is caused by our break-neck pace. . . ."[2] In the meantime they proposed to provide temporary means of communication. The lines they undertook at once were portage railways between waterways or links with American lines. Neither the Conservative nor the Liberal party welcomed public ownership in principle, but both were obliged to have recourse to it in default of an alternative; and the Liberals chose public ownership for the Intercolonial, but perhaps again from necessity. The surveys were conducted by the same person and on the same principle throughout three administrations.

Defensible as it might be in the light of the conditions and knowledge of the day, the Liberal policy of cautious advance was bound to meet one obstacle in the agreement with British Columbia. Even before the Conservative party went out of power there had been demands from British Columbia to know why construction had not been started, which Macdonald answered by saying that the survey was under way as a necessary preliminary. Even apart from accumulated irritation the Liberal party was suspect because of its determined opposition to the time limit when the terms of union were being debated. Such suspicion in British Columbia was given added strength by the known anxiety of Mackenzie to reach a compromise, and by the influence of Edward Blake which was thrown more toward financial safety than concession. The people of the province felt that the promise of a railway was the chief inducement to enter the confederation; that no real efforts had been made to implement the promise; and that the Dominion government was hostile, and attempting to evade the commitment. The Liberal government, on the other hand, faced by a period of depression, was more than ever concerned with the financial burdens which rapid construction would entail. They clung to Macdonald's argument that "ten years" was not to be taken literally – indeed it could no longer be even promised – and sought to make the best compromise they could.

A dreary period of negotiations followed. Their success was further imperilled by divisions within each party to the dispute. In British Columbia the old rivalry between island and mainland had become focused on the western terminus of the railway. By the original agreement the Dominion was bound to build only as far as the seaboard. Before the preliminary surveys had advanced far enough to justify the selection of a terminus, Macdonald had rashly fastened on Esquimalt, near Victoria. This choice complicated the issue in two ways: it led to a demand for a railway between Esquimalt and Nanaimo, to which point on the island it was expected that bridges would cross from the mainland; and it so heightened the feeling between island and mainland that any change by the provincial government in the terms of union with Canada was rendered more difficult. In the Canadian parliament there was a division of feeling in the Liberal ranks between those who followed Mackenzie in his desire for an acceptable compromise and those who followed Blake in his fear of financial commitments.

Early in 1874 J. D. Edgar was sent as Canadian envoy to British Columbia. In confidential instructions Edgar was told to make it clear that the government was anxious to construct the railway, but that it was a physical impossibility to do so within the time set by the original agreement. He was to say that the Dominion was not bound to build beyond the coast of the mainland, and that any further extension (that is, the Nanaimo-Esquimalt line) "must entirely depend on the spirit shewn by themselves in assenting to a reasonable extension of time or a modification of the terms originally agreed to." He was further to remind the British Columbia government of the terms which they had originally proposed – terms which had been increased by the federal government only as "additional means of procuring extensive patronage immediately before the general election," even though those terms were then known to be "impossible of fulfilment."[3] After some discussion with the provincial authorities, Edgar offered an immediate railway from Esquimalt to Nanaimo, a road through the mainland, and a minimum expenditure of $1,500,000 annually on the portion of the railway in the province as soon as the road and surveys had been completed. G. A. Walkem, the premier, perhaps fearing the political consequences of a decision, questioned Edgar's right to negotiate, with the result that the latter returned to Ottawa. The next step was the despatch of a protest by Walkem to the British government, rehearsing the whole story from the point of view of British Columbia. Lord Carnarvon, the colonial secretary, had, even before its receipt, stepped into the breach by offering himself as arbitrator. To Mackenzie the offer was an embarrassment which he attempted to avoid, but in the end grudgingly accepted.[4] Carnarvon's award changed Edgar's terms in two respects: the Dominion was to spend $2,000,000 instead of $1,500,000 annually and to complete the railway by the end of 1890. Mackenzie then introduced a bill for the construction of the Esquimalt-Nanaimo Railway. In the commons the measure passed, though Blake, David Mills, and Thomas Moss voted against it. In the senate the bill was defeated on a closer vote, the opposition including two Liberals.

The failure of the bill produced in British Columbia an outcry, and in Ottawa a party crisis. Mackenzie felt it necessary to bring Blake back into the cabinet to heal the division in the party, but Blake would only return on a modification of the government's policy in regard to the whole Pacific railway question. R. J. Cartwright, the minister of finance, seems to have thrown his weight in the direction of the new policy advocated by Blake. Agreement was reached in September 1875. The government was to return to the meaningless formula that the rate of taxation should not be increased; the Esquimalt-Nanaimo Railway was dropped as a federal work; and "the compensation to be given them by Canada for any delays which may take place in the construction of the Pacific Railway should be in the form of a cash bonus to be applied towards the local Railway or such other local works as the Legislature of British Columbia may undertake. . . ."[5] The amount of the bonus was fixed at $750,000, but this ingenious method of at once avoiding the building of the island railway and buying off further criticisms of delay on the main line could hardly have been expected to be palatable to British Columbia.

British Columbia at once disputed the whole position taken by the Dominion government, and appealed to the colonial office. Carnarvon once more offered himself as arbitrator, an offer which Mackenzie sought vainly to escape. Having restored unity within his party, he now found himself at odds with the governor general, who was taking an active – to Mackenzie's mind a too active – part in the unfortunate controversy. In the summer of 1876 the governor general, Lord Dufferin, went to British Columbia to judge the local situation. On his return he sought to transfer the negotiations to London, but to this Mackenzie was unalterably opposed and threatened to resign. Dufferin was obliged to come into line with the policy of his ministers, and Carnarvon threw cold water on the claims of British Columbia. In the spring of 1878 Walkem came back into office and celebrated his return by introducing into the legislature a resolution empowering the province to withdraw from confederation unless construction was begun by May 1879. Shortly after this a general election resulted in the defeat of the Mackenzie administration, and the Conservatives were faced with the solution of the problem that their earlier policy had caused. In the meantime the progress made on sections of the railway was, perhaps, greater than it appeared to the disappointed people of British Columbia. What had been done was modest indeed in comparison with the fair promises of 1870; yet through the period of economic depression and political controversy both surveys and construction on the Pacific railway had slowly but steadily gone forward.

2. GOVERNMENT SURVEYS AND CONSTRUCTION

In telling the story of the Canadian Pacific Railway, emphasis has usually been laid on the period beginning with the formation in 1880 of the company which carried the project to completion. While it is true that the five years beginning with that date saw the major part of the work constructed, and that with remarkable speed, it is proper to bear in mind the necessary spadework of the previous ten years. The heaviest burden of both surveys and construction up to 1880 fell on the broad shoulders of Sandford Fleming, a Scot who came to Canada at eighteen and entered the service of the Northern Railway, of which he became chief engineer twelve years later. After the completion of this railway he visited the Red River colony – for he was deeply interested in the future of the west – and a year later was appointed chief engineer for the surveys and construction of the Intercolonial. This task was only partially completed when he was asked in 1871 to assume the additional duties of engineer-in-chief of the Canadian Pacific Railway.

The surveys were begun promptly in 1871 and continued throughout the next several years. Fleming divided the field into three regions.[6] The eastern or woodland region was from the eastern terminus to the Red River. Much of this, like the rest of the survey, was work for the explorer as well as the engineer. "No civilized man," wrote Fleming, "as far as known, had ever passed from the valley of the Upper Ottawa through the intervening wilderness to Lake Superior. The country east and west of Lake Nipigon was all but a *terra incognita*." Nor was it country which looked hospitable to a railway. "All accounts of the country to be traversed by the railway, at least such portions of it as were, in any way, known, were unfavourable." In 1872 a favourable route was found north of Lake Nipigon, but this meant a long detour, and a line to the south was discovered in the following year. By a process of trial and error other portions of the route were provisionally located. (From Fort William east to Sudbury, Fleming's line was not much different from that adopted.) Attention was then directed from the Lake Superior area by the decision of the Liberal government to make temporary use of waterways. From Fort William the line chosen by

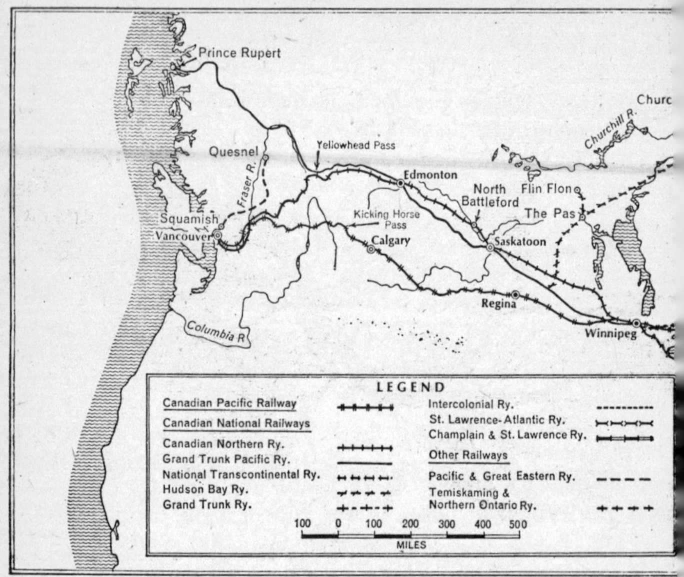

The Transcontinental Railways of Canada

Fleming ran slightly north of that eventually taken by the Canadian Pacific, and crossed the Red River at Selkirk instead of Winnipeg, as the former was thought to be the most favourable point for a bridge. In the woodland region, then, Fleming had been able to show the practicability of a line in Canadian territory, and had in fact traced the general route that was eventually followed.

The central or prairie region was that between the Red River and the boundary of British Columbia. Exploration by the imperial government indicated that no serious engineering problems would be encountered save the bridging of exceptionally wide and deep river channels. In addition to this consideration, Fleming had in mind the approach to a mountain pass, and the presence of water, timber, gravel, and land suitable for agriculture. In general he chose "the fertile belt," that is to say the northern route by the valley of the Saskatchewan River. His line at first ran from Selkirk to cross Lake Manitoba high up at the Narrows, but in 1880 this was changed to one south of the

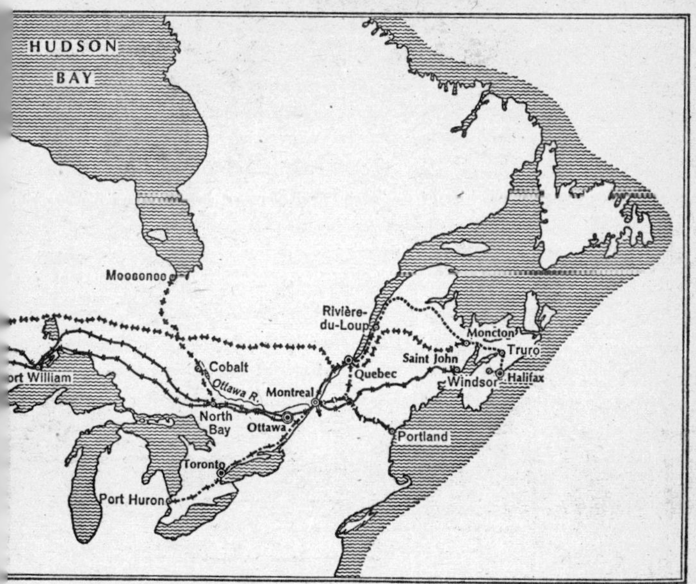

lake. From Lake Manitoba his route curved north-west to a point not far south of Edmonton, to which place it ran in a comparatively straight line. West of Edmonton he worked toward the Yellowhead Pass. Favourable gradients were found throughout. By 1880 the line through the prairie region had been sketched out, with the details of some sections to be determined. Fleming's line from Winnipeg to British Columbia was not that finally chosen for the Canadian Pacific, but blazed the trail for both the Canadian Northern and the Grand Trunk Pacific, the former following his route closely.

It was, naturally, in the western or mountain region that the greatest problems of the survey arose. They were of two kinds: one arose from local opinion which was sharply divided as to the western terminus; and the other was a straight engineering problem of how best to get from the east side of the Rockies to the Pacific coast. The chief difference of opinion in regard to the terminus was a part of the constant rivalry between mainland and island. If a southerly terminus were chosen at Burrard Inlet

(Vancouver), Victoria would lose its position as the major seaport, for only a ferry could be run across the Straits of Georgia at that point. The islanders, therefore, campaigned for Bute Inlet further north, whence bridges could be built to Nanaimo. The engineers were by no means agreed on this point. Marcus Smith, who was in charge in the British Columbia section, "found out about this Burrard Inlet mania which is a huge land job in which the minister and his friends are concerned,"[7] and over this he and Fleming had a sharp difference of opinion; but the latter remained unmoved in the decision which it will be seen he reached.

As far as is known Fleming was not influenced by local interests, and based his final recommendations on the result of years of careful investigation. The general problem is stated in his account of the first year's operations (1871).

At the commencement of the Survey, all the sources of information open to inquiry with regard to the passes through the Rocky Mountains, were consulted. After careful investigation it appeared that the two passes known as the Howse and the Yellow Head possessed advantages which, taken in conjunction with the approaches to them, as far as known, best warranted further examination.

By 1873 he could report that the Yellowhead Pass was the most eligible route yet discovered between the American border and the 53rd parallel of latitude. But the real problem was beyond Tête Jaune Cache on the western side of the pass. "It was . . . evident," he wrote, "that the obstacles which intervened between the passes and the coast of British Columbia were of a very serious character, and that the selection of a pass through the main Rocky Mountain range depended on the discovery of a practicable line across the whole mountain region." It was soon found that a line was practicable from Tête Jaune Cache by the Fraser River to the North Thompson, and probably on to Kamloops (whence Burrard Inlet could certainly be reached). Further investigation of this route, however, indicated that an "enormous outlay" would be required, and in 1872 a search was made for alternatives. The cariboo range clearly barred the direct approach to the coast, and no way could be found through it. By 1873 seven routes were reported. Parties ranged all over the mountains, finding possible variations and re-examining the early discoveries. In 1876 a winter survey was sent up the coast and found that of the various inlets or fiords, Gardner Inlet was ice-bound, Dean Inlet had been frozen for a time, but Bute Inlet not at all. By 1877 the possible routes had risen to ten. All began at the Yellowhead Pass. Two led to Burrard Inlet, one to Howe Sound, two to Bute Inlet, one to North Bentinck Arm, two to Dean Inlet, one to Gardner Inlet, and one to Port Essington (Prince Rupert).

Assuming that the Yellowhead Pass was to be utilized – and this was never seriously questioned – the routes could be reduced to two: to Bute Inlet or to Burrard Inlet. In 1878 Fleming gave his opinion.

Upon carefully viewing the engineering features of each route, and weighing every commercial consideration, I am forced to the conclusion that, if these alone are to govern a selection, if a decision cannot be postponed until further examination be made, if the construction of the railway must at once be proceeded with, the line to Vancouver Island should, for the present, be rejected, and that the Government should select the route by the Rivers Thompson and Fraser to Burrard Inlet.

He was fully conscious of the responsibility he was taking, and conscious, too, that his decision was not generally popular in British Columbia. His advice, however, was acted upon by the Mackenzie government, which, in the summer of 1878, accepted the route he recommended. Shortly afterwards Macdonald was again returned to power, cancelled the decision, and re-adopted it in 1879. Though this line by the Yellowhead Pass was later rejected for the Canadian Pacific, it was adopted by the Canadian Northern; while another route examined under Fleming's direction – that by the Fraser and Skeena rivers to Prince Rupert – was followed by the Grand Trunk Pacific. Eight years of pioneer work had not been wasted.

Before the surveys as a whole had been completed, construction began on those sections which had been finally located. The immediate purpose was to finish the parts which would, with waterways and American railways, afford access to the west, with a view to transporting materials for further construction and creating temporary facilities for commercial traffic. Thus work on the Pembina branch was started in 1874, and by 1878 the track was laid from Pembina to Selkirk, a distance of eighty-five miles. Amidst great excitement, a locomotive arrived at Winnipeg in 1877, having been brought down the Red River on barges. It had been built at Philadelphia and run by rail to Fargo, North Dakota, where it was put on board. The engine was primarily for construction on the Pembina branch, and was a welcome innovation, for all the early construction work was made more difficult by the impossibility of getting engines to the scene. Fort William was another strategic point, for from there the St. Lawrence could be reached by boat, or a combination of boat and rail. Contracts for portions of the line between Fort William and Winnipeg began to be let in 1875. The third section which was attacked was in British Columbia, the difficult and expensive section between Yale and Savona's Ferry, where tunnels and other heavy rock work were necessary. Presumably the start in British Columbia was intended as much to placate local opinion as from any other reason. By 1880 the following sections were built or under contract:

Fort William to Selkirk	410	miles
Selkirk to Emerson	85	"
West of Red River	100	"
In British Columbia	127	"
Total	722	"

Rails were laid for 136 miles west of Fort William, and 90 miles east of Selkirk. Regular trains were running from Emerson to Cross Lake, a distance of 161 miles.

Such was the progress on the Pacific railway in ten years. The Canadian government was a long way from living up to its promises to British Columbia. The slow speed of construction aroused constant criticism, not only from the Conservatives who (up to 1878) condemned the general railway policy of the Liberals, but also on grounds of incompetence and mismanagement. Charges were also made of irregularities and extravagance. To examine the whole situation a royal commission was appointed in June 1880, consisting of G. M. Clark, a judge, Samuel Keefer, engineer, and Edward Miall, assistant commissioner of the department of inland revenue, and its report was published in three volumes in 1882.[8] The conclusions may be quoted in part as indicating the views reached on the efficiency of work under the government.

That the construction of the Canadian Pacific Railway was carried on as a Public Work at a sacrifice of money, time and efficiency.

That in this work numbers of persons were employed as government officials who were not efficient in the positions to which they were appointed, having been selected on party grounds, irrespective of the question whether their engagement would be advantageous to the public interest.

That during the progress of the undertaking, delays occurred which would not have occurred, but for the necessity of staying operations from time to time until the necessary appropriations were made by Parliament.

That the examination of the country over which the line was located was inadequate, failing to give to the Government that information which could have been given, and which was necessary to enable the Government to estimate, with reasonable accuracy, the probable cost of the railway.

That large operations were carried on and extensive purchases made with much less regard to economy than would have happened under similar circumstances in a private undertaking.

That the practice which permits a Department to originate and enter upon transactions involving the expenditure of large sums of money, and, without other authority, to award the contracts under which such expenditure is intended to take place, is a disadvantage.

That the system under which the contracts were let was not calculated to secure the works at the lowest price or the earliest date; it pledged the Department to treat with tenderers irrespective of their good faith or financial strength, upon the single test of a deposit of money, so small as to be useless as a guarantee, the possible efficacy of this being neutralized by the invariable practice of returning his deposit to each defaulter. Such a system promises to every tenderer a position which he risks nothing to procure, and which he may at his option abandon, or retain, or sell if he can.

In his evidence Fleming stated that positions under him were filled by political patronage, and that the railway could have been constructed more efficiently and more cheaply by a private company. The total expenditure by the government from 1871 to 1879 had been $14,287,824, and it was shown that a number of the contracts had vastly exceeded the estimates. Fleming himself had been overworked, his health had suffered, and he had been obliged to take leave of absence. On his return in 1878 he found the staff demoralized and many branches of the work in a state of confusion.[9] He was, however, criticized, and finally (in March 1880) charges were made against him in the house. By an order in council of May 22 he was removed from office as engineer-in-chief, and refused to accept the position of consulting engineer, offered as a sop.[10] Probably Fleming must be regarded as the inevitable victim of a not very successful experiment in government construction by easy stages, though a comparison must not be too quickly drawn; for the very appointment of a commission may to some extent have been a party move to throw discredit on a previous administration.

3. THE CANADIAN PACIFIC RAILWAY COMPANY

For more than two years after coming into office the Conservative government continued the policy of governmental construction, but probably more from necessity than choice. Sir Charles Tupper, who became minister of public works in 1878 and minister of railways on the establishment of a separate department in the following year, seems to have consistently believed in private ownership. "I have, at some risk of separating myself from a portion of our press and party, persistently denounced the policy of constructing the C.P.R. as a Gov't work, and maintained that the terms of the Resolution moved by Sir G. Cartier relieved Canada from any such obligation."[11] This letter was written in 1876 while his party was in opposition, and presumably he nursed the same sentiments in the years 1878 to 1880. It is probable that the new government investigated the possibilities of a private company early in its period of office, but recognized the obstacles to this course. In 1879 the government proposed to institute a commission, including representatives of the imperial government, who should hold a very large amount of land for sale, the proceeds to pay for the construction of the railway. A mission was sent to England, but the British government was not willing to take any part. So bleak was the prospect that in April 1880 D. L. Macpherson advocated stopping work in British Columbia.

Shortly after this active negotiations began with at least two groups of capitalists. One was a partly Canadian group of which D. J. McIntyre and George Stephen were the spokesmen. The tradition is that J. H. Pope suggested to Macdonald that he should get in touch with Stephen and his associates in the St. Paul, Minneapolis and Manitoba Railway. In June McIntyre received a confidential memorandum from the government to which he suggested some modifications.[12] The government, however, stuck to their terms, and McIntyre declared that negotiations were for the time being closed. The chief point of difference was that the government offered a subsidy of $20,000,000 while the capitalists they were dealing with asked for $26,500,000. Meanwhile an English group, headed by the Earl of Dunsmore and Puleston, Brown and Company, were also seeking a contract. They proposed to build the portions of the line not yet under contract and to own and operate the whole for a subsidy of $9,500 and 16,000 acres per mile.[13] The government, however, refused to come to any decision and it resolved to send a delegation of Macdonald, Tupper, and J. H. Pope to England, to receive any tenders and discuss terms. Sailing on July 10, they interviewed Sir Henry Tyler, president of the Grand Trunk, on arrival and proposed that his company should undertake the completion of the Pacific railway. Tyler, however, would not consider the proposal if it included a line from Fort William to Lake Nipissing, while the Canadians were determined to have a through rail route.[14] He clung to the old Grand Trunk argument for a line (their line) south of Lake Superior.

While the delegates were in London both the other groups of capitalists reopened negotiations. (Macdonald referred vaguely in the house of commons to other groups, but refused to disclose their identity.) The English group, who announced themselves associated with the French firm, the Société Générale, now offered to replace the subsidy with a bond issue of $65,000,000, each $100 bond to carry the right to 160 acres of farming land, the Dominion government to guarantee interest at four per cent for twelve years.[15] Apparently, however, the offer was not acceptable as nothing more was heard of it. In August McIntyre produced new terms by which he and his associates agreed to build the railway for $25,000,000 cash and twenty-five million acres of land for the 2,000 miles.[16] A confidential letter from Stephen to Macdonald, written just after the failure of the negotiations in Ottawa and just before Macdonald sailed for England, emphasized his attitude.

There are two ways which you can get the road built and operated: one by getting up a financial organization such as Allan contemplated and such as Jay Cooke & Co. got up for the construction of the Northern Pacific Railway – with what result I need not remind you. A scheme of this nature involves the issue of a large number of Bonds . . . the outcome of a plan of this character is that the real responsibility is transferred from the Company to the people who may be induced to buy the Bonds, while the Company or the projectors pocket a big profit at the start out of the proceeds. This, in the rough, is I fear the method any English financial organization is likely to follow. . . . The other plan, and the one I should have followed . . . would have been to limit the borrowing of money from the public to the smallest possible point . . . to have looked for a return of our own capital and a legitimate profit entirely to the growth of the country and the development of the property. . . .[17]

The government accepted the terms offered by McIntyre in London, and before the end of September the draft of the agreement was on paper. The contract was signed on October 21, and on December 10 brought down to parliament for approval. The quality of the railway was to be that of the Union Pacific as first constructed. The gauge was set at four feet eight and one-half inches. Those sections already built were to be handed over to the company, while others under contract – that is, from Kamloops to Port Moody and parts between Lake Superior and Selkirk – were to be completed by the government. The remainder was to be built by the company, and the whole was to be finished by 1891. Subsidies were to be on the terms suggested in the previous summer: $25,000,000 and 25,000,000 acres of land, both payable in instalments on the completion of each twenty miles of line; but the subsidies were unevenly distributed according to the difficulty of construction. The land granted was to be in alternate sections of 640 acres each, 24 miles deep on either side of the railway between Winnipeg and Jasper House. Land not fit for settlement was to be replaced elsewhere. Additional privileges were accorded to the company. Land for the road bed, shops, stations, and so on was to be granted. Materials for original construction might be imported free of duty. The railway with its grounds and buildings, "rolling stock and appurtenances" used for construction and operation, and the capital of the company were to be forever free from any taxation. The land grants were not to be taxed for twenty years, unless sold or occupied in the meantime. For twenty years no railway should be authorized south of the Canadian Pacific, except a line running south-west, but such a line might not continue to within fifteen miles of the border. Finally, the company was empowered to issue $25,000,000 in bonds secured upon the land granted. These bonds were to be held by the government, which might sell all but one-fifth and hand the proceeds to the company. By an attached schedule the Canadian Pacific Railway Company was incorporated with a capital stock of $25,000,000.

Montreal was heavily represented in the new company. The president was Sir George Stephen, who resigned as president of the Bank of Montreal to take the leading position in the railway. R. B. Angus, general manager of the same bank, became a member of the executive committee. The vice-president was D. J. McIntyre, manager of the Canada Central Railway, and his inclusion marked a further victory for Montreal since it indicated that the terminus of the Canadian Pacific would be at that city rather than at Toronto. The syndicate included no one from Ontario. There was, however, an important American connection. Both Stephen and Angus had made fortunes out of a startlingly successful enterprise in Minnesota, the St. Paul, Minneapolis and Manitoba Railway. Two of their associates in that railway, Donald Smith and J. J. Hill, were members of the original Canadian Pacific group. Smith was not at first a director because of a political quarrel with Macdonald, but he had great influence with Stephen, and continued in the councils of the company. Hill was for a time an influential director, but he never threw in his lot completely with the

Canadian Pacific. His prime motive in becoming a member of the syndicate was to secure business for the Minnesota railway. From the start he opposed the construction of a line to the north of Lake Superior,[18] and when this became a reality, he found it impossible to ride two horses at once and withdrew from the Canadian railway to create the Great Northern.

There is a superficial parallel between the connection of Sir Hugh Allan with the Northern Pacific group in 1872 and of Stephen with the St. Paul, Minneapolis and Manitoba railway in 1880. The most valid objection to the first was a fear that the interests of the Americans would lead them to treat the Canadian railway as a feeder rather than as a through line. It is not known exactly what their intentions were; nor is it known whether there is any reason to suspect that such motives existed in the syndicate of 1880, except in so far as Hill may have had some such purpose in mind. It is obvious, however, that the balance of power between the Canadian and American interests was different in 1880 from what it had been in 1872; and to preserve that balance the charter provided that the majority of the directors, of whom the president was to be one, were to be British subjects. Donald Smith was born in Scotland and was only temporarily a director of the Minnesota railway. J. J. Hill was born in Canada, but remained primarily interested in American railways. Through his Great Northern he carried on a vigorous rivalry with the American-born Van Horne, champion of the Canadian Pacific. W. C. Van Horne was born in Illinois. He became a telegraph operator in the Illinois Central at the age of fourteen; clerk in the Michigan Central; and ticket agent and telegraph operator in the Chicago and Alton. In this railway he rose rapidly, and was appointed superintendent of a new subsidiary, the St. Louis, Kansas City and Northern, with his headquarters at St. Louis. From this he became president and general manager of a bankrupt pioneer railway, the Southern Minnesota. Having restored this railway to health, he returned to the Chicago and Alton as superintendent, and thence to the Chicago, Milwaukee and St. Paul. There can have been few railwaymen in the United States with such a record of unbroken success in management. In 1881 he was recommended by Hill, whose territory touched Van Horne's, as the most suitable man to be general manager of the Canadian Pacific.

It was a choice which was to be richly justified. Several other members of the original staff were brought from American railways, their experience being of value to the Canadian Pacific which was built and operated under similar conditions. But the use of Americans on the Pacific railway did not originate with the syndicate, for Andrew Onderdonk had received the government's contract for the British Columbia section. Neither in executive officers, contractors nor financiers did Great Britain play a part in the Canadian Pacific similar to that in the Grand Trunk. London, however, was represented financially by Morton, Rose and Company, and the continent by Kohn, Reinach and Company of Paris and Frankfort, and the Société Générale.

The introduction of the agreement into the house of commons in December 1880 was the signal for a long debate.[19] Tupper, who as minister of railways introduced the subject, sought to show that the terms were the best that had been obtained in the history of the Pacific railway, and by a long series of quotations from earlier speeches by leading members of the opposition attempted to take the ground from under their feet. In reality, however, no exact comparison could be made owing to the fact that a portion of the railway was built or being built by the government – a point that for some reason was not stressed by the opposition. On other grounds the Liberals strenuously opposed the bill. Edward Blake, now leader of the opposition, characterized it as "not merely fraught with great danger, but certain to prove disastrous to the future of this country." His attitude was not inconsistent with his previous alarm about committing the country to an immediate realization of the Pacific project. He remained opposed to a line north of Lake Superior, arguing that it was wiser to make use of American territory, just as Americans shipped goods through Canada. On the whole, however, the Liberals were hampered in debate by their act of 1874, and could only oppose individual sections of the terms under discussion. They proposed amendment after amendment, each of which was voted down with machine-like efficiency by the serried ranks of the Conservatives.

One or two of the points raised in the debate have more than passing importance. An objection that was bound to arise was to the position given to Montreal not only in the personnel of the company, but also in the use of the Canada Central which would give direct connection with Montreal. The old division of 1872 between the interests of Ontario and Quebec was revived, and again a rival company – the heir of the Inter-oceanic – was organized. Its directorate included many men prominent in business, principally in Ontario: Sir William Howland, A. R. McMaster, William Hendrie, J. P. Proctor, G. W. Cox, P. Larkin, and a number of others. They offered to build the railway for $22,000,000 and 22,000,000 acres of land, and to forego exemption from duties on materials, from taxation on lands, and the clause forbidding construction south of their line. On the face of it, it was a much better offer, but the government claimed that it was purely a party move, and that it was too late to change. (In this connection it may be noted that the government had consistently refused to reveal anything concerning the negotiations with the chosen syndicate or any other group.) The only modification that Ontario could secure was a clause allowing to the Ontario and Pacific Junction Railway – which corresponded in Ontario to the Canada Central – "all reasonable facilities . . . when their railway shall be completed to a point of junction with the Canadian Pacific Railway and the Canada Central Railway for the receiving, forwarding and delivering of traffic upon and from the railways of the said companies." It may be deduced from this episode that the Conservative government of 1880 could charter a Quebec group when the Conservative government of 1873 could not. Or was it that the American bogey was the real obstacle standing between Allan's company and the charter? It is an interesting political study.

A side of the agreement that was to have more obvious repercussions in the future was the use of large-scale land grants in lieu of additional money subsidies, or guarantee of bonds. The Liberals fulminated against the exemption of the lands from taxation, but that was only part of a larger issue. The effect of the grant of land to the Canadian Pacific, added to the already large grants made to the Hudson's Bay Company, was to remove from the control of the government an enormous area which might have been used either for the free homestead system or as a source of revenue. It is not surprising that the vast area of the west seemed unlimited: and it was easy to argue that the land granted would be sold at low rates to settlers, whose coming in any case hinged on the existence of a railway. All this might be true, but a large portion of the fertile land found its way into the possession of two private companies.

The Liberals could not criticize the system of land subsidies as such, for this system had become an accepted method of dealing with the Pacific railway. The origin of the land subsidy policy, like not a few things connected with Canadian railways, is to be found in the United States,[20] where the idea of land grants in assistance of railways had first been put into practice about the middle of the century, and in the following twenty years some 150,000,000 acres had been granted to western railways. Opinion slowly veered against the policy, however, and by 1871 it was abandoned. This was just the time when it was first adopted in Canada, for, although grants had been passed for railways, none had actually been made. With a view to grants to both the Hudson's Bay Company and the Pacific railways, power over the natural resources of Manitoba and the North West Territories was vested in the Dominion. Macdonald's Railway Act of 1872 allowed for the granting of 50,000,000 acres in aid of a Pacific railway, but the lands were to be located in large blocks instead of in alternate sections as had been the practice in the United States. The Canadian Pacific of 1873 (the amalgamated company) was also to receive 50,000,000 acres, and was for the first time permitted to refuse any land "not of the fair average quality of land in the sections of the country best adapted for settlement." Mackenzie's act of 1874 provided for the granting of 20,000 acres per mile of railway in smaller blocks, but it never became operative. On returning to power in 1878 the Conservatives obtained from parliament power to appropriate 100,000,000 acres in aid of the railway, but this act also became a dead letter. In the meantime the plan for allotting the land was made similar to the American practice of alternate sections.

Such was the background of the land subsidy policy which was first carried into effect in 1881. It is probable that no other expedient could have been found at the time. Apart from the importance of their land holdings to the Canadian Pacific Railway Company, the origin of the land-granting system is important, for it was carried much further before it was abandoned. But no later through line, as such, received grants of land.

The debate on the agreement with the syndicate, long as it was carried on, ended only with the passage of an act embodying the terms, virtually unchanged. In one sense it was regrettable that the Liberals, by their continued criticisms, should have been judged as hostile to the Canadian Pacific Railway Company, for out of this was to come much evil: charges of undue influence in elections, and a growing feeling in the Liberal party that a counterweight to the Canadian Pacific Railway must be found. Yet the results of their opposition were not entirely negative, for in the next twenty years they were to develop a Liberal railway policy which in some respects reflected their criticisms made in 1880.

4. COMPLETION OF THE PACIFIC RAILWAY

The tale of the completion of the Pacific railway by the company is one that has more than once been told in terms of hardships faced and problems overcome.[21] That such an approach has incidentally tended to shadow the no less great hardships and problems of the surveys and construction carried out by the government's engineers is unfortunate; but the slow progress made in the years 1871 to 1880 must pale as a story beside the dynamic energy and rapid achievement of 1881 to 1885. The rocks and marshes north of Lake Superior, the chasms of the prairie rivers, and the forbidding mountains of British Columbia were obstacles that offered battle to the stoutest hearts. Perhaps the surveyor, beset with flies and mosquitoes, hacking a way for the transit and chain, the construction gang toiling in the heat of a Canadian summer, or the superintendent harassed by shortage of supplies, may have failed at the time to see the romance of their tasks. Yet romance it was; and even these men, so beset by immediate discomfort and difficulty, must have paused at the end of a day to look upon their work and see that it was good. But since the adventurous side of the building of the railway has been told, and well told, it will be best to look at the period from somewhat different and more prosaic angles.

The contract of 1880 provided that the route to be followed was that already chosen by the government: from Callander at the east end of Lake Nipissing, over the north shore of Lake Superior to Selkirk, via Edmonton to the Yellowhead Pass, and through the North Thompson and Fraser valleys to Port Moody on Burrard Inlet. Actually only a part of this was adopted by the Canadian Pacific, and even where it was followed in general, considerable changes were made in detail. Van Horne's biographer states that Hill and Stephen had not intended that the Lake Superior section should be built as early as the rest, if at all; that in the meantime they planned a connection with a branch of the St. Paul, Minneapolis and Manitoba at Sault Ste. Marie; that it was Van Horne who encouraged the government to proceed with the Lake Superior section at once; and that it was this decision that led Hill – who had hoped to have virtual control of the Canadian Pacific – to withdraw from the company.[22] If this interpretation be true of the period after the first signing of the agreement, it can only be assumed either that Hill (and perhaps Stephen) hoped to avoid building the Lake Superior section for an indefinite period, or intended to secure a change in the charter later. Either move might have received support from a number of Liberals, but it seems improbable that parliament or public as a whole would have agreed to anything but an all-Canadian route. The Conservative delegation to England in 1880 had broken off negotiations with the Grand Trunk on that issue. There is little evidence to settle the point. In making comments on the contract, McIntyre, Angus, and Abbott dealt with the need of protection from foreign railways, and pointed out that traffic must run east and west. Any lines to the boundary, they wrote, would only be to draw traffic to the Canadian Pacific Railway.[23] Stephen, who was indignant at the attitude of the opposition in parliament, wrote to Macdonald that "the real control and government of this enterprise will be in the hands of Angus, Kennedy, McIntyre and myself, and I think personally I can carry with me the support of our London and Paris associates, so you see there is no danger of the control getting into the hands of our St. Paul friends."[24]

Whatever may have been the internal dissensions within the syndicate, or their private plans, it is certain that work was begun on the line west from Callander in 1882. The company's engineers found it desirable to relocate in detail a considerable portion of this section, authority for which was secured by periodic orders in council. In 1882 some eighty miles of the way were located, a few miles of line laid, and some bridges built; but still there was suspicion that the company was not serious about its work.

I am well aware [wrote Stephen] *of the* pretention *to uneasiness on the part of the (friends) of the Gov't. in Press and elsewhere, not excluding the Cabinet, lest we should turn out a pack of rogues and "lie down" on the Lake Superior section having made a lot of money out of the construction of the line in the central section, leave the Gov't to furnish the Lake Superior section and the Rocky Mountain section and so get rid of the thing. . . .*

I take it for granted that our worst enemy will not pretend to say we have not pushed the work on the main line with energy. The Globe *says we are building it too fast. I claim we have been equally energetic on the eastern section and have relatively accomplished as much work – real work though it does not "hulk" in the public eye. You will not forget that we had to begin de novo. The locations and surveys of the Gov't were useless to us, and I have learnt enough of Railroad building to appreciate this fact, that the moment your line is finally located, your money is gone, that is, it has only to be paid out. The amount is settled by your engineer when he has located the line. . . .*[25]

Following Fleming's advice, the Canadian Pacific Railway chose a line near the shore of the lake, rather than on the height of land. It was difficult country, rocky and marshy, and without local traffic, but allowed for rapid construction by its proximity to water transportation. Added to other difficulties was that of transportation of supplies, which Van Horne solved by shipping materials by rail to Owen Sound and thence by water. In winter rough roads were used. The progress of the Canadian Pacific Railway in the whole eastern section (Callander to Winnipeg) can best be seen from a few figures.

1883: 100 miles completed west of Callander; 35 miles completed near Port Arthur; trains running between Port

Arthur and Red River (the government-built section).
1884: track laid for 403 out of 657 miles between Callander and Port Arthur; 193 miles in addition graded; train service between Callander and Sudbury.
1885: rail completed in May; passenger service in November.

The central or prairie section, from Winnipeg to Kamloops, was constructed almost entirely by the company. Here the change in route was complete, consequent on the decision to adopt a southerly line. One of the reasons given for the change was that the line could in this way be shortened, but a more fundamental consideration was the desire to be closer to the American border. Such a position would bring two benefits: it would enable the company to compete for American traffic, and protect its American connections after the twenty-year restrictions had run out. It is also possible that Donald Smith's influence was thrown in favour of a southern route in order to protect the northern fur country from invasion. Furthermore, the company may have been influenced by the consideration that the grains then available would not ripen quickly enough to make a safe crop in the more northern part of the prairies. Thus the line was directed toward Calgary rather than Edmonton. It was commonly supposed to be a comparatively simple task to build a railway over the prairie – and was simple compared with other sections – but Stephen claimed that conditions were not so easy as they had been represented to be: "The so-called Prairie section is not prairie at all, it is a broken, rolling country, with a great deal of heavy work, and the line we are building is a very different thing from the standard fixed and costing double the price of a poor Prairie road."[26] Large parts of the prairie, however, were easy going, and the company was able to show quick results. In the first summer, 1881, only a modest hundred miles were completed, but in the second season the company was determined to build five hundred miles – an objective which seemed impossible to attain. In the summer of 1882 five thousand men and seventeen hundred teams were at work. Night gangs were put on the bridges, and to bring up the rails and lumber. The five-hundred mark was not quite reached that year, but by June 1883 the track was laid as far as the summit of the Rockies.

The choice of a southern route necessitated the abandonment of the Yellowhead Pass. In 1881 this change was decided on, and in 1882 an act was passed enabling the company to build through a pass other than the Yellowhead, provided it was not less than one hundred miles from the boundary (45 Vict., c. 53). The junction with the government-built section would, as before, be made at Kamloops. To reach this point it was necessary to cross two ranges of mountains – the Rockies and the Selkirks. Through the first a comparatively satisfactory pass, the Kicking Horse, had been found. It entailed a grade that was heavy compared to the easy ascent at the Yellowhead; but the company was willing to accept this added cost of operation rather than go so far north. But on the other side of the Rockies lay the great rounded slopes of the Selkirks, through which no way had yet been discovered. Major Rogers, an American engineer, was sent to reconnoitre, but 1881 passed with Rogers optimistic but unsuccessful. In the meantime the railway was approaching the mountain, and unless the Selkirks could be pierced a long detour by the Columbia River would have to be taken. In the summer of 1882, however, Rogers at last found the pass (named after him) and it became possible to follow the direct line.

A good deal of heavy work – tunnels, trestles and blasting – was unavoidable through the mountains. To hasten the completion of the line the company was empowered to construct a temporary line for some nine miles. Of Van Horne, who was furiously working to get the line completed, a characteristic story is told which may be repeated here. A locating engineer was called to his office, and pointing to a profile, Van Horne said, "some infernal idiot has put a tunnel in there. I want you to go and take it out." Asked how long it would take to build, the engineer suggested a year or eighteen months. "What are they thinking about?" roared the general manager, "Are we going to hold up this railway for a year and a half while they build their damned tunnel? Take it out." Another way was found.[27]

In October 1885 the line was open for traffic up to the east slope of the Rockies, and by November rail connection was established from Montreal to Port Moody (2,893 miles). From Kamloops to Port Moody was the section constructed by the government, and part of this, near Yale, had been difficult and heavy work. During the early eighties, therefore, the British Columbia section was being constructed partly by the company and partly by the government. The whole was, of course, to be operated by the company: the government-built section to be handed over as part of the original agreement, the company accepting it "subject to the adjustment and correction by the Government of any defects or deficiencies in the construction thereof, if any, according to the specifications and conditions of the contracts therefor, except, in so far as the same were modified by the Government prior to October twenty-first, 1880." When the section was duly handed over the company protested that it had not been built according to specifications, and to settle the dispute that arose an arbitration board was set up by order in council in January 1888. Van Horne asserted to the board that the road was not safe for use,[28] while Schreiber, the government's chief engineer, admitted, according to Van Horne's account, that the road was not as described in the contract or specifications.[29] The government, however, contended that their section was better built than that of the company; but nevertheless J. H. Pope (minister of railways) insisted that it should be examined, in accordance with the Railway Act. The arbitration proceedings dragged on until 1891, the delay, according to Stephen, being engineered by the government "to put the Company to all the loss and inconveniences that delay involves."[30] The award was made in October 1891 and named $579,255 as the sum payable by the government, representing the cost of work that should have been done on the road. The Canadian Pacific Railway had claimed $12,000,000.

While Van Horne had been directing the work of construction on the spot, and Shaughnessy[31] was in charge of sending out the enormous amounts of supplies that were needed, Stephen and Donald Smith were struggling to provide the sinews of war. Owing to the speed of construction the sums of money annually required by the company were very large and not easy to raise. Since it had been decided not to finance construction by the sale of bonds, there were left four main sources of revenue: sale of lands, sale of land-grant bonds, sale of stock, and the government subsidy. Had the first three of these consistently realized good prices there would have been no great problem, but they were far from doing so. There were a number of factors operating to depress prices: a lingering suspicion of Canadian railway securities; stories of the inhospitable climate, poor soil and doubtful future of the Canadian west; and the bankruptcy of the Northern Pacific in 1883. Enemies of the Canadian Pacific did their best to exploit such factors with a view to smashing or crippling the new railway. In England the wide influence of the Grand Trunk was once more directed against a potential rival, and the English public, who were more interested in Barnum's elephant, Jumbo, than in Canada, were supplied with news tending to show that the west was unsuitable for settlement.[32] (It is ironic that poor Jumbo was later killed by a Grand Trunk engine.) "The worst feature for us in Canada is that there is hardly a newspaper in the whole country which is in a position to say a word against the G.T.R. no matter what it may say or do against the country – without losing Hickson's advertizing."[33] At the same time the New York market was hostile, it is said because of the propaganda of Hill's and the other railways of the American north-west. The stock dropped from par to forty. Various expedients were adopted to keep going, but by the end of 1883 Stephen was almost in despair. "Things have gone to the d – l in New York," he wrote, "something must be done at *once* to put the company out of discredit or we better give up and let the govt step in and carry on the business of the company. . . . Things have now reached a pass when we must either stop or find the means of going on. Our enemies here and elsewhere think they can now break us down or finish the C.P.R. for ever."[34]

The cost of construction was mounting far beyond the estimates. Ten years earlier Fleming had put the cost of construction and equipment at $100,000,000, but it had become obvious that this would not nearly meet the bill. The company was thus thrown back on the government for support; and while in his more depressed moments Stephen bitterly reproached Macdonald for lack of support, the company would have failed time after time if it had not been carried over crises by public funds. But it was no simple matter to provide constant loans. The cabinet was divided in regard to the Canadian Pacific Railway. Tupper was a staunch believer, but Campbell, McLelan, and Mackenzie Bowell were, at least on one occasion, opposed to further relief.[35] Parliament was equally uncertain, and Macdonald could not assume an automatic majority for Pacific loans. An influential section of the press, too, constantly sounded warnings of the danger of unlimited credit to the company. There were suspicions that the recurrent crises in the finances of the Canadian Pacific were magnified in order to induce further governmental assistance. In the end the government always made the required loans, but it seems that Macdonald grew wearied of Stephen's constant importunities and was not willing to move until he was sure that it was necessary. Tupper, on the other hand, appears to have been more ready to accept the company's account of its own position; and when the time came for putting loans through parliament, he was invaluable. At the end of 1883 he was hurriedly called back from England, and obtained from the commons a loan of $22,500,000 for four years at four per cent, secured by a first lien on the main line. The company subsequently (March) agreed to complete its line by 1886 instead of 1891 – a declaration which was valuable to stem the rising tide of opposition. In the meantime the company was living from hand to mouth. Large advances from the Bank of Montreal had to be covered by collateral security put up by Stephen and Smith, and Stephen said that he was afraid to ask for more lest there should be "a bear raid on the Bank stock, on the ground of heavy advances to the C.P.R. without adequate cover."[36]

One financial crisis succeeded another. The heavy expenses of 1884 brought the company once more to the end of its resources. In December the men struck for their pay at Port Arthur. More money was needed. Macdonald was alarmed at further demands, for the previous loan was to have been the last, and too much pressure on parliament would mean the collapse of the government – and with it the C.P.R. He talked over the situation in London with Tupper, now high commissioner, and Tupper wrote a reasoned statement to the minister of finance, Sir Leonard Tilley, in which he confessed that he was disappointed that further assistance was required, but argued that either the government must take over the road and run it – to which he was opposed – or "meet the difficulty caused by the complete collapse of the credit of the Co." He advocated cancelling the $35,000,000 of unissued stock, and providing for

$40,000,000 of first mortgage bonds, taking $30,000,000 in payment of the loan, giving $5,000,000 to the company and holding the remaining $5,000,000 for future needs of the road.[37] Sir John Rose gave much the same advice, pointing out that it was not a good time to raise money.[38] Stephen was afraid that "the patient will die while the doctors are deliberating on the remedy to be applied," but managed another advance from the bank, secured on his and Smith's securities.[39] In March he reported that the company was still in the "greatest straits," and in April Van Horne telegraphed that he had no money with which to pay wages.

All during the spring it seems to have been touch and go. The Bank of Montreal's last loan had covered the April dividend, but the stock was driven down to 34, and complaints were being made of wages unpaid. In March Stephen formally wrote to the prime minister asking for terms very similar to those sketched out by Tupper, and including the $5,000,000 loan. Macdonald was undecided. Could he again persuade parliament? A sign was needed, and happily provided in the ability of the Canadian Pacific Railway to transport troops to put down the North-West Rebellion. Until navigation opened on the lakes there was no feasible means of getting troops rapidly to the west. Seeing the possibilities of the situation, Van Horne offered to transport troops from Ottawa to Qu'Appelle in eleven or twelve days. It was the kind of problem of organization in which he revelled, and, although there were still gaps in the line, he had two batteries at Winnipeg in four days from the time they left Ottawa. Whether it was because of this demonstration or other influences within the cabinet, the government finally acceded to the company's request. Macdonald got the measure through the caucus, with the loss of A. W. McLelan, minister of marine and fisheries. In July the bill was finally passed. The terms were somewhat more favourable than Tupper had first suggested. The stock in the hands of the government was cancelled, and $35,000,000 of first mortgage bonds created in its place. Of this $15,000,000 was credited to the company, and the balance held against an equal amount of the companly's debt to the government. The remainder of the debt – $9,880,000 – was secured on the unsold and unpledged lands of the company. Of the company's share $8,000,000 was held by the government against a loan of

$5,000,000 cash. The financial standing of the company was strengthened by the purchase by Barings of $3,000,000 of bonds at 90; and while only about one-half of these were taken by the public, the fact that Barings and their friends were holding the rest was not disclosed. The price was maintained at about 96.[40]

It had been a near thing, but at last the company was out of the woods, and in the summer of 1886 the entire debt to the government was paid off. With the knowledge of later years it was easy to cast scorn on the doubts of those who opposed the Pacific railway in the form in which the Conservative government had begun it, and easy to criticize those – Liberal and Conservative – who lost heart while construction was making ever-increasing demands on the exchequer. But to all but a few enthusiasts it was always, or became, a hazardous experiment. A thinly populated east throwing a railway over two thousand miles of almost uninhabited country was not to be taken lightly. And it is only fair to remember that the same controversy arose over the later transcontinental lines, and while the optimists again won the day, the country was later bitterly to regret a Pyrrhic victory. No little credit is due to the Canadian Pacific group – or to those of them who stuck to their task – led by Stephen, Smith, Van Horne, and Shaughnessy, who had the courage to risk their fortunes and their reputations in what not once, but many times, seemed a hopeless cause. And credit, too, is due to the government which (in the face of strong opposition, and under the shadow of disastrous failure) made it possible for the railway builders to complete their work. Perhaps it was partly fear of the political consequences that led the majority in the cabinet to keep their hand to the plough; yet Macdonald, with as keen a political sense as has been seen in Canada, feared a hostile vote in the house of commons. The completion of the most daring enterprise undertaken by the Dominion was made possible only by a successful (if somewhat tempestuous) marriage of private enterprise with public support. Without the first the railway had languished: without the second it must have crashed into bankruptcy.

November 7, 1885. "The first train from Montreal is approaching Yale, within a few hours of the Pacific coast. The last spike was driven this morning by Honourable Donald Smith at Craigellachie, in Eagle Pass, some 340 miles from Port Moody.

On reaching the coast, our running time from Montreal, exclusive of stoppages, will be five days, averaging twenty-four miles per hour."

And so a prophecy was fulfilled. By the writer, surveyor, navvy, politician, financier, and engineer, it was brought to pass that they should have dominion from sea to sea.

CHAPTER 5

Consequences of the Pacific Railway

1. EFFECT ON THE GENERAL POSITION

The first train that ran from Montreal to the Pacific coast was the herald of a new era in the history of Canadian railways, an era that was marked by two main characteristics: the development of transcontinental traffic across Canada; and active competition between large companies, which in the course of that competition absorbed the smaller lines. From these twin impulses came a growth in railways that was all the more remarkable in that it came under conditions which were far from being uniformly favourable. Broadly speaking, the period from confederation to the turn of the century saw a series of economic depressions, the spaces between which were all too brief. Population increased at a sedate pace from 3,689,257 in 1871 to 4,833,239 in 1891. The number of immigrants, which was only 27,773 in 1871, and never reached high figures in the next ten years, jumped to over 100,000 in each of 1882, 1883, and 1884, that is, the years in which the main work of construction on the Canadian Pacific Railway was under way. Canada was still predominantly an agricultural country, sixty-eight per cent of the population living outside towns in 1891. The area of occupied farms increased from 36,046,401 acres in 1871 to 58,997,995 in 1891 – the increased rate of settlement corresponding to the rise in immigration, both of which were primarily due to the opening of farming areas in the west. By 1891 the annual value of mineral production was still slightly less than $19,000,000, and the lumber trade was steadily advancing. Although the larger part of the population was still rural, the chief change that was taking place in the Canadian economy was the gradual increase of urban areas and of the industrial concerns on which they depended. The "national policy" of 1878 was designed to raise the tariff against imports sufficiently to protect infant industries, and this policy was modified rather than altered by the Liberal administrations after 1896. In the twenty years from 1870 to 1890 the gross value of manufactured goods mounted from $221,617,773 to $481,053,375.

The growth of railways did not spring from an existing prosperity but from a belief, generally held, that Canada could progress only if an adequate transportation system was built up. This belief was translated into concrete terms by the willingness of the legislatures to render financial assistance. Cities made substantial grants. The provinces of Quebec and Ontario adopted, in 1869 and 1871 respectively, policies of subsidies to local railways, either in money or in land. In 1882 the Dominion government introduced its own subsidy policy, which in effect replaced those of the provinces. The measure provided for a grant of $3,200 a mile (the cost of steel rails) to selected railways distributed amongst the four original provinces. Two years later the system was extended to the western provinces, land taking the place of cash. Payments made under the subsidy policy, which were in some cases higher than the general rate, averaged one million dollars a year. A drawback to this method of encouragement was that it tended to be directed by sectional or party interests rather than by genuine needs. A further objection was that investors were mistakenly reassured by the stamp of government approval apparently involved in a subsidy. A company which received $400,000 in subsidies stimulated the sale of $500,000 of its bonds in England by a statement that the capacity of the road was taxed to the utmost. The equipment of the company consisted of two engines, one passenger car, two box cars, fifteen flat cars, and a snow-plough![1]

Government support, however, did not mean government ownership. The experience of governmental construction on the Pacific railway had not been a happy one, and for a time discouraged all further experiments except in additions to the Intercolonial. Both the Grand Trunk and Great Western offered to sell out to the government, but their offers were firmly refused. "We have a sufficiently big elephant in the Pacific Railway," wrote Blake, "without undertaking to become the proprietors of other lines. . . . Mr. Childers [president of the

Great Western] may be right in his view that Canadian credit will suffer somewhat by calamities overtaking private corporations, but I am sure it would suffer much more by our purchasing great railways which are known to be in very great straits."[2] The tendency was toward private companies assisted by public funds. Such companies, however, were subject to an increasing degree of regulation. The first federal statute applying to all railways chartered by the Dominion, the Railway Act of 1868 (31 Vict., c. 68), was modelled on the province of Canada act of 1851. In addition to provisions similar to those of the latter, the act of 1868 included new ones: any company might make special traffic arrangements with another, but must also afford reasonable facilities to the remaining companies without discrimination. The interests of the country in a national emergency were protected by a clause which reserved for the government, when necessary, the exclusive use of both telegraphs and railways. Various penalties were provided for persons interfering with or damaging the property of a railway, and for officers of the company who contravened its by-laws.

For the continuous supervision of the private railway companies a special body was set up, the railway committee of the privy council, to consist of not less than four members, and whose particular duty it was to ensure the safe operation of the railways. No railway or portion of railway might be opened for traffic without a month's notice to the committee, which might then have an inspection made by the department of public works, and if necessary the opening of the line could be delayed. The committee might also have any railway examined when in operation, and – with the consent of the governor in council – condemn all or part of it. The inspecting engineer might also on his own authority stop the operation of a railway and report his action to the committee. Every railway was to contribute an amount, to be fixed by the committee and not to exceed $10 a mile, to the railway inspection fund. It must also make returns twice a year of all accidents. In 1886 the control of rates, which up to that time had been left to free competition (with the exception of maxima set in some of the early charters), was assigned also to the committee.

For the first twelve years after confederation there was no separate minister or department within the federal government to deal with railway matters, which were in that period handled by the department of public works. With increasing mileage, however, and particularly with the construction of the Pacific railway, the work became important enough to justify the establishment of the department of railways and canals in 1879, with a minister holding that portfolio alone.

The progress of railway building in the generation after confederation was rapid, though not nearly so rapid as the granting of charters. In 1867 the total mileage of railways operating in Canada was 2,278, having increased by only 200 miles in ten years. By 1881 it had risen to 7,331, which included the Intercolonial, but only a small part of the Canadian Pacific Railway, and by 1900 it was 17,657. More than 15,000 miles of railway were brought into operation in thirty years. Increased traffic led to the necessity of double tracks and the acceptance of a standard gauge (four feet, eight and one-half inches). Larger engines were procured, and coal was gradually adopted as a more efficient fuel than wood. Snowploughs reduced the loss of time due to drifts, and night travel was made more attractive by the introduction of Pullman sleeping cars in 1870. More elaborate stations were built to take care of growing traffic, such as the Union Station at Toronto (later replaced) – an unhappy example of the architecture of the age – which was opened in 1873, and described as "capacious and elegant."

Running through this general story of growth may be seen the attempt of the Canadian Pacific Railway to secure control of a complete transcontinental line, and to make that line pay by providing enough traffic for it. In the pursuit of this aim the company was determined to secure some hold over southern Ontario and Quebec, the area in which railway activity was already most conspicuous. Companies, large and small, were adding to their mileage; but already the tendency was for the absorption of the smaller by the larger. The picture there is important both in itself and as the main field of battle of the two great companies. In the western part of Ontario the Wellington, Grey and Bruce was built in 1870-1874 from Guelph northward, breaking into two forks to the ports of Southampton and Kincardine on Lake Huron. On completion it was absorbed by the Great Western. A railway with a similar name and in the same area was the Toronto, Grey and Bruce, the main line of which ran (1873) from Toronto to Owen Sound, thus covering the portage route between the lower lakes and Lake Superior. A branch ran north-westerly to Teeswater on the Wellington, Grey and Bruce. From Wingham, near Teeswater, the London, Huron and Bruce ran south-west to London. The Hamilton and North Western was built in 1878 from Hamilton to Barrie and thence to Midland on Georgian Bay. In 1879 it amalgamated with the Northern. A railway which was important because of its place in the C.P.R.-G.T.R. struggle was the Credit Valley from Streetsville to Orangeville, and the longer line from Toronto to St. Thomas (1881). These, with the lines of the Grand Trunk, the Great Western, and the Canada Southern, made up the chief railway services in the western part of the province.

In central Ontario there were two important railways in addition to the Grand Trunk: the Northern and the Midland, the latter of which had only reached Lindsay before 1867. It was carried on past the east side of Lake Simcoe to Midland. The Northern, a railway built before confederation as far as Collingwood, expanded into a considerable size in the seventies and eighties. Taking over the Hamilton and North Western in 1879, its name was changed to the Northern and North Western (which was perhaps just as well as its affairs became so suspicious that a royal commission was appointed to examine it in 1876, and found that improper payments had been made from its funds). Its tracks were from Port Dover, through Hamilton and Barrie to Collingwood and Meaford; and another line from Toronto to Barrie, where it forked to Midland and Gravenhurst. In 1884 it had 377 miles in operation. In 1886 it reached North Bay.

Between Port Hope and Kingston there were few railways except the main lines of the Grand Trunk and Canadian Pacific. From Kingston the Kingston and Pembroke ran north into Lanark County. The Brockville and Ottawa was extended to connect with the latter city, and, as the Canada Central, to the north-west as far as Callander (1882), just after having been purchased by the Canadian Pacific Railway in the previous year. Across eastern Ontario, from the Ottawa River to Georgian Bay, was the Ottawa, Arnprior and Parry Sound Railway (1896), taking a northerly line through a sparsely settled part of the province.

In the province of Quebec a new railway with an imposing name and an important strategic position was the Quebec, Montreal, Ottawa and Occidental. The North Shore, as this was more briefly called, was a combination under the provincial government of two private companies which had failed to raise enough capital to carry on construction. One of the reasons for failure was the opposition of the Grand Trunk, actuated by the knowledge that the whole scheme was intended to draw western traffic to the city of Quebec. By 1879 the line was complete from Quebec to Ottawa, and branches were added in the next few years. An important pioneer and lumber road was the Quebec and Lake St. John, which ran nearly two hundred miles north from Quebec to Roberval on the shore of the lake. Completed to that point in 1888, it was extended eastward to Chicoutimi on the upper Saguenay in 1894. To the south of the St. Lawrence the Atlantic and North West, which absorbed the International, ran from Lachine through Sherbrooke and Megantic to the border of Maine, and thence easterly to Mattawamkeag. Leased from 1886 by the C.P.R., it became a part of the Short Line to Saint John. From Sherbrooke to Lévis was the Quebec Central (1884).

Such were the most important railways in the central provinces, with the exception of three which have a peculiar interest. In western Ontario the Great Western was the pioneer trunk line. One of its purposes was to handle local traffic in a well-settled country, and to carry out this policy it expanded its lines built in the fifties by absorbing the London and Port Stanley (1875), the Wellington, Grey and Bruce, and the London, Huron and Bruce in 1876, and the Brantford, Norfolk and Port Burwell in 1878. But the search for local traffic was the least of the ambitions of the Great Western, for it was designed, too, to act as a trunk line serving not only Canadian, but also American through traffic. In this it met two obstacles: the competition of the Grand Trunk, which had invaded its territory, and a further threat from an American railway, the Canada Southern, completed from Windsor to the Niagara River in 1873. The prospectus of the Canada Southern explains that the railway is "to form with other Roads a cheap line of Traffic between Chicago and New York, so located and constructed as to reduce the cost of transporting the products of the Interior to the lowest limit." The line is said to be "practically level and straight to tide water." It is to connect with other railways at each end, and "will thus be a connecting link between two great systems of roads, which can now supply to it, at either end, a traffic equal to its utmost capacity." This reads strangely like the original prospectus of the Great Western. To meet this last challenge the Great Western built an "air line" (that is, one taking a comparatively straight course) from Fort Erie, near Welland, and cutting across the southern part of the peninsula to join up with the main London-Windsor line at Glencoe. The air line, however, was not a panacea. The Great Western, and the Grand Trunk as well, began to suffer heavy losses from rate wars with each other and with competing American lines. In 1869 the two Canadian companies agreed to maintain equal rates and to pool competitive Canadian traffic; but this, with other similar agreements, did not prove to be lasting. Following the failure of the attempt of each company to sell out to the government, amalgamation of the two roads began to be discussed in 1876, but it was not until 1882, when competition from the C.P.R. created a pressure, that it was accomplished.

The condition of the Grand Trunk, which had been so critical in the sixties, was still such as to give alarm to its directors and shareholders. In general the position had not materially altered: revenues were low, expenses high, shareholders clamorous for dividends, and a crying need for expenditure on the property. It is unfortunate that most of the available comments on the history of the Grand Trunk are from hostile or at least unsympathetic pens, but the causes of what was a general unpopularity are not far to seek. Although the railway had done essential pioneer work in the development of Canada, it had never been a Canadian enterprise. Foisted on a dazed legislature and public by the ingenuity of Hincks and the spell-binding of Jackson, its management had been steadily removed from Canada, while at the same time it had called – and successfully called – for privileges and subsidies from the Canadian government. On the other side of the Atlantic the Grand Trunk was conceived of as a distant enterprise for earning dividends on the capital that had been poured into it; and when it failed to earn dividends it met with no sympathy.

The Grand Trunk had a heavy capital structure, and while an effort had been made by the Arrangements Act of 1862 to reduce the bonded indebtedness, there was constant pressure to take the scanty operating profits for dividends instead of improvements, and to add further issues of stocks or bonds. Secondly, the railway had been built at great expense, but defects were constantly appearing in the line itself and the equipment, and the executive were never able to secure sufficient funds to repair these weaknesses. The revenues from operation were not enough to justify the expensive machine that had been built up. The Grand Trunk was primarily designed for through traffic, but had never been able to secure a sufficient volume. The plan of using its road as part of an American through route was, as has been shown, not a success; and the Grand Trunk consistently refused to build into the Canadian west unless allowed to go south of Lake Superior. Finally, it may be noticed that the directors in England were handicapped by a lack of understanding of Canadian conditions, and the divided rule introduced a complicated relation with executive officers resident in Canada. The Grand Trunk was served by individuals of considerable ability, but from the circumstances of its organization was never able to develop an *esprit de corps* or a continuous personnel: the latter partly because of periodic and acute differences of opinion between presidents, general managers, directors, and shareholders.

After one such difference, Sir Edward Watkin retired as president in 1869, and was succeeded by Mr. Richard Potter, chairman of the Great Western Railway of England. Potter spent three months of the year of his appointment in Canada, going over the property. On his return he stated his belief that "the only safe and prudent course as a matter of account keeping and as a matter of policy is that when a railway is maintained all renewals which do not add to the extra accommodation of the railway properly belong to revenue."[3] He pointed to ballasting, new rails, and new cars as proper objects for the scanty surplus. But Potter received little support, and the revenue was still diverted to dividends. In 1872 the president inspected the road in company with Mr. Allport, general manager of the

Midland Railway of England; and Allport's impression was gloomy: "I am bound to say that it has not been my experience, I think, ever to have gone over a worse line, – a line in a worse condition than a great portion of the Grand Trunk."[4] To the heavy expenses of laying steel rails in place of iron ones, re-ballasting, and other necessary works, was added a new financial difficulty. The Arrangements Act of 1862 created a "suspense period" of ten years during which the first and second preference bonds and stocks would pay only five per cent, and no legal action could be taken in respect of these securities. In 1872 that period would come to an end and the capitalization of dividend and interest would cease.

Potter's comments on the state of the road were as grave as Allport's. He reported that some six hundred miles of the line were in a dangerous condition, and that two hundred and fifty miles did not pay working expenses. The whole position of the company he regarded as critical, and – after consultation with the board and some of the proprietors – made the following suggestions for financial adjustment: that there should be issued an additional £600,000 of equipment mortgage bonds, a reissue of £410,000 of Atlantic and St. Lawrence guaranteed stock, and an extension of the Arrangements Act. To this Mr. Baring and Lord Wolverton had agreed, after a last attempt to protect the bondholders. There now appeared on the scene a syndicate who were ready to issue a large amount of common stock. The men concerned were Alexander McEwen, a Scot, and Baron (Albert) Grant, both of whom had had colourful financial careers. Whether they first approached the Grand Trunk, or the Grand Trunk them, is not clear; but it is certain that they offered to issue £10,000,000 of common stock.[5] After an agreement had been reached between the Grand Trunk executive and the syndicate, an act was passed through the Canadian parliament in 1873 (36 Vict., c. 18), extending the suspense period for three years, but raising the rate of interest to six per cent. The company was empowered to issue second equipment mortgage bonds up to £1,100,000 and common stock to a maximum of £10,000,000. The bonds and preference stock were again rearranged so as to create stock instead of bonds, and thus postpone a reckoning. The effects of the reorganization of 1873 were twofold: on the one hand important improvements were made in the road in the laying of steel rails and new ballast, and changing the gauge to standard; and on the other the capital structure was made even more top-heavy. It was apparently a year or so after the act of 1873 that the company was offered for sale to the government, so that it was not yet in smooth waters.

Potter was not long to remain in office to watch the effects of his planning, for in 1876 he was forced to retire after a break with Joseph Hickson (the new general manager) and the board. The new president was Sir Henry Tyler, an engineer who had been a member of the Grand Trunk board. In the year in which Tyler took office, General M. B. Hewson, an engineer with Canadian and American experience, set out to find the causes of the difficulties of the Grand Trunk. The trouble, he believed, was not due to over-building, for Ontario had less mileage of rail in proportion to population than Maine or Michigan, half that of New Hampshire, and one-third of that of Minnesota. Nor was the climate more rigorous than that of several American states. The receipts from traffic per mile compared favourably with American roads, but not the working expenses. The following comparison illustrates the latter point:

	MILEAGE	OPERATING RATIO
All lines in Michigan	1,904	62.5%
Great Western of Canada	444	59.7%
Grand Trunk	1,377	80.4%

Finding no other cause, the author attributed the troubles of the Grand Trunk principally to faulty management, citing such instances as the building of the Victoria bridge, leasing the Buffalo and Lake Huron Railway, leasing the bankrupt Montreal and Champlain Railway and the Atlantic and St. Lawrence on unfavourable terms. He calculated that the Grand Trunk had hired 4,291 freight cars while needing only 1,222. Finally he criticized the centralization of the management at Montreal, arguing that it was impossible for the general manager to exercise real supervision over the whole road.[6]

Yet, if the Grand Trunk was suffering from problems of finance and management, it did not pause in its growth. By 1881 the Rivière du Loup section had been disposed of to the government and a line to Chicago acquired. Amalgamation with the

Great Western in 1882 gave it valuable new lines and obviated expensive competition. The addition of the Midland and other smaller railways gave a total mileage of 2,856 in 1884. The company began to lay double tracks on its main line in 1888, and completed the work between Toronto and Hamilton in 1892, between Montreal and Toronto, and Hamilton and Suspension Bridge in 1903. The important communication with Michigan was greatly improved by the boring of a tunnel under the St. Clair River, from Sarnia to Port Huron, begun in 1889 and completed two years later. Such growth and improvements were largely inspired by the threat from the expanding Canadian Pacific Railway.

2. EXPANSION OF THE CANADIAN PACIFIC IN THE EAST

The charter of the Canadian Pacific provided for the construction of a railway from Callander on Lake Nipissing to the Pacific Ocean, but it was manifestly impossible that a railway could remain poised in mid-air in northern Ontario: the question was how connections were to be established with the ports and industrial areas of eastern Canada. The terms of the charter also empowered it to acquire the Canada Central and "to obtain, hold, and operate a line or lines of railway from Ottawa to any point at navigable water on the Atlantic seaboard, or to any intermediate point." With these comprehensive powers, the company began a rapid and calculated policy of eastward expansion. The Canada Central was bought in 1881, and its completion taken in hand. In the same year the Brockville and Ottawa was acquired, and in 1884 the St. Lawrence and Ottawa – the latter being a direct line between Ottawa and Prescott.

By these means the Canadian Pacific Railway had reached two important river ports as well as the capital, but it was also considered essential to extend to Toronto and the south-western part of the province on the one hand, and to Montreal and tidewater on the other. The first object was secured by building a line (at first under the name of another company) from Smiths Falls on the Canada Central through to Toronto. The territory west of Toronto was covered by the acquisition of the Toronto, Grey and Bruce, the Credit Valley from Toronto to St. Thomas, and an extension from there to Windsor. To reach Montreal the C.P.R. bought from the province of Quebec the western section of the North Shore Railway (from Ottawa to Montreal), and later – by threatening to build a parallel road – the eastern section to Quebec from the Grand Trunk.

It remained to secure a direct line from Toronto to Sudbury, to tap the eastern townships, enter the Maritime Provinces, and secure a winter port. For a time the company contemplated following the example of the Grand Trunk and acquiring a line to Portland. That municipality was ready to sell its interest in the Portland and Ogdensburg Railroad, and so in the autumn of 1883, Stephen and Abbott (the company's solicitor) visited Portland and discussed with the city council the possibility of purchase by the Canadian Pacific Railway. "It is not unnatural," Stephen said to the council, "having reached Montreal, and, as you are well aware, Montreal being only a six-months port, we should be looking to the question of reaching the Atlantic, and it is not unnatural that our eyes should be cast upon the most direct way. . . ."[7] Nothing came of the negotiations, however, and as an alternative the company proceeded to secure a route to the American border only. In 1883 they obtained possession of the South-Eastern Railway, which ran from Farnham to Newport, just across the border; and from Farnham to Montreal opened a new line. At Newport connections were made with American railways to Boston and Portland.

Access to American ports over American railways was not enough for the Canadian Pacific, or to satisfy opinion in the Maritime Provinces. In a letter to Tupper, Van Horne wrote that "we were pressed into the 'Short Line' scheme by the Government to meet the wishes of the people of the Maritime Provinces,"[8] but it seems improbable that the company would in any case have been content to leave the Atlantic provinces untapped, or to be without a direct line to a winter port. It was part of the scheme that the Canadian Pacific Railway line to the Maritimes should run in conjunction with a new and fast Atlantic service of steamships. It may well be, however, that it was the pressure from the government and from public opinion that led to the choice of Saint John rather than Portland. The Short Line, as it was called, was planned to cut across Maine, and so avoid the long loop by the northward. The route which it should take was the subject of a controversy only less active than that over the Intercolonial. The rival claims of Halifax and Saint John as termini were put forward by chambers of commerce and city engineers, and various alternatives and compromises were suggested. Finally it was decided that the line should take advantage of railways built or in course of construction; that the terminus should be at Saint John; but that running rights should be secured to Halifax. The lines acquired by the Atlantic and North-West Company, described above, were leased in perpetuity to the Canadian Pacific Railway, which thus reached Mattawamkeag in Maine. The eastern section of the Short Line was made by the New Brunswick system of railways, leased for 999 years to the C.P.R. In 1890 the Canadian Pacific reached the port of Saint John.

The company, however, was dissatisfied, or affected to be dissatisfied, with its latest extension. The line of fast steamships did not materialize. Construction of the new sections was more expensive that had been anticipated and business was light. The company – rightly or wrongly – attributed this unhappy state of affairs to sins of omission and commission by the government. The Intercolonial was accused of discouraging passengers from going by the Short Line, of making connections as inconvenient as possible, and of charging excessive rates for the haulage of C.P.R. cars. Stephen expressed his woes in a characteristic letter to Macdonald.

As to the "Short Line," you know what the influences were that induced me to touch it. Tupper had a political object to serve; Pope had, in addition to that, a personal advantage to gain; and that, I am free to say, weighed with me quite as much as the former. Further, at a meeting of the Maritime Members,— which I have since learned originated with Pope,— under the threat that they would not support one of our life-and-death measures then before the house unless I agreed to build the Short Line, Tupper and Pope repeatedly said, by way of inducement to undertake the work, that, on the opening of the Short Line, the I.C.R. would be run as a local road, that the through business would all come over the Short Line, that the I.C.R., worked as a local road, would be just as useful to the people of the country traversed by it; and the annual loss to the Government would be much less than by operating it as an expensive fast through line; – and much more to the same purpose. Can any sane man suppose I would have touched the Short Line unless I felt certain that the C.P.R. would have every facility for its short line trains reaching Halifax and doing business there as well as at all intermediate points along the line between St. John and Halifax? In this, as in many other things, I have been the victim of my own credulity and of my criminal confidence in the Government, – especially in the then Minister of Railways – and the C.P.R. is to-day suffering the consequences.[9]

This, and a similar letter from Stephen a week later – embracing other sore points as well as the Short Line – brought a cool answer from Macdonald. "I shall do my duty to the country according to the best of my judgment, and suffer even the threatened hostility of the Company, if need be." Stephen, who had used phrases about a possible breach in the friendly relations of government and company, hastily denied that there was any threat implied in his words. He was not blaming the government for the lightness of traffic on the Short Line: only asking for a fair share of what there was.[10] Some twenty years later an independent outlet to Halifax was secured by the lease of the Dominion Atlantic Railway, and a steamship service from Saint John to Digby.

The expansion of the Canadian Pacific Railway into central and eastern Canada necessarily brought with it competition with the Grand Trunk: a competition, which, while it was in large part inevitable, was bitterly resented by the older company. In Stephen's view, there was bound to be competition as soon as it was decided that the C.P.R. should build from Montreal north of Lake Superior, for the C.P.R. would naturally try to take the western business over their line, and the Grand Trunk to take it by way of Chicago.[11] The first phase of Grand Trunk opposition had taken the form of an attempt to discredit the whole project of a railway through Canadian soil to the Pacific, and an embarrassingly successful blockade of the London money market against Canadian Pacific loans. Such activities were, of course, never admitted by Grand Trunk officials, but there can be little question that they took place; and certainly they were not forgotten by the harassed management of the Canadian

Pacific. Overlapping these moves, and carried out in the open, was a campaign to prevent the Canadian Pacific Railway from cutting into Grand Trunk business east of Lake Superior. The Grand Trunk executive took the attitude that the C.P.R. should be confined to its line from Callander west, and tacitly argued that it should find an outlet over the lines of other companies. More especially were they opposed to C.P.R. expansion between Toronto and Windsor, an area in which the Grand Trunk was already trying to remove competition by absorbing the Great Western and other smaller companies. The Grand Trunk argument was that construction of additional competing lines was extravagant and unnecessary; that their cost fell both on the Grand Trunk and the taxpayer; and that the C.P.R. was being enabled by public money to compete with a private concern.

For years a literary warfare was waged by the partisans on both sides. Shareholders were informed of the iniquities of the rival company; pamphlets on the subject poured from the presses; newspapers took up the issue; and the heads of both companies deluged the prime minister with statements, cajolements, and veiled threats. The chief spokesman for the Grand Trunk was Joseph Hickson, who had succeeded Brydges as general manager. He claimed that his company was not unfriendly to the Canadian Pacific as long as the latter kept within its legitimate sphere, but that it was being allowed to trespass beyond that sphere.

It seems to me not only the height of folly, but vicious, and in the highest degree detrimental to the interests of Canada to have two Railways built alongside each other for eighty miles and practically within the same fences – Mr. Stephen and his friends are building a road from the neighbourhood of Peterboro to Perth, alongside the Midland Railway practically constructed. . . . Mr. Stephen and his friends with the power of the Government at their back, and with the funds which they are obtaining from the Government, are constructing the Ontario and Quebec line to the serious injury of commercial investments, and perhaps without much benefit to themselves in the long run. . . .[12]

Macdonald sent the letter on to Sir John Rose in New York, where Rose was trying – vainly, as it proved – to reconcile the claims of the two companies. He was not altogether happy about the extent of the commitments in "collateral projects" which Stephen was making, but vigorously denied Hickson's statement that Stephen was fighting the Grand Trunk with public money.[13] Hickson, however, continued to harp on that theme. In forwarding a cabled protest from his directors against subsidizing lines outside the Canadian Pacific charter, he took occasion to enlarge on the argument in a letter which was later printed.

If that Company [Canadian Pacific] had been incorporated and its transactions conducted on the ordinary basis of a Joint Stock Corporation, it is probable that the Directors of the Company would not have thought it necessary to address any remonstrance to the Government, as the usual conditions attaching to the investment of private capital would have afforded them all the protection necessary, or that they could expect:— but as practically the money to build the railway is being supplied out of the public revenues, largely increasing the burdens of this Company, which is directly and indirectly at present the largest separate taxpayer within the Dominion, the operations of the Canadian Pacific Company assume an entirely different aspect. When in addition the fact is taken into consideration that the funds provided by the Canadian Government, more than sufficient in themselves to complete the Pacific line, and the resources of the Canadian Pacific Company, obtained through the assistance and credit of the Government, have been and are being diverted to the promotion of lines in direct antagonism to the company,— lines which are either not needed in the public interest, or where needed should be supplied entirely by private enterprise,— it becomes a duty incumbent upon those who have charge of this Company's affairs to protest against the course being pursued.[14]

The whole stand of the Grand Trunk in the matter of public assistance was, of course, disputed by the Canadian Pacific. Writing in 1890, when the controversy was still active, Van Horne attempted to turn the argument by showing that the Canadian Pacific Railway had spent, since 1882, a total of $28,296,000 on lines toward which no subsidy had been granted. On the other hand, he said, not a single important work had been carried out by the Grand Trunk in the same period without governmental assistance. As an extra dig, he added that the

Grand Trunk had no more reason to complain of the original subsidy to the Canadian Pacific Railway than the latter had to the loans made to the Grand Trunk, which "became practically a gift."[15]

The phrases used by both sides have a modern ring, and a modern parallel which will be easily recognized. In reality, of course, the parties in the case were both private companies, both heavily indebted for their success to the assistance of the state. If on the one hand the Grand Trunk was seeking to prevent what it held to be improper competition, on the other hand the partisans of the Canadian Pacific raised the cry of monopoly (a cry of which they were soon to tire in another connection). The Grand Trunk, Stephen told his shareholders, cannot monopolize railway enterprise in Canada. And from Toronto came a blast from E. B. Osler, addressed to the members of parliament representing that city, protesting against the attempt of the Grand Trunk to establish a railway monopoly in Ontario by blocking the C.P.R. Once that was accomplished, the company "could, and would, at once put up rates from one end of the country to the other."[16]

Where did the Conservative government stand in the face of this fire from both sides? To Hickson and to Stephen, Macdonald long protested that the government was impartial, and the subsidies show that both companies were generously assisted. But when pushed too far he was forced to remember that the Canadian Pacific Railway was a child of the Conservative party. "My own position as a public man," he wrote to Stephen, "is as intimately connected with the prosperity of the C.P.R. as yours is, as a railway man."[17] And a few months later: "We have been showing such preference for the C.P.R. that Hickson has declared war – what we will, I dare say, survive."[18] The Canadian Pacific Railway, on its side, remembered the affiliation when election time came. "Our canvass is nearly complete and the C.P.R. votes will be practically unanimous – not one in one hundred even doubtful. My letter to Drummond was intended to show our men on which side their interests lie and it has had the intended effect with them." An enclosure from the general manager of the Dominion Express Company (a subsidiary of the C.P.R.) was also encouraging: "I have all hands at work, two men I sent west of Toronto changed thirteen votes yesterday. I have no fear of our men and think they will all work for the Company's interest when they have the way pointed out to them."[19]

Honours were pretty equally divided between the two companies, and in the following years the process of competitive expansion continued both by new construction and the absorption of smaller railways. The effect was to leave two great companies in possession of the greater part of the railway mileage in Canada. In central Canada they served roughly the same areas, but on the east the Grand Trunk cut down to Portland, while the Canadian Pacific ran through to Saint John. On the western side the difference between their positions was more significant. The Grand Trunk, by extending to Chicago, consistently followed the theory that the approach to the west should be to the south of Lake Superior. If it could secure a direct connection with the Canadian west by the Red River Valley, that would be a serious threat to the C.P.R. The position in the west, then, was that the Canadian Pacific was free from the rivalry of the Grand Trunk and was partially protected from competition. As long as it could maintain an uninterrupted flow of traffic over the Lake Superior section its pioneer venture was likely to be increasingly fruitful.

3. COMPETITION OR MONOPOLY IN THE WEST

A dominating theme in the project of a Canadian railway to the Pacific had always been that of a line through Canadian territory, reaching both Atlantic and Pacific ports, and serving as a link in a British route from Europe to the Orient. Despite early differences in the syndicate concerning the Lake Superior section, the company officially took over this whole conception of its purpose, adding a private rider that it would one day have its own steamships on both oceans. To carry its plans into effect, the company bought and built its way to the ports of Montreal, Quebec, and Saint John on the east, and to Vancouver and Victoria on the west. The completion of the transcontinental line, together with the necessary feeders, would produce a railway which would have the benefit of through traffic, and would be able to pay its way in spite of the existence of unprofitable sections.

From the first the chief officers of the company took the attitude that they must be enabled to reach the more populated areas of central and eastern Canada, and that they must be protected – for a time at least – from competitors tapping their main line at any point. Both these demands were partially met in the charter. To enable the company to extend eastward from its specified terminus at Callander, the clause was inserted which permitted acquisition of the Canada Central and other railways. As defence against the inroads of rivals, the "monopoly clause" read as follows:

For 20 years from the date hereof, no line of railway shall be authorized by the Dominion Parliament to be constructed south of the Canadian Pacific Railway, from any point at or near the Canadian Pacific Railway except such line as shall run South-West, or to the Westward of South-West; nor to within fifteen miles of latitude 49. And in the establishment of any new Province in the North-West Territories, provision shall be made for continuing such prohibition after such establishment until the expiration of the said period.

Such was the wall built round the Canadian Pacific Railway by the original charter. In general an attack might be expected at one of several points: in northern Ontario, at Sault Ste. Marie, in the Red River Valley, or on the Pacific coast. In any case the object of the attack would be the same: to tap the long trunk line of the Canadian Pacific and divert traffic to rival roads. The company held that any such attack was not only dangerous, but that it was unfair: dangerous because it threatened their ability to make the whole line carry the sections with no local traffic, and unfair because they claimed to have built north of Lake Superior only on the understanding that they should not be attacked from the rear. The attacks came, however, and each varied according to the area.

In northern Ontario the Canadian Pacific main line ran to Callander, this point having been chosen so as to favour neither Montreal nor Toronto. The C.P.R. succeeded in obtaining its own approach to Montreal over the Canada Central and North Shore, but in regard to Toronto they were forestalled by the

Grand Trunk, which, by absorbing the Northern and North-Western, gained control of what had been the Northern and Pacific Junction from Gravenhurst to North Bay.

The objects [wrote Stephen] *which the G.T.R. have in view in securing the control of the Northern and Nor Western Railways are now clear to me, and may be so to you. Having secured the control of the Northern System they thereby cut off the C.P.R. connection with Ontario. Seventy-five per cent. of the C.P.R. business to and from the Nor West is with the Province of Ontario, and to save a share of that business it is perfectly clear to me that the C.P.R. will be forced to build a line of its own from Toronto to Sudbury.*[20]

It was not, however, until some years later that the Canadian Pacific Railway was able to counter by building its own line.

The second vulnerable point was at Sault Ste. Marie, where the transcontinental line first ran near to American territory. The C.P.R. had early planned to connect the Canada Central with Sault Ste. Marie, with the immediate purpose of reaching Lake Superior navigation while their main line was under construction, and with the further purpose of drawing in traffic from the neighbouring state. The problem was to make sure that their "Soo" line was drawing in rather than letting out business. The only way to secure this end seemed to be to gain control of adjoining American roads.

Smith and I are off this afternoon to New York and to try and devise means of saving the line from the "Soo" to Minneapolis from falling into the hands of the Vanderbilt system. If we fail, the result will be the loss for ever of that traffic to the St. Lawrence route to Europe, and the permanent diversion of the traffic into the existing American channels. The Minneapolis traffic including that of the Nor Western States would be captured by the Michigan Central Line, which on reference to the map you will see runs direct north from Detroit to the Straits of Mackinaw, at which point there is a railway transfer ferry in operation, and the whole traffic taken east to the seaboard over the Vanderbilt lines, without a pound of it ever getting on the Canadian lines at the "Soo." ...

There was even worse to come, as Stephen read the signs of

the times, for the Grand Trunk spectre was also to be seen.

. . . The G.T.R. with the Northern in their hands will at once build a line from some point on their line between Gravenhurst and Callander, westwards to the "Soo," connecting at the "Soo" with the Duluth and South Shore line which runs direct along the lake shore from the "Soo" to Duluth, where a connection will be made with the Northern Pacific and with the St. Paul and Manitoba lines, both of which will sooner or later have independent connection with Winnipeg as well as with other points westward on the C.P.R., and so giving the G.T.R. a through connection with the whole Nor West to the Pacific Ocean through American territory.[21]

There was the rub. If Stephen and his fellow officers allowed this Grand Trunk scheme to go through they would lose not only their anticipated American traffic, but also the traffic of the Canadian west. These alarming results, however, never came: rather the boot was on the other foot, for the C.P.R. at that time began to establish a very powerful position in the middle western states. They bought control of both the Minneapolis, St. Paul and Sault Ste. Marie Railway and the Duluth, South Shore and Atlantic Railway Company. On completion of the system, the C.P.R. had a line from Sault Ste. Marie, through Duluth to Winnipeg; and another from Sault Ste. Marie to St. Paul, and north-west to meet the main line at Moose Jaw. Together with branches, these railways made a network which formed an ample barrier against the invasion of rivals – Grand Trunk or American.

So far the Canadian Pacific had registered one failure and one success in the struggle to protect its trunk line. The battle waged at the third point of danger had less definite but more far-reaching results. For some years the chief outlet for Manitoba had been south by the Red River valley to the border of Minnesota, where use could be made of American railways. The news of the formation of the syndicate in 1880 was received with mixed feelings in Manitoba. In general there was satisfac tion that progress in the building of the Pacific railway was to be made, but the personnel of the syndicate was not altogether acceptable. The presence of a group from the St. Paul, Minneapolis and Manitoba Railway suggested a connection with

American lines, and a consequent lack of competition which might keep down freight rates. To create the competition that it wanted, the province began to charter railways itself: the Winnipeg South-Eastern, to run to the American border; the Emerson and North-Western Railway Company, from Emerson (on the border of Minnesota) to the western edge of the province; and the Manitoba Tramway Company.

Such action was bitterly resented by the Canadian Pacific Railway Company, which had, even before the charter was discussed in parliament, given notice that they could not have any competing line running to the border, for this would "strangle" them.[22] The federal government then disallowed the charters. The reason given for this and later disallowances was that railways to the American border would divert traffic from the C.P.R. At first it was said in parliament that this policy would be continued only until the C.P.R.'s line north of Lake Superior was completed, but in practice the policy was retained for some three years longer. This change of policy, together with the earlier statements that Manitoba had the right to charter railways, led to a long controversy between the provincial and federal governments. Disallowance was not on the ground that the Manitoba charters contravened the act chartering the Canadian Pacific, for that, being a Canadian act, could not override the British North America Act. The disallowance was rather based on the fact that the federal government had power to veto provincial acts which were not in the general interests of the Dominion. Legally this power was indisputable, but in practice it was continually opposed by Manitoba.[23]

The force behind the resistance of Manitoba was resentment against the freight rates charged by the Canadian Pacific Railway. The freight rates were undoubtedly high in comparison with those either in Eastern Canada or on American railways. The difference was defended on grounds of higher cost of operation, to which it was answered that the C.P.R. had been subsidized just because it was not at first expected to pay. Moreover, the rates were increased in 1883, and it was felt that the whole development of the province was being retarded by the high cost of moving commodities. A few figures taken from a pamphlet issued by the Winnipeg Board of Trade illustrated the difference in freight rates on wheat between east and west.

LOCAL RATES

C.P.R., Brandon to Winnipeg	133 miles	20 cents per 100 lbs.
G.T.R., Stratford to Bowmanville	131 miles	13 cents per 100 lbs.
C.P.R., Moose Jaw to Winnipeg	398 miles	34 cents per 100 lbs.
G.T.R., Brantford to Montreal	403 miles	17½ cents per 100 lbs.

THROUGH RATES

C.P.R., Winnipeg to Toronto	1,287 miles	50 cents per 100 lbs.
G.T.R., Ingersoll to Halifax	1,283 miles	31½ cents per 100 lbs.

The rate on wheat on the St. Paul, Minneapolis and Manitoba Railway from St. Paul was 10 cents for 100 miles and 30 cents for 525 miles; on the C.P.R. from Winnipeg, it was 17½ cents for 100 miles, and 39 cents for 525 miles. J. H. Pope, who was not unfriendly to the C.P.R., wrote that ". . . Stephen and Hill . . . are charging such exorbitant rates from St. Paul to Emerson that it is almost ruinous to shippers and operates very much to prejudice the public against our policy, as they say if you had allowed another road to be built from Winnipeg to the boundary there would have been a competing line to the St. Paul and Emerson road."[24] No matter how conscious the people of Manitoba may have been of the advantage of having a transcontinental railway, and even of the problems of operating it in a sparsely settled area, it is not surprising that they continued to protest against the cost of transportation. They believed – not altogether correctly – that the high cost was due to a monopoly, and a monopoly based on an unreasonable use of federal powers. They therefore proceeded to break the monopoly by the establishment of competing lines.

Stephen claimed that the agitation for another railway was really for the benefit of speculators who did not care about the province, and that there was an annexation element in it; but there seems to be every indication that the campaign against monopoly, led by the *Winnipeg Free Press,* represented a very wide body of opinion. More convincing was the argument that the real danger lay in the continued opposition of the Northern Pacific to the Canadian Pacific, and a threat to divert the traffic of the Canadian west to the south at Winnipeg. "Now if he [Villard] can manage to tap our traffic from Winnipeg West before it has become fully developed or got into its own proper channel we might as well give him the line east of Winnipeg to Thunder Bay and save our money on the North Shore Line."[25]

The Ottawa government was impressed by the general danger to the C.P.R. and for a time held to its policy of disallowing the provincial charters on grounds of general interest. In the meantime the legislature of Manitoba grew more determined. Not content with railways to the border, it chartered and subsidized a railway to Hudson Bay, of which forty miles of track were actually laid. It then turned back to the border railway. The Manitoba Central, Winnipeg and Southern, and Red River Valley companies were all chartered in 1887, and all disallowed. The first of these was designed to connect with the Northern Pacific, and on the act being disallowed the government determined to carry on the undertaking itself. On the constant buying and selling, chartering and disallowing of Manitoba railways there is no need to dwell in detail. The point of importance was the clear-cut issue between the province and the Dominion as to railway policy. Feeling ran high, and at one moment there was danger that the struggle might end in tragedy. The provincial government was building a branch of the Red River Valley Railway from Portage la Prairie to Winnipeg, and to do so had to cross a branch of the C.P.R. Van Horne ordered resistance. An old engine was ditched in the line of the oncoming track and two hundred and fifty men were brought by the C.P.R. superintendent to hold the fort. A volunteer army of three hundred men was rushed from Winnipeg and took up a position near by. In the night a "diamond" crossing was laid, and promptly torn up by the defending force. Reinforcements were brought by both sides, and it was only a growing sense of reasonableness in both groups of partisans that prevented a fight.

For a year or more the struggle continued to be waged between the Dominion government and the Canadian Pacific Railway on the one hand and the province on the other. The British North America Act, the charter of the Canadian Pacific Railway, and Hansard were read and re-read, interpreted and re-interpreted. The C.P.R. claimed that the attempt of Manitoba to divert traffic to the south was a breach of faith, and threatened to transfer its western shops to Fort William. The executive council of Manitoba formally protested against the policy of the federal government, and the latter answered with a charge that Manitoba was acting against the general interest of the Dominion. Macdonald privately told Rose that Manitoba was running toward bankruptcy, and asked him to discourage the floating of her government's loans in London.[26] In Ottawa, however, it was gradually being recognized that the game was not worth the candle. Thomas White, the minister of the interior, advised Stephen that the policy of disallowance was a mistake.[27] The Winnipeg Conservatives clamoured for the abolition of the policy, and formed an association to present their views. In the meantime the Canadian Pacific officers found that the agitation against the company both in Manitoba and Ontario was destroying their credit. Stephen told Tupper and Macdonald that the Canadian Pacific Railway could not remain in the position of an unpopular monopoly, and would have to face competition. But there was an urgent need of cash – "$15,000,000 will be required within the year 1888. . . . If the capital cannot be secured the company must collapse and go into bankruptcy...." Lack of revenue made the need acute.[28]

The government, by adding two and two together, found the solution to an intolerable situation. By an act of 1888 (51 Vict., c.32) the monopoly clause was repealed, the policy of disallowance was implicitly abandoned, and the government was empowered to guarantee the interest on a loan of $15,000,000 to be issued by the company. The battle was over, but who had won the victory? The federal government got peace, the C.P.R. fifteen million dollars, and Manitoba freedom to build or charter other lines. But the real object of the struggle was not gained by the province, for the freight rates remained much as they were. The Northern Pacific built a number of lines in Manitoba, but instead of conducting a rate war with the C.P.R. divided the traffic with that company. Continuing complaints from the west led to a series of inquiries into freight rates.[29] A royal commission of 1888 reported against any fundamental changes and its views only led to increased powers in the railway committee of the privy council. Another commission was appointed to investigate the question, but this reported in 1895 that the C.P.R. gave lower rates than American railways operating under similar conditions; and that, while local rates were higher than in the east, they were necessary on account of the greater cost of transportation. No relief came to the west until 1897 when the Crow's Nest Pass agreement was made between the Dominion government and the Canadian Pacific

Railway. In consideration of a subsidy to a line through the pass the company agreed to a general reduction.[30] Finally, comprehensive consideration was given to the whole question of rates in an inquiry made by Professor S. J. McLean. His two reports, presented in 1899 and 1902, made definite criticisms of the railway committee on the grounds that it was political as well as administrative, was not sufficiently permanent or expert in personnel, and did not travel about the country.[31] He also proposed an alternative method of handling consideration of freight rates, a plan which was written into the Railway Act of 1903 (3 Edw. vii, c.58). There was to be a board of three (later six) commissioners appointed by the governor in council for ten years. To this board a permanent staff of experts was attached. The commission took over all the powers of the former committee, but, unlike the committee, its activities were largely in the regulation of rates, and for such purposes it was to act as an informal court of law. Appeals from its decisions lay to the governor in council, while appeals on points of law might, with the consent of the commission, be carried to the supreme court of Canada.

A less tangible result was the continuing and rooted objection to railway monopoly which existed in Manitoba and in the west generally. Whether or not the Canadian Pacific had taken advantage of its monopolistic position, and whether or not the appearance of other Canadian and of American lines in the west affected the height of freight and passenger rates, there was a very strong feeling that never again must the west be exposed to the monopoly of a single railway. It was the existence of that sentiment, which, probably more than any other single factor, set opinion in the west against any amalgamation of the Canadian Pacific and the heir to the other railways, the Canadian National.

The cancellation of the monopoly clause in the Canadian Pacific charter hastened a struggle that had already been foreseen with American roads. The old bogey was the Northern Pacific, but the Northern Pacific expanded into the prairies and did no great harm. In any case it was a failing force. After his phenomenal success in the St. Paul and Pacific and the St. Paul, Minneapolis, and Manitoba, Hill for a time was associated with the Canadian syndicate, but before long withdrew and devoted his great energies to the building up of a new transcontinental line, which he called the Great Northern. It was primarily this railway which Van Horne had to fear when, in 1892, he became president on the resignation of Lord Mount Stephen (as he now was). The two men – Hill and Van Horne – the one a Canadian in charge of an American railway, and the other an American in charge of a Canadian railway, were worthy antagonists. Indeed, their love of battle might have led them further than interest demanded had it not been for the shock-absorber put in by Mount Stephen and Strathcona, both of whom had remained at once influential directors of the Canadian Pacific Railway and large shareholders in the Great Northern.

There was a clear clashing of interest between the American and Canadian roads, for both hoped to penetrate beyond the national boundaries and draw business in to their main lines. Both believed in the offensive as the best form of defence. The personal attitudes of the presidents toward the struggle may be illustrated by two remarks. Hill, on hearing that Van Horne was determined to build the Lake Superior section, had burst out – "I'll get even with him if I have to go to hell for it and shovel coal." And Von Horne, in connection with Hill's intention of invading Canada, had remarked, no less picturesquely: "Well, if he does, I'll tear the guts out of his road."[32] Van Horne's measures of protection were, in the main, two. The Minneapolis, St. Paul and Sault Ste. Marie was joined up with a branch running north-west to meet the Canadian Pacific main line at Moose Jaw. The object of this was to make a shorter route between the Pacific coast, St. Paul, and Chicago. The extension from Port Moody to Vancouver also assisted in the development of traffic with the Orient, a side of their business which the Canadian Pacific were anxious to encourage. A mail subsidy from the British government in 1889 was followed by the building of Canadian Pacific steamers, and the full operation of a trans-Pacific service by 1891.

The second measure of defence was to run lines through the southern part of British Columbia, that is, in the boundary or Kootenay country, into which the Great Northern had made its next raid. In the late nineties the Crow's Nest Pass line was begun, partly by acquisition of local railways and partly by construction. Running close to the border the new line, together with branches, forestalled serious incursions of the Great Northern, and at the same time enabled the Canadian Pacific to take advantage of the development of mining in the boundary country. In British Columbia as in Manitoba the cry of "monopoly" was raised. In 1897 the provincial government announced an impressive number of subsidies to be granted, one of them for a railway into the Kootenay country. In 1898 the government made a contract with Mackenzie and Mann for a railway from Vancouver to Penticton, on Okanagan Lake, and on to Midway, east of Rossland. The election of the same year led to the cancellation of the contract. Nothing further was done until the accession of the Dunsmuir government in 1901, when it appeared that the Canadian Pacific Railway was to receive the contract, and in public meetings and in newspapers protests were voiced against monopoly and against the influence of the Canadian Pacific in politics.

Broadly speaking, the Canadian Pacific had succeeded in protecting its trunk line against the threats of either American or Canadian rivals. Theoretically it gave up its monopoly in 1888, but the absence of any real competition for many years rendered that concession nugatory. It was not until the opening of the new century that the tardy appearance of the Grand Trunk Pacific and the formation of the Canadian Northern showed that the days of the absolute rule of the Canadian Pacific in the west were numbered.

CHAPTER 10

The Later Transcontinental Railways

1. THE COMING OF PROSPERITY

With the turn of the century there came the long-awaited prosperity in Canada. The years from 1898 or 1900 to 1913 saw a rapid recovery throughout the world from the doldrums of the nineties, and the economic expansion which resulted was nowhere so marked as in North America. In spite of all efforts, Canada – and particularly the Canadian west – had only progressed in short spurts, though there was a rooted belief throughout the country that it was only a question of time before Canada would grow in population and wealth as she had already done in territory. That belief seemed to be justified when the new century brought a flow of immigrants, capital, and orders for foodstuffs. It was seen as the dawn of a new day. Since, it was argued, the land of the American west was nearly taken up, the tide of European emigration must be diverted to Canada, which would then go through a similar stage of rapid development. Out of such comforting thoughts arose the expression, "Canada's century." It was in this atmosphere of optimism, and with tangible signs of better days, that the third great forward movement of Canadian railways was imagined and begun.

The basic need of the Dominion was for more people. Immigration, which had materially increased in the eighties, owing principally to railway construction and the opening of the west, had fallen off badly in the nineties and reached a low mark of 16,855 in 1896. From there it began to recover, passing 50,000 in 1902, 100,000 in 1903, 250,00 in 1908, and reaching a maximum of 400,870 in 1913. Allowing for emigration, there was a loss until 1901, and while emigration remained important, there was a net gain of over 200,000 persons in 1913;[1] and the rate of growth of population in the years 1900-1910 – thirty-five per cent – was higher than in any other country. The United Kingdom quota of immigrants was in most years the largest, with the United States second. Other European countries contributed, too, more especially when the search for immigrants by the Canadian government, led by the energetic minister of the interior, Clifford Sifton, was definitely extended into Europe, in the belief that the English-speaking countries alone could not provide all the people that were needed. Eastern Canada absorbed a portion of the newcomers; but they migrated chiefly to the scantily populated prairies. Those settling in the east found their livelihood in the industries which were springing up up or increasing, and helped to swell the movement to the towns, and the consequent relative gain of urban over rural population; and those going to the west were absorbed in wheat-growing or ranching, and so participated in the production of foodstuffs for export. Many of these latter newcomers found temporary or seasonal work in railway construction – sometimes supplementary to independent farming.

Imports of capital on a large scale accompanied immigration. Since only a small amount of capital could be found within the country, public and private bodies turned to the United Kingdom, the United States, and European countries. After a long period of industrial expansion England was possessed of a large amount of exportable capital. The general prosperity of the early twentieth century brought a willingness to lend large sums abroad, while the bright prospects in Canada, combined, perhaps, with the revival of imperial sentiment, created an almost unlimited credit for Canada in London. The United States was the second largest lender, and other countries combined to make a poor third. The total investments in Canada in the period 1900 to 1913 have been calculated as follows:

Great Britain	$1,753,118,000
United States	629,794,000
Other countries	162,715,000
	$2,545,627,000[2]

This capital financed new railways and the industrial and agricultural development of which railways were at once the cause and result.

The heavy expenditure on railways in the early twentieth

century was defended partly by glowing phrases about the future and partly on the grounds of tangible needs. For the former, illustrations will be found in plently in the orations of the day; for the latter, a few figures may be quoted to indicate the rate and distribution of economic progress, though it must be remembered that in the period covered, railway construction synchronized with, rather than followed, the development of agriculture and industries.

	1901	1911
Area of occupied farms, in acres	63,422,338	108,968,715
Production of wheat, in bushels	55,572,368	132,077,547
Value of livestock	$268,651,026	$615,457,833
Exports of wood and wood products	$33,099,915	$56,334,695
Mineral production	$65,797,911	$103,220,994
Gross value of manufactured products	$481,053,375	$1,165,975,639[3]

Agriculture gained slightly or remained stationary in the eastern and central provinces, but showed a marked increase in the west, where the rapid expansion of livestock and wheat-farming strained the resources of the existing railways. Manufacturing was centred almost entirely east of Lake Superior, and its growth signified urbanization and a more mixed economy. The industries which increased most rapidly were those connected with building materials, iron and steel, and transportation equipment.

The prime motives in building the two later transcontinental railways were to provide more adequate transportation facilities for the west, and – on the part of the companies concerned – to share in the traffic that was being created there. Such traffic was both in the exports of the west and in the carriage of supplies, lumber, and other goods to the settlers. "Railways and continually improving transportation were as essential as rain and sun to progressive settlement on the Canadian prairie. Nearness to railways and to projected railways was of first importance to the settler."[4] In the prairies and foothills grain and livestock could be raised for export. Since it has been calculated that, under most circumstances, grain could not be profitably hauled more than ten miles to a railway,[5] main or branch lines were needed if the west were to have more than a narrow belt of settlement. Railways and immigrants went together to the west, each dependent on the other. The following table indicates the growth of population.

PROVINCE	1901 TOTAL POPULATION	IMMIGRATION	1911 TOTAL POPULATION	IMMIGRATION
Manitoba	255,211	11,254	461,394	34,289
Saskatchewan	91,279 ⎫		492,432	40,076
Alberta	73,022 ⎭	14,160	374,295	44,091
British Columbia and Yukon	178,657	2,600	392,480	52,786
Totals	598,169	28,014	1,720,601	171,242

Canada had a great pioneer area – "the last best west" – for neither the United States nor any other country could any longer offer free lands to large numbers of immigrants, and every effort was made to exploit this advantageous position. No further grants of land were made to railways after 1896, and the land was used instead for the free homestead system. Federal and provincial governments, railway companies, and private organizations sent agents and literature to the United States, England, and the continent of Europe to advertise the attractions of settlement in western Canada, and to make smooth the path of the immigrant. By 1912 there was little land still available for homesteads in the southern half of the provinces. Added to those who came from the United Kingdom and foreign countries were thousands of others from Ontario and the eastern provinces.

Farming was the chief occupation of new and old settler alike, and wheat played the leading part. Manitoba, as the first part to be settled, was for some years the chief centre of wheat production. A crop of a little over a million bushels in 1880 rose to nearly seven millions in 1885, to eighteen millions in 1900, and to nearly thirty-three millions in 1905. Alberta and Saskatchewan, meanwhile, had passed the Manitoba total, increasing from five million bushels in 1900 to thirty-five millions in 1905. These are small figures compared with those of ten years later, but they already represented a considerable surplus for export and at times strained the existing railway system. In the late nineteenth and early twentieth centuries the variety of wheat most commonly grown in the west was Red Fife; but as settlement spread northward it became increasingly necessary to develop another type which would ripen earlier and so escape the frosts. The result of a long series of experiments was a cross-named Marquis, which was first distributed in 1909, and soon came to be the dominant variety.

Wheat was by no means the only crop, but it produced the acute problem for the railway. Oats and barley were grown in considerable quantities, and cattle raising was an important industry, the latter especially in Alberta where the foothills of the Rockies offered ideal conditions. The largest part of the wheat crop had to be moved to eastern ports shortly after it was harvested. The period involved was very short, and every box-car and engine that could be spared had to be put into this service. Gaunt elevators rose at intervals beside the track, and whether on the main or on local lines, had to be cleared by the railways, and the crop started on its long trip eastward. At the beginning of the century the grain had to be moved from Winnipeg, the hub of the system, over the single line of the Canadian Pacific Railway to Fort William, where water transport began. In that link there were stoppages in 1901 and 1902, and the movement of grain was interrupted, a state of things which affected all those who were directly or indirectly concerned with the sale, financing, and export of the crop. It needed no more than one or two such examples to cause a re-examination of the railway situation in the west.

At the turn of the century the only railway with any considerable mileage west of Fort William was the Canadian Pacific. From its main line branches ran north to Saskatoon and Prince Albert in Saskatchewan and to Edmonton in Alberta. South of Winnipeg were a number of branches running to the border or parallel to it. From Calgary a line ran south to Macleod, and Lethbridge, on the Crow's Nest Pass line, was reached from the main line further east. In addition there were numerous shorter branches. Besides the Canadian Pacific there were only the lines of the Great Northern to the south and west of Winnipeg, the nucleus of the Canadian Northern, and a few other local railways.

Faced by the rapid growth in the population and traffic of the west, the Canadian Pacific made efforts to keep pace with the demands upon it, and further branches were continually thrown out. These branches in turn threw a heavier burden on the main line. It was not, however, to be the fate of the Canadian Pacific to maintain a virtual monopoly in the west. There was an obvious need for greater mileage. Not only did the over-loading of the Winnipeg–Fort William line indicate the necessity of duplication, but also the frontier of settlement was steadily being pushed northward. With the discovery of great tracts of good agricultural land and the perfection of varieties of wheat maturing early enough to escape the frosts, the incoming settlers moved to more northerly districts until they reached the rich Peace River country. The current view was that, as the settled belt was widened, railways should be established to serve the new areas as the Canadian Pacific served the longer-settled area in the south. All degrees of optimism were evinced as to what the future of the west would be, but there was general agreement that the one railway was not enough.

The opportunity for new business was seen by other railway companies as well as by detached observers. The Canadian Pacific, instead of failing to pay for its own axle grease, had been a financial success. So long as the west developed slowly there was, perhaps, no room for another railway to share in the same harvest, but now that prosperity had come others might expand into that field. There were two companies interested: the Canadian Northern, possessed of a few small lines in the prairies, but with unlimited ambition; and the Grand Trunk, which, having failed to confine the Canadian Pacific to the west, was now thinking in terms of transcontinental traffic. Both companies were under energetic and enterprising management.

Lastly, the pressure for additional railways came from the people of the west themselves. They wanted, naturally, to ensure adequate facilities for the export of wheat, and lines to be extended as settlement spread; but they did not want the whole transportation system of the west to be in the hands of one corporation. The memories of the struggle over monopoly in Manitoba were fresh. That province had never ceased to exhibit a readiness to charter and assist independent companies, or even to operate railways as public works. Throughout the west, too, there continued to be dissatisfaction with the rates charged and a belief that they could be lowered through competition. Shippers claimed that they were in the hands of a monopolistic company which charged whatever the traffic would bear and which gave little thought to their convenience. It was, therefore, certain that further railways would be built. Whether there should be one or more, where and how they would find outlet in the east, and how they were to be financed, were all matters to be decided.

2. THE LIBERAL RAILWAY POLICY

The policy adopted at the beginning of the century, of allowing the construction of two additional transcontinental railways, marks a turning point and crisis of Canadian railway development. After a long sojourn in the wilderness, the Liberals came into power in 1896, on the eve of the great years of prosperity. With a rapidly filling treasury and a good working majority in parliament, the government was in a strong position to carry out the popular policy of rapid expansion of railways. It was also in a strong position to steer a judicious course between a timorous refusal to bank on the growth of the west and a prodigal disregard of caution. No Liberal government had held office at Ottawa since that of Alexander Mackenzie. The memories of that administration and of the opposition as led by Edward Blake would, in so far as they concerned railways, have been willingly forgotten by the Liberals of the twentieth century. The cautious policy of Mackenzie and Blake had as its fruits the slow and partial construction of the Pacific railway; while the criticism of the arrangement with the syndicate of 1880 had been popularly interpreted as opposition to the whole plan. The Conservative government had then, by taking a risk on the success of the syndicate, completely eclipsed anything that had been done by the Liberals, wiped out the memory of the Pacific scandal, and gained the credit for the completion of the much-desired Pacific railway. It came to be accepted by both the government and the Canadian Pacific Railway Company that they were mutually dependent; and it was not surprising that the company formed a tacit alliance with the Conservatives in the years immediately following the completion of the road.

It is not an unreasonable deduction that the Liberal administration was ready to sponsor a fresh railway enterprise which would cancel their former mistaken, if honest, belief in the inability of the west to maintain a railway. They were now in prosperous days instead of in days of depression. They had in

Wilfrid Laurier a leader who could catch and exploit the public optimism in the future of the country. Moreover, it had been demonstrated that there was room and business for another railway across the west. All the signs, in fact, pointed to action: the question was as to the exact form that that action should take.

There was not, as there had been a generation before, a clean sheet on which the government could write a new railway policy, for there existed two powerful companies, neither of which had a transcontinental line and both of which felt it necessary to secure the benefits of long-haul traffic. The Grand Trunk had a network of lines throughout Ontario and Quebec, a seaport at Portland, and an entry to the middle west at Chicago. Although the company had more than once refused opportunities of building into the Canadian west on Canadian soil, its officers and directors had now become satisfied that such a step was necessary. The Grand Trunk had not been able to settle its relations with the Canadian Pacific on the basis of a division of territory, and therefore turned to the alternative of competition as a through road. A much younger railway, the Canadian Northern, was geographically in the opposite position: it had lines in the west but none in the east. With a number of lines in Manitoba and Saskatchewan, it had (in 1902) built to Port Arthur, where the wheat which it gathered on the prairies could be delivered to lake boats; but it had no other access to the east, and was anxious to remedy the defect.[6]

The logical solution for the problems of both companies was amalgamation or co-operation. Negotiations to this end were conducted, but such a veil of mystery shrouds them that it is impossible to know the whole truth. It is said that the Grand Trunk offered to purchase the Canadian Northern in 1902, and that the latter eventually agreed to sell on a basis of about $30,000 per mile – a price which the Grand Trunk refused to pay.[7] In evidence before the royal commission of 1917, E. J. Chamberlin, president of the Grand Trunk, threw some further light on the negotiations:

They [the G.T.R. executive] *tried to buy the Manitoba lines, but they could not get together, Mr. Hays told me at one time, and Mr. Wainwright told me also. I asked him why they did not* *buy out the Canadian Northern. They said they had had meeting after meeting with them, and that the best terms they could get were that they assume all obligations, all bonds and everything else, and give $25,000,000 for the common stock for that little bunch of lines up around Winnipeg.*

But Sir Donald Mann's later account of the situation, given in evidence before the arbitration board (1918) does not entirely bear out the statement that the Canadian Northern was willing to sell.

> *Both companies [C.P.R. and G.T.R.] wanted to buy us out and neither was friendly. Of course the Grand Trunk made no bones about it. The Government sent for us and we had a session at Ottawa, and they (the Grand Trunk) wished to buy us out and always were in the hope they would buy us out. We offered to build a joint section from Port Arthur to North Bay, and we would develop the west and they would develop in the east. That was before the Grand Trunk Pacific was built and they refused and would not do anything but buy us out. We were too young and ambitious to sell out at that time. That was the year they got their charter . . . and we were running to Port Arthur at the time.*[8]

Another attempt to bring the railways together was made, apparently in the winter of 1902-1903, by Laurier, who called the heads of the two roads to Ottawa and suggested a general plan by which each company should be the complement of the other, the Canadian Northern in the west and the Grand Trunk in the east. It is fairly clear that the reason for the failure of discussions was the refusal of both sides to give up their separate ambitions. It is not at all clear, however, why the government gave way, since neither railway could proceed without a charter and financial assistance from parliament. Various explanations of the weakness of the government in this connection may be guessed at: divisions in the cabinet; fear that too much pressure would result in no railway at all; a failure to appreciate the significance of the issue. To the last may be added the excuse that the general optimism of the period supported an almost unlimited expansion of railways. The government of the day was no more foolish and − unfortunately − no wiser than the public, the companies themselves, and business men, eminent and otherwise, who were using extravagant terms about the boundless possibilities of Canada and the necessity of double-tracking all the railways. Nevertheless the willingness of the government to take the line of least resistance committed the country to a system of railways that was ill designed for its needs and greater than it could support without strain.

After the failure of the negotiations for co-operation the government turned to alternatives, the first being the plan proposed by the Grand Trunk. In November 1902 that company offered to build a railway from North Bay (its terminus in northern Ontario) to the Pacific coast, at or near Port Simpson, and asked a subsidy of $6,000 and 5,000 acres per mile, with tax exemptions. This represented half the amount of land and three-fifths the cash paid to the Canadian Pacific syndicate, but the offer was not acceptable. Judging by the generosity of later subsidies it is evident that the amount was no obstacle, although it would have had to be wholly in money since no more large land grants were to be made. The chief reason given for the refusal of the terms was that the traffic gathered by the road would be carried to Portland instead of to a Canadian port. The Grand Trunk's expressed willingness to connect with the Intercolonial was apparently not credited, and the government was still labouring under the delusion that grain would be carried to the sea by rail by way of the direct line that they proposed.

During the greater part of 1902 and 1903 the cabinet may be imagined as wrestling with the railway problem. No doubt there were frequent consultations of all sizes, involving ministers, railway officials, and financiers. No doubt there was the usual lobbying by interested parties. But what came out of it all was that the railway fathered by the Liberal party was to be no mere extension of the Intercolonial and Grand Trunk into the west, but a completely new transcontinental line stretching from New Brunswick to the Pacific. The change from the original Grand Trunk proposal to the plan adopted was explained by W. H. Biggar, the company's solicitor, in a letter written to the royal commission of 1917.

In the early months of 1903, conferences were from time to time held between Mr. Hays and Mr. Wainwright on behalf of the company and Sir Wilfrid Laurier and members of the Cabinet, as a result of which Mr. Hays was asked to have the Bill amended to provide for the construction of a line from North Bay to Quebec. Not only do I personally know this to be the fact, but it is corroborated by a letter written to Sir Charles Rivers Wilson by Mr. Hays on March 16, 1903, in which he stated that at the request of the Government we have amended our Grand Trunk Pacific charter, taking powers to build a line from Quebec to North Bay. . . . When the Bill first came up for discussion before the Railway Committee of the House of Commons, such strong opposition developed that practically no progress was made at that meeting nor, in fact, at several subsequent meetings of the committee. While the Bill was thus under consideration, several members from the Maritime Provinces insisted that the eastern terminus of the line should not be Quebec, but a point in the Maritime Provinces. So strongly was this view pressed that in the end the Government acquiesced and directed that the Bill be further amended to include the construction of a line from Quebec to Moncton. . . . Moncton was decided upon as a compromise, regard being had to the fact that both Halifax and St. John could be reached from there by the Intercolonial. . . . That his [Hays's] original intention was not carried out was, to my personal knowledge, not due to a change of view on his part but because he came to the conclusion that the Government aid essential to the construction of any Grand Trunk Pacific line could only be secured upon the terms set forth in the agreement of July 29, 1903.[9]

Laurier was unable to secure unanimous approval by his cabinet of the plan which was finally adopted. A. G. Blair, his minister of railways and former premier of New Brunswick, resigned in July 1903 rather than agree to the proposed railway. The announcement of Blair's resignation, which Laurier made to the house of commons on July 16, was the first official word on the government's railway policy, although it was known that plans were afoot. It was not a happy beginning to have to tell the house that the minister most directly concerned felt so strongly against the measure that he was determined to leave the government. Although it was not revealed at the time, Clifford Sifton was also opposed, and before leaving for England on the Alaska boundary case had given to the prime minister a memorandum in which he urged that the Canadian Northern and Grand Trunk should be "required" to come to an arrangement by which the two formed a "perpetual traffic contract," neither building into each other's territory, the boundary of which would be at Port Arthur. But, because he was in England when the decision was reached, Sifton swallowed the unsavoury bill, being able to distinguish, as a friend remarked, a hearse from a band waggon.[10] Blair's arguments, as expressed by his and Laurier's speeches in the house and by their letters printed in the *Debates*, are clear as far as they go.[11] His "decided preference" was for "a Government owned and government operated railway across the continent." This he was prepared to forego, but was opposed to a "hybrid scheme involving the compromise of two antagonistic principles." In particular he disbelieved in the Lévis to Moncton section, which, he held, would parallel the Intercolonial; and in building the Quebec to Winnipeg section before the character and conditions of the country had been more fully explored. He accused Laurier of discussing with other ministers, and allowing those ministers to discuss with Grand Trunk officers, plans for the transcontinental railway without informing him, although he was the minister of railways. Laurier's answer to this last charge was put in such general terms as to be an admission of its truth. This is most suggestive, for it seems to indicate either a general lack of confidence between Laurier and Blair or else a fundamental difference on railway policy. It has been asserted that Blair was more friendly to the Canadian Northern than to the Grand Trunk;[12] yet it is curious that Blair made no reference to the Canadian Northern in his letters to Laurier – curious because the paralleling of lines was the weakest joint in Laurier's armour, as Blair himself made clear in reference to the Intercolonial. Sifton had expressed himself vigorously about the avoidance of such overlapping. Either Blair failed to appreciate fully the significance of this point, or else he hoped that the government would come to terms with the Canadian Northern rather than with the Grand Trunk: that is to say, he would adopt the Machiavellian tactics of scotching the first plan and then producing the second. Again, however, there is mystery about the motive.

In spite of the protests of the opposition, nothing further was revealed concerning the new railway policy until July 30, when the prime minister moved for leave to introduce a bill for the construction of "a National Transcontinental railway,"[13] thus again arousing resentment amongst members of the opposition, who had not yet seen the bill. The scheme was an ambitious one, envisaging a completely new transcontinental railway from Moncton in New Brunswick to the Pacific coast. The eastern section from Moncton to Winnipeg (the National Transcontinental) was to be built by the government and on completion leased to a new corporation, the Grand Trunk Pacific. The route was to be from Moncton to Edmundston, near the American border, and thence midway between the border and the St. Lawrence to Quebec. The western section, to be built by the Grand Trunk Pacific, would follow a northerly route to Winnipeg and thence through the Yellowhead Pass to Port Simpson.

In introducing the measure Laurier emphasized the necessity of immediate action.[14] Unless Canada could provide for the trade of her own west it would be captured by "an ever vigilant competitor." This led up to the theme of the national character of the road, which was his chief defence of the section east of Quebec. The Intercolonial followed too circuitous a course, and the Canadian Pacific line went through Maine. The old bogey of abolition of the bonding privilege was once more trotted out, and the words of Andrew Carnegie and President Cleveland (in 1888) quoted to show the sinister intentions of the United States. Against the Quebec-Moncton section the opposition protested time after time. Blair, who took a leading part in the debate, denied that the Intercolonial was unsuitable for through traffic and claimed that the National Transcontinental would be a parallel and unnecessary road. From the experience of the Canadian Pacific, R. L. Borden, leader of the opposition, argued that little grain would be moved by rail east of Port Arthur. He also sought to show that the Grand Trunk would secure virtual control of the Intercolonial, whose lines it would need to use from Moncton to Saint John or Halifax. Or, as J. G. Haggart, minister of railways in the former Conservative government, put it:

*With the experience we have had in connection with the Inter-
colonial Railway – an expenditure on capital account of nearly
$43,000,000 and a loss to the people for the last six years,
putting it at a moderate amount, of $2,500,000 per year – we
are asked to build a road which will destroy the traffic of the
Intercolonial Railway from Quebec to Moncton . . . for the purpose of saving a distance of fifty or sixty miles in the carrying
of traffic from the North-West Territories and Manitoba to St.
John and Halifax. Did a more insane idea ever take possession
of any one? The ports of the North-West and the ports of
Manitoba are at the head of Lake Superior, and I believe will
in the future be at Hudson Bay.*

The remaining part of the National Transcontinental, from
Quebec to Winnipeg, was to be in northern country which was,
for the most part, unexplored. There were two obvious arguments in favour of this: to provide a direct line for through
traffic, and to widen the area available for agriculture, mining
and lumbering. The validity of the first hinged on the volume
of through traffic, which was, to say the least, problematical. In
regard to the second, one can either praise the optimism or
question the temerity of building a colonization railway to the
standard of the best trunk lines. It is said that Laurier was
induced to choose Quebec city as the St. Lawrence terminus
by political pressure from the province; and, further, that the
province was willing to accept the National Transcontinental
in lieu of a projected railway to the northern area. In any case,
given Quebec rather than Toronto or Montreal as the chosen
point on the east, it was inevitable that the line should run rather
far to the north, rather than slant down toward Montreal and
Ottawa. The National Trancontinental from Moncton to Winnipeg was to be constructed out of public funds under the
supervision of a board of three commissioners appointed by the
governor in council, but the Grand Trunk Pacific Railway
Company was to approve of the specifications. On completion,
the National Transcontinental was to be leased to, and operated
by, that company, on terms of no rent for the first seven years,
and three per cent per annum on the cost of construction for the
remainder of the fifty-year term.

The situation was paradoxical. On the one hand the government section was to be built as part of the Grand Trunk Pacific, would be operated by the company, and to all intents and purposes would become a part of the Grand Trunk system. On the other hand, to the National Transcontinental was ascribed the role of a common highway for those western railways which had no eastern outlet. It was in these terms that Laurier described it to the house of commons.

But why did we keep this section of the road in our hands? Why did we not give it to the company to build as the other section? We did it because we want to keep that section of the line which is to be the exit of the productive portion of the west, in our own hands so as to be able to regulate the traffic over it. The prairie section will be teeming with business, as we know; it will be teeming with activity as we know. Already there are three lines of railway, the Canadian Pacific Railway, the Great Northern and the Canadian Northern; and this one will be still another. Other roads are going to be built there to meet the increasing wants of the people. The Canadian Pacific Railway has its exit on the north shore of Lake Superior; those other railways have no exit. It is our intention that this road shall be kept and maintained under our supervision, so that all railways may get the benefit of it, so that the Canadian people may not be compelled to build another road across that section of country.

This is a curious statement. In the first place, the government undertook construction only because the Grand Trunk was either unwilling or unable to do so; in the second place, the Canadian Northern had completed its line to Lake Superior; and in the third place the line was to be handed over to one, not all, of the western railways. Moreover what the house of commons should first have been discussing in 1903 was whether Canada could maintain two transcontinental railways in addition to the Canadian Pacific. In the previous session, in 1902, an act (2 Edw. VII, c. 50) had been passed allowing the Canadian Northern to extend its lines from Port Arthur to Montreal, Ottawa, and Quebec. And yet in 1903 the prime minister (who had failed to bring the Canadian Northern and Grand Trunk together) was talking about a common highway to Winnipeg! Yet no real consideration was given to this preliminary problem, although Laurier had seen the unwisdom of two additional lines north of Lake Superior.

Members of the Conservative opposition were free to point out the weak spots in the government's plan. This they did at considerable length: the debate in the commons occupies several hundred pages of Hansard. Speaker after speaker attacked the Quebec-Moncton line from every possible point of view. Further criticisms were levelled at the decision on the construction of the Quebec-Winnipeg section without adequate surveys. A number of members showed the unlikelihood of grain being carried to seaboard by rail. The financial burden of the whole project on the country was viewed with alarm by others. On the whole relation of the great Canadian railways to one another there was less clarity. Haggart and others called in question the arrangement by which any company might have running rights over the National Transcontinental, holding that this was in principle no exceptional privilege, and in practice would be unworkable. Members on both sides of the house were strikingly silent about the future of the Canadian Northern. At one stage of the debate Borden suggested that the government should buy the Canadian Pacific line from North Bay to Fort William, improve it, and allow running rights to the Canadian Pacific, Canadian Northern, and Grand Trunk Pacific. Similarly he suggested that the latter two companies should build one common line through British Columbia to the coast. He added that the Intercolonial should be extended to Georgian Bay.

In the light of later events it is easy to conclude that it was this failure to see the railway question as a whole that was the weakness of the plan of 1903 – a failure that was to bring much trouble to the next generation. It is hard now to recapture the optimism of that period, when parliament, the press, and businessmen all were thinking in terms of progressive prosperity and rapid expansion. It was this spirit which gave a grandiose character to the plan for providing additional railway facilities; and some additions, it must be remembered, were genuinely necessary. The nature of the plan adopted was determined not only by this general attitude but by a number of special considerations as well. The Conservatives were associated with the Canadian Pacific whose national character coincided with the federalist tendencies of that party. If new railways were to be built the interests of all the provinces had to be considered, more especially as the Liberal party leaned toward the support of provincial rights. The main pressure in this connection came from three sources: the opposition to monopoly in the west, the insistence by Quebec on a colonization railway in her northern territories, and the determination of New Brunswick to obtain as her part a line through the centre of the province.

Having failed to secure voluntary co-operation between the Grand Trunk and the Canadian Northern, and being unwilling or unable to force that co-operation, the government was then driven toward a compromise scheme which had both advantages and disadvantages. It had the weakness of a plan designed to satisfy all parties. The National Transcontinental was needlessly expensive for a colonization railway and proved to be too heavy for the Grand Trunk to carry, while in New Brunswick it imperilled the through traffic of the Intercolonial. The west secured unlimited competition at the cost of over-building. For scores of miles west of Edmonton the Grand Trunk Pacific and Canadian Northern were built side by side, only to be unified in a later day. While, therefore, the nature of the railway policy of 1903 may be understood, its defects are glaring. The Canadian railway problem did not begin in 1903, but it was greatly accentuated by the decisions taken at that time.

3. THE GRAND TRUNK PACIFIC

The Grand Trunk Pacific was the Grand Trunk writ large. The old company, in spite of a staggering debt and periodic crises, had amazing powers of recovery. One period of recovery happily began just before the early nineties had run their gloomy course. In 1895 Sir Henry Tyler retired from the presidency after an exciting but expensive period of office. He was succeeded by an even more exciting and considerably more expensive régime. The new president was Sir Charles Rivers Wilson, who, as an eminent civil servant, had significantly had charge of the national debt and been a member of the international commission of liquidation for Egypt. As general manager, Wilson immediately secured the services of Charles M. Hays, an American, who in his early thirties had pulled the Wabash

Railway out of difficulties. With the exception of a year when he returned to the United States Hays was general manager of the Grand Trunk until 1909, and president from then until he was drowned on the *Titanic* in 1912.

The new administration began to show promising results. A valuable rental was obtained from the Wabash for the use of some five hundred miles of Grand Trunk tracks; similarly running rights over the Toronto-Hamilton line were leased to the Canadian Pacific. The Chicago extension, a separate company, was put into receivership, and reorganized as the Grand Trunk Western with a considerable reduction of interest charges. By these and other measures an operating deficit was changed into a respectable surplus in 1902. Not that this was of much help to the general manager, for any revenue that could thus be collected went into the insatiable maw of the bond- and stockholders. During twelve years under the new management the business of the company had grown substantially. Compared with 1896 gross earnings were up by 99 per cent, net earnings by 85.7 per cent, and total tonnage moved increased by 111.9 per cent, in 1907.[15] In 1902 and 1903 curves were reduced and grades improved in a number of places, thus reducing the cost of operation. Engines and rolling stock were increased in numbers, size, and power. The lighter rails were replaced by others weighing eighty or a hundred pounds per yard.[16]

The most far-reaching plan of the Grand Trunk was to tap the growing business of the west and secure the advantages of a long haul. Now that the Canadian Pacific had had such good success, and the west was beginning to fill up, Hays was anxious that no more opportunities should be let slip. For purposes of construction and operation a new company was incorporated, known as the Grand Trunk Pacific Railway Company, with a capital of $45,000,000. This company was to construct the "western division," from Winnipeg to the Pacific, and to complete it in five years. It was to be built to a standard "not inferior to the main line of the Grand Trunk Railway Company of Canada between Montreal and Toronto, so far as may be practicable in the case of a newly constructed line of railway." The decision to achieve immediately the standard of a first class railway was based on the belief that the cost of original construction would be more than offset by lower operation and maintenance charges, a policy in marked contrast with that of the Canadian Northern.

No such railway could, of course, be built without generous assistance from the public exchequer. Although the government were not willing to provide land or cash subsidies, they were ready with guarantees and – later – with loans. On the prairie section, from Winnipeg to Wolf Creek, Alberta, the government guaranteed first mortgage three per cent bonds to the amount of $13,000 per mile, and on the mountain section, that is, the remainder, similar bonds to the extent of seventy-five per cent of the total cost, whatever that might be. For seven years the government was to pay the interest on the bonds which it had guaranteed. The balance of the cost of construction was to be met by the sale of bonds, these to be guaranteed by the parent company. The Grand Trunk also was to acquire and hold not less than $24,900,000 of the common stock of the Grand Trunk Pacific.

The eastern division, from Winnipeg to Moncton, was to be built by the government, on the same high standard that was set for the western. When completed, the eastern division was to be leased for fifty years to the Grand Trunk Pacific, rent free for the first seven years, and at the rate of three per cent per annum on the cost of construction thereafter. The whole line, from Prince Rupert to Moncton, was to be equipped with "modern and complete rolling stock," and to be operated by the Grand Trunk Pacific. The agreement also provided that the lease of the eastern division should contain articles designed to implement the general principle of the government that the whole railway was to have a national character. The articles were to reserve power to the government, in respect of publicly owned railways, of running rights over both the eastern and western divisions; and power to grant running rights to any railway company over either division. How these provisions might have been worded in the lease, or how effective they might have been, is a debatable question, for, as it proved, the lease never came into operation. At the time they were treated with scant ceremony by the opposition in parliament on the grounds that they secured little more than was already in the Railway Act, and that the rights which they seemed to convey could not in practice be exercised. A further clause was included in the agreement of 1903 which read as follows:

It is hereby declared and agreed between the parties to this agreement that the aid herein provided for is granted by the Government of Canada for the express purpose of encouraging the development of Canadian trade and transportation of goods through Canadian channels. The Company accepts the aid on these conditions, and agrees that all freight originating on the line of the railway, or its branches, not specifically routed otherwise by the shipper, shall, when destined for points in Canada, be carried entirely on Canadian territory, or between Canadian inland ports, and that the through rate on export traffic from the point of origin to the point of destination shall at no time be greater via Canadian ports than via United States ports, and that all such traffic, not specifically routed otherwise by the shipper, shall be carried to Canadian ocean ports.

The proposed railway was to run through a greater proportion of unsettled and presumably unproductive territory than either the Canadian Pacific or the Canadian Northern, both of which cut down into southern Ontario as soon as possible. Therefore it was designed for through traffic to the sea, either at Quebec or at Saint John and Halifax. What goods could be carried? The chief export of the west was grain, but grain, as had been demonstrated over and over again, would take the cheaper transport by lake carriers. There is some question as to whether the last quoted article was intended to cover combined land and water transport. As far as grain was concerned, the real pull away from Canadian ports was not to Portland, but to American ports by way of Buffalo. It seems a reasonable conclusion, therefore, that the ports of the Maritime Provinces would benefit no more from the National Transcontinental than from the Intercolonial; for the small saving in mileage would not materially affect the movement of grain. From the company's point of view Chamberlin claimed (in evidence before the royal commission of 1917) that it was impossible to carry freight to Halifax at the same rate as to Portland or Boston, and that it had always been recognized as impossible.

The work of construction on both the eastern and western divisions began in 1905. The criticisms of the Moncton-Quebec section had no deterring effect and the line was built as planned. At Quebec the St. Lawrence had to be bridged. The Dominion government undertook to provide a bridge independently, without charge to the railway, and engaged a firm of engineers to erect it. The plan was ambitious, calling for the longest cantilever bridge in the world, and providing for electric railways, a road, and pedestrians as well as for the trains. Construction began and about half the bridge was in place, when in August 1907, with only slight signs of weakness showing, the completed portion collapsed so suddenly that the men on it were carried into the river. This catastrophe, bringing with it a terrible toll in lives and money, led to a modified and less ambitious plan, which was carried out at a cost of $22,616,898, and the bridge was opened for traffic in 1917.

From the city of Quebec the railway followed its lonely course through northern Quebec and Ontario, unconnected by branches with Montreal or Toronto, except with the latter by the Temiskaming and Northern Ontario. Shunning Lake Superior, the main line ran to the north of Lake Nipigon, with a branch to Fort William. No railway surveys had previously been made and no accurate maps existed, so that the engineers were also explorers. Much of the country through which the line ran caused difficulties in construction. The first contract was let in 1905 and the battle began with the rock and muskeg (swamp) of the north.[17] The last spike in the eastern division was driven late in 1913, but at that time the Grand Trunk Pacific refused to carry out the agreement by which they were to lease the road, being not unnaturally staggered by the fact that the cost exceeded the estimate by approximately one hundred million dollars, or two hundred per cent.

No friend of public enterprise can fail to be embarrassed by some aspects of the story of the National Transcontinental. Charges of widespread corruption in the letting of contracts were never proved, but the public continued to believe that fire existed as well as smoke. The opposition in the house of commons was vigilantly looking for irregularities in contracts. In 1909 a minor sensation was caused when the chief engineer of the National Transcontinental, H. D. Lumsden, resigned on the grounds that the assistant engineers were not following his instructions. He charged them with showing more rock-cutting than existed. In the debate that followed in the house, Houghton Lennox pointed out a number of contracts in which common excavation had been turned into rock-cutting – to the profit of the contractors, and hinted at collusion with the commissioners.[18] The cost of the road was so enormous – about $88,600 a mile – that a royal commission was appointed to investigate. It reported that neither the Transcontinental Railway commission nor the Grand Trunk Pacific had encouraged economy; and that the instructions for low grades had been laid down without information as to the real cost of construction.[19] A more legitimate reason was the rise in cost of materials and labour.

The western section, that built by the Grand Trunk Pacific, followed in general the route long since chosen by Fleming. Running somewhat south of the Canadian Northern, it passed through Edmonton, pierced the Rockies at the Yellowhead Pass (although it had been earlier intended to use either the Peace or the Pine River Pass), and took one of Fleming's alternative routes by the Fraser and Skeena rivers to the Pacific, where a new port was established at Prince Rupert. The whole division was opened for traffic in September 1914. By that time, however, the Grand Trunk Pacific was in such a parlous condition that it could not long stand on its own feet.

4. THE CANADIAN NORTHERN RAILWAY

Unlike either the Grand Trunk or the Canadian Pacific the Canadian Northern Railway began not with a trunk line, or any plans for a trunk line, but with a few small and local roads. That it grew rapidly into the third of the great railways of Canada was due to the ambition and enterprise of its two architects, William Mackenzie and Donald Mann. After experience as contractors on the Canadian Pacific and other railways, the two men formed a private partnership under which they operated until 1902 when they incorporated a joint stock company, Mackenzie, Mann and Company. From the beginning of their acquisition of railways they associated with them Z. A. Lash, who, besides being their solicitor, became a director in the company. The interest in the company was equally divided between Mackenzie and Mann, Lash holding a qualifying share.

In 1896 Mackenzie and Mann bought their first railway, the Lake Manitoba Railway and Canal Company — or rather, bought a charter passed by the legislature of Manitoba in 1889 but never acted on. The times were propitious. The spread of settlement in the west offered opportunities for such grain-gathering railways as the partners first acquired. The sentiment of Manitoba, too, was friendly towards railways in competition with the Canadian Pacific. The position at that time, as he saw it, was later summarized by D. B. Hanna, one of the first employees of the Canadian Northern.

The Canadian Pacific Railway . . . then [1896] *practically controlled the province* [Manitoba] *in its operations, and it might be said that it entirely controlled it regarding any traffic moving between the East and West of Canada. It is true that the Northern Pacific and Manitoba, a subsidiary of the Northern Pacific of St. Paul, Minnesota, had a few hundred miles of railway in operation in that province, but there was a friendly arrangement between the two companies — not necessarily put on paper, but in such a way as to be a gentleman's agreement . . . that the traffic coming to the West from Eastern Canada should not be poached on by the Northern Pacific, and in the same way the Canadian Pacific Railway respected the territory of the American line for business passing into the United States. So that to all intents and purposes the province of Manitoba at that time was subject to the control of the Canadian Pacific Railway. So that it follows that any demand that might be made for reduced rates or fair treatment received the usual consideration when one enterprise has the traffic by the throat.*[20]

The charter of the Lake Manitoba Railway already carried a valuable federal land subsidy of 6,000 acres per mile for 125 miles, and to this the provincial government added a guarantee of bonds up to $8,000 per mile for the same distance. The charter gave authority to build to Hudson Bay, but its new owners began in a modest way. From Gladstone (thirty-six miles north-west of Portage la Prairie) they built to Lake Winnipegosis by way of Dauphin. Running rights over the Manitoba North-Western enabled them to come as far south as Portage la Prairie. Operation began in 1897 as a pioneer road, with mixed trains twice a week, using second-hand or borrowed cars, and stopping wherever there were passengers or freight.[21] East of Winnipeg construction was started on the Manitoba and Southeastern Railway, the first section of which – forty-five miles from St. Boniface to Marchand – paid its way by hauling firewood. In the next few years additions were rapidly made in both directions. By 1902 there was a through connection between Winnipeg and the Dauphin country, and in the same year the Canadian Northern (as it was called after 1899) reached Port Arthur by construction under the charters of the Manitoba and Southeastern and the Ontario and Rainy River railways, and by the acquisition of the existing track of the Port Arthur, Duluth and Western. In 1901 the Canadian Northern secured the Northern Pacific lines in Manitoba, which had been taken over by the provincial government on a 999-year lease, and were sought by both the Canadian Pacific and the Canadian Northern railways. The latter paid to the government a sum equal to the rental paid to the Northern Pacific, and gave reductions in freight rates, which, for competitive reasons, led to a similar reduction by the C.P.R. The most important of the lines thus added were those from Winnipeg to Emerson, and from Morris, on that line, to Brandon. In all the new mileage totalled 350.

In 1901, also, the first move was made in eastern Canada by acquiring a three-mile line from Parry Sound to a junction with the Canada Atlantic Railway. Two years later development in the east began in earnest. In Quebec the Canadian Northern absorbed the Great Northern Railway of Canada and the Chateauguay and Northern Railway. The principal lines thus obtained were from Rivière à Pierre Junction to Hawkesbury, Montreal to Joliette, and the Montfort branch. Taken together, these formed the nucleus of the Ottawa-Montreal-Quebec line. In Nova Scotia the company acquired the Central Railway, from Lunenburg to Middleton (that is, across the peninsula), and a branch to Caledonia. The Canadian Northern had 344 miles of track in eastern Canada at the end of 1903, and a total of 1,706 in east and west together.

At the time of the parliamentary debates on the new railway policy the Canadian Northern was rapidly extending its lines in both eastern and western Canada. What reason was there to suppose that it would grow into a transcontinental railway?

There was the charter of 1902, but that might have been interpreted as a precautionary measure rather than as a definite intention. The Canadian Pacific and the Grand Trunk Pacific both announced their intentions at the outset. Sir Donald Mann was questioned on this point by the counsel for the Canadian Bank of Commerce, and the following answers were elicited.

Hellmuth: . . . perhaps you would tell me about the time when you came actually to consider and eventually accomplish the building of the road through to the Pacific coast?

Mann: That was much after this date [1903] *we were considering it; but I always maintained we should not build east or west until we had about five thousand miles in operation in the prairies, which would feed the lines east and west; and my judgment then was that there was sufficient through traffic to make the road pay. . . . I discussed it with the late Mr. Hill. . . . We were in the west and we were bottled up; anything we had to send there or get from the east had to go over our rivals' railway.*

Commissioner Harris: The Canadian Pacific Railway?

Mann: Yes. I tried many times to make a satisfactory arrangement with them, but they were not friendly and could not do it.[22]

The fact that Laurier attempted to persuade the Canadian Northern not to build eastward, and – still more – that it refused to consider the suggestion, indicates that the final objective was a transcontinental railway.

Whatever may have been their views as to the final position of the Canadian Northern, there is no doubt that Mackenzie and Mann continued their policy of expansion. By the end of 1905 the Canadian Northern ran from Winnipeg to Edmonton, and from Winnipeg almost to Prince Albert. To the eastward there was through connection to Port Arthur, and beyond that the lines between Ottawa and Quebec. To make a connected system two long and expensive sections would have to be filled in: from Ottawa to Port Arthur, and from Edmonton to Vancouver. In other words Mackenzie and Mann had devoted their attentions first to the areas where construction was relatively cheap and a paying business might be expected. Such a procedure was in accord with their general principles. They built relatively inexpensive lines which were intended to make some revenue before being improved to the condition of a first-class road. Freight was always the chief concern of the Canadian Northern, and its passenger traffic was never heavy. The Lake Superior and mountain sections would involve expensive work and run through country where there was little or no local business.

In 1908 surveys were begun through the Yellowhead Pass to Vancouver, following the line traced out by Fleming. Building had begun toward the pass from Edmonton when it was found that the Grand Trunk Pacific, which had seemed to be heading for either the Pine or Peace River Pass, also was making for the Yellowhead. To avoid the duplication of expensive construction, Mann suggested to Hays that the Canadian Northern should get trackage rights from the Yellowhead Pass west, and the Grand Trunk Pacific similar rights from Port Arthur to north of Lake Nipigon. He also, he said, offered rights from North Bay to connect with the main line. Hays, however, refused without giving any reason.[23] Thus the two railways ran side by side through the pass, although the Grand Trunk Pacific continued westward to Prince Rupert while the Canadian Northern turned down the valley to Vancouver. Good grades were obtained throughout the mountain section, enabling trains to be pulled through without the aid of extra engines. This condition was particularly desirable in that the heavy grain trains could be hauled over the mountains without great expense. The Pacific ports, being open throughout the year, were valuable outlets for the export trade. In distance Vancouver was 1,237 miles nearer to Saskatoon than was Saint John by land.

During the same prosperous years before the war the greater part of the Lake Superior section was built. To avoid the long detour by Toronto, a straight line was followed from Ottawa to Capreol, and thence in a northerly curve – between the Canadian Pacific and National Transcontinental – to Port Arthur. In September 1915 the last spike was driven in the transcontinental line, and before the end of the year a regular passenger service was established from Quebec to Vancouver. While the main line was under construction a considerable number of branches were added, especially in the west. One – based on an acquired railway – ran from Prince Albert down through

Saskatoon and Regina to Brandon. From near Edmonton another was built down to the coal mines at Drumheller, and thence to Saskatoon. A single invasion of American soil was made by a branch from Fort Frances to Duluth. In 1915 the Canadian Northern, with its affiliated companies, possessed 9,362 miles of track.

In spite of some unfortunate results, it is hard to avoid admiring the performance of the Canadian Northern group, for the creation of the railway was the most astonishing feat in the history of Canadian railways. A pioneer in the northern parts of Manitoba with a total staff of thirteen, it ended as a line from tidewater to tidewater. Two peculiar features have already been mentioned: the patchwork way in which it was put together, and the cheapness of the original construction. It had been said that the track had a regrettable tendency to jump up and hit the trains from behind, but much might be forgiven to a pioneer. A third feature of the Canadian Northern – and one that was to bring grey hairs to many an accountant – was its original and tortuous methods of finance. The methods of raising capital for construction and equipment for the other two transcontinental railways may readily be understood, but the Canadian Northern had no such virtues of simplicity. In the first place it consisted of a number of companies separately incorporated, which gave to its accounts a striking variety. The sources of its capital were many. There were cash subsidies from the federal, provincial, and municipal governments. A second source of funds was in grants of land; for, although the policy of making land grants to railways was abandoned shortly before the Canadian Northern was started, some of the old charters which it acquired carried such grants with them. Thirdly, the Canadian Northern obtained loans from the Dominion government. Its fourth, and main, source of revenue was the sale of bonds, of which there were a large number of issues, a considerable portion being guaranteed by the federal and provincial governments. It will thus be observed that the Canadian Northern received substantial assistance from public bodies, although such assistance was rendered piecemeal over a period of years. Few railway builders have had more success than the Canadian Northern group in extracting financial aid from governments, though for the most part they were fortunate enough to make their appeals in times of optimism and prosperity. However badly they may have been in need of funds from time to time, Mackenzie and Mann never parted with their common stock, by the possession of which they retained control of the voting shares.

The Canadian Northern, with the Canadian Pacific and Grand Trunk Pacific, made three transcontinental railways in Canada. The two later ones belong to the period of rapid economic expansion in the early twentieth century, a period which came to an end as abruptly as it began. At the end of 1913 and in the early part of 1914 the pace slowed up and signs of a change were unmistakable. In the summer the war broke out; and while this led in time to an artificial stimulation of industry, at first it did nothing but harm to the new railways, then incomplete. Immigration ceased, British investment stopped, and the new railways – outward and visible signs of the belief in the Canadian millenium – were left stranded without sufficient funds or traffic. From the vantage point of later years the mistakes in policy seem clear enough. First in importance was the decision to build two additional and complete transcontinental railways, instead of adopting one of the compromises suggested. Secondly, the expensive construction of the Grand Trunk Pacific and National Transcontinental, and the route of the latter, were hostages to fortune. These were, indeed, mistakes which were to cost the country dear, and to form one of the most important contributory causes to what has come to be called "the railway problem."

CHAPTER 11

Nationalization of Railways

1. RAILWAYS AS A PUBLIC PROBLEM

The early years of the twentieth century saw a rapid development of railways in a period of marked prosperity. The total
mileage in operation almost doubled in the years from 1900 to
1914; and in that period two great transcontinental systems
were added to the older one. Between these three companies
there were significant differences. The Canadian Pacific Railway
had overcome its earlier financial difficulties and was able to
carry out a policy of gradual expansion built on a foundation
that was strategically sound. The report of the company for
1913-1914 showed an operating surplus of some eighty million
dollars, and — after making provision for replacements and
contingencies — a large surplus on the total account. A handsome
profit was being made on the company's lands, for in that year
259,371 acres were sold at an average price of $17.80 an acre.

An early dream of the Canadian Pacific directors was realized
when the company's steamships plied on both Atlantic and
Pacific, joining Canadian ports with England on the east, and
Japan, China, and Australia on the west. Whether or not the
ocean steamships were independently profitable, their prime
purpose was to feed the transcontinental railway; for Canadian
Pacific officials never forgot that their success or failure depended on that long line, to protect which they had fought many
a battle. Increased traffic made it necessary and possible to
effect improvements. On the east the position of the C.P.R. was
strengthened by the lease of the Dominion Atlantic Railway
in 1912, which, with a steamship service between Saint John
and Digby, gave access to the port of Halifax, and also made
possible a steamship connection from Yarmouth to Boston.
Increased business in the prairies brought the steady building of
branches, and the traffic from these, together with larger through

traffic, made it desirable to double-track the main line, most of the section between Winnipeg and Swift Current being so improved by 1914. Heavier traffic in the west put further pressure on the rest of the main line. The section between Winnipeg and Fort William carried not only through rail traffic, but also the grain and other goods that followed the rail and water route, and consequently was double-tracked in 1907. A start was also made on the section from Fort William to Sudbury, which, however, carried lighter traffic. From Sudbury there were two main routes to Montreal: the older and more direct line by the Ottawa River, and another line by way of Toronto. This latter was connected with the Great Lakes transport by a branch from Port McNicoll on Georgian Bay to Bethany Junction near Peterborough (1910). There was now an additional strain on the Toronto-Montreal line, which was relieved by an additional and more southerly track from Toronto to Glen Tay, and double tracks from there to Montreal. In the far west improvements were made by running a connecting link from the main line by way of the Columbia River valley to the Crow's Nest line, and by reducing the grades through the Rockies by means of spiral tunnels between Hector and Field.

For railway companies, as for armies, the offensive may be the best means of defence. The Canadian Pacific was now carrying on a war on two fronts, with American and with Canadian rivals. To broaden its front on the Pacific it secured running rights through Spokane to Portland, Oregon. To compete with the Canadian Northern and Grand Trunk Pacific in the northern area a branch was cut off the main line at Portage la Prairie and extended to the Calgary-Edmonton line, just south of the latter city. Between this new line and the American border the network of rail was steadily filled in. By means of its control of the Minneapolis, St. Paul and Sault Ste. Marie Railway and the Duluth, South Shore and Atlantic, the C.P.R. could retain some command over the two southern routes between the Canadian prairies and eastern Canada, by way of Sault Ste. Marie and Chicago – the latter being made possible by a lease of the Wisconsin Central to the Minneapolis, St. Paul and Sault Ste. Marie, and by traffic arrangements between Chicago and Detroit. The practice of utilizing existing lines was also followed in southern Ontario. Control of the Kingston and

Pembroke Railway made a connection between Lake Ontario and the transcontinental line at Renfrew, and the lease of the Tillsonburg, Lake Erie and Pacific Railroad gave access to Lake Erie at Port Burwell.

The other great private companies were in a very different position from the Canadian Pacific. At the outbreak of the war in 1914 neither the Grand Trunk Pacific nor the Canadian Northern had completed the laying of rails, far less had an opportunity of improving the new line, building branches, or in general establishing the traffic which was their life-blood. Apart from the fact that some sections of the Canadian Northern had been in successful operation for some years, the two new transcontinentals may be compared to the Canadian Pacific of twenty-five years before. They were, in fact, approaching that stage, found in many enterprises, in which a heavy capital expenditure must soon be relieved by income. It was the misfortune of both companies to reach the final and most expensive stage in their development at an unfavourable time – most expensive because they were carrying the accumulated burden of borrowed capital and were engaged in construction in the mountains of British Columbia.

A steady rise in wages since the beginning of the century increased the labour costs of the railways during the period of construction, but there was an ample supply of men.

INDEX NUMBER OF WAGES (1913=100)[1]

1901	67.8	1916	105.7
1906	78.7	1917	117.5
1911	92.5	1918	139.8
1914	101.4	1919	160.4
1915	101.4	1920	192.1

Materials for construction, rolling stock, and equipment of all kinds increased in price. The index number of wholesale prices shows a rise from 84.5 in 1901 to the basic 100 in 1913, to 102.3 in 1914, 109.9 in 1915, and to much higher levels in later years.[2]

The rise in wages and prices was accompanied by a corresponding increase in prosperity, and by private and governmental optimism which made railway construction accepted as part of the general progress of the country. Apart from the first panic at the outbreak of hostilities, the war stimulated rather than depressed business. Unemployment and other indications of depression that existed in 1914 were soon cured by an increasing demand for men and goods. Immigration fell off, and production was encouraged by the sudden demand for natural products and manufactured goods in Europe. The effect of the war on traffic and income of all Canadian railways is evident in the following table.[3]

YEAR (ENDING JUNE 30)	PASSENGERS	FREIGHT (TONS)	GROSS EARNINGS $	OPERATING EXPENSES $	RATIO OF EXPENSES TO RECEIPTS %
1911	37,097,718	79,884,282	188,733,494	131,034,785	69.43
1912	41,124,181	80,444,331	219,403,753	150,726,540	68.70
1913	46,185,968	106,992,710	256,702,703	182,011,690	70.90
1914	46,702,280	101,393,989	243,083,539	178,975,259	73.63
1915	46,322,035	87,204,838	199,843,072	147,731,099	73.92
1916	43,503,459	100,659,088	261,888,654	180,542,259	68.94

The height of the good years before the war came in 1913 and income declined in 1914 and in 1915. The ratio of expenses to receipts scarcely changed in the first year of the war, (1914-1915), and went down materially with better traffic in 1916.

The last spike in the National Transcontinental was driven in November 1913. The Grand Trunk Pacific refused to implement the agreement by which it was to lease that railway, and it was operated by the Canadian Government Railways from June 1915. The Grand Trunk Pacific, from Winnipeg to Prince Rupert, was opened for traffic in September 1914. The rail on the Canadian Northern was completed in January 1915, and passenger traffic established by November. For both of the latter railways a large amount of work on the track remained to be done, and the Grand Trunk Pacific particularly required extensive branch lines.

At this critical time in the history of the two companies the flow of capital began to diminish. The London money market had for some years been ready to meet their needs, but in 1912 began to be less responsive, and a Canadian Northern issue raised in the spring of 1914 proved to be the last. The company was then obliged to turn to New York, but loans could only be floated at low prices and higher rates of interest.[4] Parliament had long been a main source of capital, and in 1914 it again made loans to one or both companies. When in 1916 it was proposed that further advances should be made, it became apparent that it was time to take stock of the position of the government in regard to these railways and to consider the formulation of a policy for the future. Sir Thomas White, the minister of finance, told the house of commons that,

with improving financial conditions and with better earnings in prospect, it was hoped that no material assistance would be required in addition to the aid which was given in 1914, but it is now clear, from the statements presented by the railway companies in question, . . . from the financial conditions which still prevail, and from the fact that the war is still raging, that relief is absolutely necessary if these two railway companies are to continue as solvent and going concerns. It has been the policy of the Government since the outbreak of the war to maintain stability and to promote confidence in the financial and economic condition of Canada. We have, therefore, . . . looked with growing concern upon the financial condition of these two great transcontinental enterprises whose affairs have become so intimately connected with the public credit both of the Dominion and of the provinces of Canada. Securities to the amount of several hundred millions of dollars have been issued by both these companies and have found their way into the hands of investors in Great Britain, the United States, and Europe. Any financial crisis in their affairs could not but react seriously upon the general credit of the Dominion in the eyes of the outside world.[5]

The minister went on to examine in detail the financial position of both railways, in the course of which he quoted from a letter from A. W. Smithers, chairman of the Grand Trunk, in which Smithers stated that "we are at the end of our tether with regard to Grand Trunk Pacific financing." Having laid bare the facts, White then sketched the three alternative policies which might be followed. The first was to withhold aid and allow the companies to go into receivership. Such a course would endanger the position of the Grand Trunk itself; would, in his opinion, be a serious threat to the credit of public and private bodies in Canada; and would result in the dismemberment of the Canadian Northern, the provinces taking over the constituent companies which they had guaranteed. The second alternative was

to permit and take physical possession of the two railway systems in question; that is to say, foreclose the mortgage which we hold. In that event the Dominion Government would take over the mortgaged premises and hold them as it does the Intercolonial railway. If it continued to hold them and operate them without a receivership or liquidation it would mean that it would have to pay all the interest on all the securities of these companies at present outstanding. It would have to provide the amount of temporary aid which we are now proposing and in addition it would have to provide for the future financing of these roads.

The third alternative, and the one which the government advocated, was to give such temporary financial assistance as would enable the two companies to continue operations, and to delay any decision on policy until an investigation of the whole railway situation had been made by experts. A royal commission was appointed in July 1916, consisting of A. H. Smith, president of the New York Central Railroad (chairman), Sir Henry Drayton, chief commissioner of the board of railway commissioners for Canada, and W. H. Acworth, an English authority on railways. (Mr. Acworth was appointed to replace Sir George Paish, who had resigned on account of ill health.) The terms of reference covered the general problem of transportation in Canada, the status of the three transcontinental railways, and reorganization or acquisition of any of these. In the case of acquisition, the commissioners were to give an opinion on the most effective system of operation. During the autumn the commissioners toured Canada, taking evidence as they went. At the same time they had a physical examination of the Canadian Northern and Grand Trunk Pacific made by engineers under the supervision of Professor G. F. Swain of Harvard.

The commission reported in 1917, Drayton and Acworth presenting a majority, and Smith a minority, report.[6] The disagreement between them was not on the necessity of governmental aid, but as to the extent and character of that aid. All commissioners agreed that the Canadian Pacific was able to stand on its own feet and needed no governmental assistance.

The only way in which this railway entered into any plan that might be adopted was in relation to the avoidance of discrimination against it, for example, by means of uneconomic rates. The majority of the commissioners recommended that the Grand Trunk, Grand Trunk Pacific, and Canadian Northern "be assumed by the people of Canada." Having decided on this, they considered "how this control should be exercised."

In our judgment it is not in the interests of Canada that the operation of its railways should be in the hands of the Government. We know no country in the world where a democratic state owns and operates its railways, in which politics have not injuriously affected the management of the railways and the railways have not had an injurious influence on politics. We do not think Government ownership of the Canadian railways would tend to reduction of rates, but rather in the contrary direction.

Somewhat paradoxically, the commissioners maintained, as an argument especially applicable to Canada, that government ownership and operation of other railways would be unfair to the Canadian Pacific, since rates might be lowered; so that, if the Dominion operated the other railways, "it would be morally bound to offer to purchase the Canadian Pacific also." A second particular argument against government operation was adduced from the fact that the railways in question had a considerable mileage in the United States; and a third was that Canadian resources were fully needed for the conduct of the war.

The commissioners, it appears, objected not only to government operation, but to government ownership. At the same time, the three companies were to "pass into other hands," but not by way of receivership, for that course would involve danger to Canadian credit.

We think the question, whether there should be one body or more, is answered by the facts that we have already recited. The Canadian Northern is weak in the East. The Grand Trunk, with the inadequate prairie branches of the Grand Trunk Pacific, would be almost powerless to compete in the West with the Canadian Northern and the Canadian Pacific. The natural tendency of the Grand Trunk and Canadian Northern organiza-

tions, if left separate, would be for each to invade the territory of the other. Remaining separate, the Canadian Northern system would need to spend many millions of dollars to obtain an adequate hold on the East in competition with the Canadian Pacific and Grand Trunk. Remaining separate, the Grand Trunk and Grand Trunk Pacific system would need to spend many millions of dollars on new branches in the West, in order to hold its own with the Canadian Pacific and the Canadian Northern. And this money would be needed at once, for till it was spent neither organization would possess a complete system. Canada cannot afford all these new railways, and does not need three competitive systems. We recommend therefore that the three undertakings, the Canadian Northern, the Grand Trunk, and the Grand Trunk Pacific be united in one system.

It had been suggested to the commission that the Canadian Pacific should acquire the other roads and operate them as partner with the government, and again that the government should acquire all the roads, including the Canadian Pacific, and operate them as a unit, but both of these suggestions were rejected in the majority report, largely on the grounds of opposition to monopoly on the one hand and to state ownership on the other. Believing that a commercial company could not be formed to take over the three railways which were in trouble, the commissioners then turned to the solution which they favoured. A board of five trustees should be constituted by parliament and incorporated as "The Dominion Railway Company," in which the ownership of the Canadian Northern, Grand Trunk and Grand Trunk Pacific railways was to be vested. The Intercolonial (including the Prince Edward Island Railway) and the National Transcontinental were to be "handed over" to the company, and the whole five to be operated as a single system. For its part, the government was to assume responsibility for the payment of interest on existing securities.

In order to secure its independence, the board of trustees was to be permanent and self-perpetuating. It should be made up of experts in railways, finance, and labour, and must not even be suspected of assuming a political complexion. This was the great danger that the majority commissioners saw in their plan, and time after time they reiterated their opposition to state operation. "We do not recommend the transfer of the three companies at all," they wrote, "unless our recommendations as to the method to be followed are also substantially accepted."

In a brief but able minority report, A. H. Smith explained the reasons for which he differed from his colleagues.

They insist that this board is to be permanent and self perpetuating. I do not know by what means one Parliament can bind its successors to a given policy, especially in so simple a matter as changing the organization of a government board. My friends seem to avoid government ownership and operation, in fact condemn it as inadvisable, but propose a plan which contains so many elements of danger in the direction which is sought to be avoided that I am unable to join them.

Their plan, he added, would add about a billion dollars to the Canadian debt. It left out some of the railways, and discriminated in the methods by which properties were to be acquired. Centralization of control, Smith believed, would not ensure good service. In place of the plan suggested, he proposed another, which he summarized as follows:

Let the Canadian Pacific alone; let the Grand Trunk operate the eastern lines now held by that company and the Canadian Northern; let the Canadian Northern operate the western lines, now held by that company and the Grand Trunk Pacific system; let the government operate the connections or procure their operation by private companies.

Smith realized that his plan would not do away with the continuance of public aid to some of the railways, but believed that that aid would be reduced to a minimum, and would be concentrated on those lines which were not self-supporting and could not, for many years, be expected to be self-supporting.

2. NATIONALIZATION OF THE CANADIAN NORTHERN

The report of the royal commission was presented to parliament in the spring of 1917, and at the beginning of August the government announced its policy.[7] The gravity of the situation, as portrayed by the report, was accepted; and it was assumed that some steps must be taken immediately which would ensure the maintenance of an adequate transportation system, avoidance of a dislocation of credit, protection of the governmental investment in the companies, and some degree of permanence in the solution. In regard to the Canadian Northern the policy was simplicity itself. The government should be empowered to acquire that portion of the common stock of the railway which it did not already hold, the value of the stock to be determined by a board of arbitration. Holding the common stock, the government would then be in a position to control the company, whose credit would be restored by the very fact of acquisition.

The debate on the plan was long and, at times, bitter. After two weeks of debate G. P. Graham, who, as a former minister of railways, naturally became chief spokesman for the opposition, moved an amendment that parliament should take over the Canadian Northern without any compensation to the holders of common stock. The amendment was lost, but the issue continued to be debated. Objections to the bill were based on a number of grounds. Some members objected to it because they disbelieved in government ownership on principle. A more consistently expressed argument was that, since the Drayton-Acworth report had found the stock to be valueless, the proposed arbitration was unnecessary. A number of members sought to show that the government was influenced by financial interests. Persistent questioning elicited from the minister of finance the fact that, of the $58,614,000 of common stock standing in the name of Mackenzie, Mann and Company, $51,000,000 was pledged to the Canadian Bank of Commerce against advances. The minister, however, was not prepared to state the amount of those advances. One member asked baldly: "Would not the object [of the bill] also be to save from bankruptcy the Canadian Bank of Commerce, which is said to be responsible for all the Canadian Northern's liabilities since its very inception?" A second member, though making no charge, said that "the conclusion is borne in upon the mind of any man who thinks that unless this stock is given some value the Canadian Bank of Commerce may have trouble in getting repayment of their loan."[8]

Again and again the bill was attacked and defended. The debate ran through the whole of August, and it was only by vigorous use of the closure that the government was able to bring it to an end before another month began. The act (7 & 8 Geo. V, c.24) was brief indeed as a result of such major campaigning. It empowered the government to acquire the 600,000 shares which it did not already hold, at a price to be determined by arbitration. When the transfer of shares had taken place, the government might assist the Canadian Northern to the extent of $25,000,000 without further authority from parliament. In the agreement of October 1, 1917, between the government, Mackenzie, Mann and Company, and the Bank of Commerce, for the purchase of the shares, it was stated, under the authority of an order in council, that no more than $10,000,000 should be paid for the stock.[9]

The die was cast, and it only remained to determine the value of the shares. The board of arbitration as appointed consisted of Sir William Meredith, chief justice of Ontario, as representative of the government and chairman of the board; Wallace Nesbitt for the stockholders; and R. E. Harris, justice of the supreme court of Nova Scotia, as the neutral member. The hearings began at Toronto on January 18, 1918. A galaxy of legal talent was ready to argue the case: W. N. Tilley for the government, Pierce Butler, of the Minnesota bar, for Mackenzie, Mann and Company, I. F. Hellmuth for the Canadian Bank of Commerce, and F. H. Phippen for the Canadian Northern Railway, were the leaders. The hearings continued, with some protracted breaks, until the middle of May, and covered and re-covered almost every possible aspect of the value and operations of the Canadian Northern. The mass of evidence brought forward, together with previous examinations of the railway, afford an opportunity of analyzing the position of the Canadian Northern system at that time.

The Canadian Northern was built at a low cost with the intention of effecting improvements as income permitted. That this was in general the case was never seriously questioned by its friends or its critics. Both D. B. Hanna and Sir Donald Mann, men who knew the road intimately, in evidence before the board of arbitration, argued that the Canadian Northern was in all essentials the best transcontinental railway in Canada. They referred to the superior grades and curvatures which had been obtained; and Mann, when questioned about the relative standards of the Canadian Northern and Canadian Pacific, pointed out that people had forgotten what the latter was like when first built. He admitted that the Canadian Pacific in 1917 was better in some places than the Canadian Northern, but that difference, he said, could be made up: on the other hand the Canadian Pacific could never get such a favourable route through the Rockies or between Nipigon and Sudbury. Other witnesses told of deficiencies which they had found. G. R. Balloch, one of the engineers employed by Swain, made the general comment: "It is the cheapest line. The most cheaply-constructed line, with more temporary structures which will depreciate in time, rapidly in fact. The time is maturing now for a lot of things and in another fifteen or twenty years will mature on the others."[10] In detail he said that the roadbed was narrow in places; that the line was undulating; that the ballast was in some cases inadequate; and that light or worn rails were not uncommon. He pointed to wooden bridges, trestles, culverts, and water-tanks – all of which would have to be replaced. H. A. Drury, engineer for the board of railway commissioners, stated that he had found the line along the Kaministiquia River to have a dangerously narrow embankment, and a track that was rough and out of line.

Further impressions may be gained from the report drawn up at the request of a group of New York financiers by a commission composed of E. E. Loomis, president of the Lehigh Valley Railroad, and J. W. Platten, president of the United States Mortgage and Trust Company, and employing as consulting engineers the New York firm of Coverdale and Colpitts. In the report, dated March 1917, it is said that "the entire transcontinental line is well located and well built. As to grades and alignments, it is superior to its competitors. ... ." The roadbed on both main and branch lines was described as "adequate," but portions of the latter were said to require ballasting. The only real criticism was directed at the inadequate supply of locomotives and rolling stock. As compared with other evidence, the Loomis report seems to give too favourable a picture. Leaving this as one extreme and the stories about trains sinking into the mud as the other, it may probably be taken that the Canadian Northern was well planned and located, and economically built, but maintenance had been inadequate, and it contained a good deal of temporary work that would sooner or later have to be replaced. The amount of replacement necessary had an important bearing on the value of the property.

All those who examined the Canadian Northern, whether officers of the company or not, laid stress on the route it followed, not only as regards grades but also in relation to the traffic which it either had or might expect to have. The line, with its feeders, through the northern wheat belt had proved a great success. Besides grains, forest products and coal were carried in satisfactory amounts, as well as the usual freight of a settled area. In the prairies, where the Canadian Northern had originated, adequate branches and terminals existed; but in 1917 such developments had not been more than started in the east and far west. Lack of terminal facilities at Vancouver meant that little use could be made of the railway for exporting wheat. In the east the situation was worse. Terminals had yet to be established at many centres, notably at Montreal. Spur lines to factories did not exist in sufficient numbers to allow competition on even terms with the other railways which were in a position to secure freight and route it over their own lines. Another weakness was the lack of American connections. The company intended to build west from Toronto, *via* Hamilton to Niagara Falls, but had not yet been able to do so. Largely to this condition was attributed the small amount of passenger traffic, especially in the east. Over the whole system the revenue from passenger traffic was very slight: in 1915 the Canadian Pacific's earnings per mile on passengers were $2,468, while the corresponding figure for the Canadian Northern was $843.[11]

As seen from the Canadian Northern point of view the problem was that financial considerations made it impossible to complete a programme by which it had been hoped to create a profitable railway; and it was lack of capital rather than a breakdown in operation that caused the crisis of 1917. Part of the difficulty of disentangling the accounts of the Canadian Northern arises out of the number of companies that made up the system as a whole. In order to secure provincial aid, separate companies had been created in almost every province. The transcontinental line was made up of the Canadian Northern Pacific, Canadian Northern, Canadian Northern Ontario, and Canadian Northern Quebec, and in addition there were a score or more affiliated companies. The cost of construction was met by the sale of bonds and debentures, of lands granted in aid of construction, and by direct subsidies. The common stock of both the Canadian Northern proper and of the affiliated companies was held almost entirely by Mackenzie, Mann and Company, in payment for their services as contractors and promoters and in exchange for lands which they had received as contractors on the roads making up the early Canadian Northern.

As owners of the voting shares Mackenzie and Mann were able to control the policy of the Canadian Northern, and to act quickly without notice to the public. Such a position was valuable, for example, in the case of the acquisition of a railway which rival interests might want. Although no dividend was ever paid on the common stock, their ownership of it was the only means by which Mackenzie and Mann could expect a return on their expenditure of time and money. The arrangement by which all expenses were met out of securities calling for a fixed interest was advantageous from the point of view of management, but it had drawbacks in other ways. This was a point emphasized by Tilley in his argument before the board of arbitration.

The Canadian Pacific Railway [he said] *has a certain flexibility to its capital because it has the shareholders' money, and if they cannot pay a high dividend they can pay a lower dividend. They can get some return, but with the Canadian Northern you have the whole expense of the road in its fixed charges, you have got no flexibility at all. If you do not get the money, you just accumulate your debts, and instead of being able to say to the shareholders, now, we will cut off your dividend, the debt keeps on accumulating and piling up, because everything is in that fixed charge, and it goes on, and that must be paid. . . . The capital stock itself represents no cash investment. Nothing has gone into the property for it.*[12]

The last remark is hardly accurate, because in fact Mackenzie and Mann never charged the company with their services as contractors; but the main point is an important one. Mackenzie and Mann had followed a financial policy directly contrary to that followed by the Canadian Pacific, with its small fixed charges, and they ran into difficulties. On the other hand, the use of bonds for construction expenses may be partly explained by the willingness of both federal and provincial governments to guarantee such bonds in preference to helping the company by land grants – a change of method which dates from after the building of the Canadian Pacific.

In a small compass it is impossible, even if it were otherwise practicable, to recount the intricate financial history of the Canadian Northern. As an indication of the trend, however, a portion of D. B. Hanna's evidence in 1918 may be quoted.

. . . for 18 years up until the 30th June, 1914, the road not only paid all its fixed charges, interest on all its equipment purchases, but it did something more, it paid for four years dividends out of its net income after paying all its fixed charges, dividends on the 5 per cent. income charge convertible debenture stock. That stock was sold subject to dividends based upon net income, and in 1911 that stock sold to the extent of 15 million dollars. It paid out of its surplus income after all fixed charges, including interest on equipment securities, $312,892.05. The surplus for that year before paying these amounts out being $1,007,696.80. In 1912 the surplus after paying all fixed charges, including interest on equipment securities, was $1,250,200.99. It paid out that year on income charge account $674,804.11. In 1913 we had sold the additional 10 million dollars of the 5 per cent. income charge convertible debenture stock increasing the amount to 25 millions. That year the surplus was $1,832,943.78, after paying all the fixed charges and equipment securities interest; and they paid out of that surplus on income charge account, $988,214.49. In 1914 the surplus for that year was $1,554,505.41. Out of that surplus the railway paid $1,250,000 on income charge convertible stock. . . . In 1914 . . . the depression came along, and the war aggravated that situation, and business fell away, and we have not paid anything since 1914.[13]

The financial stress forced the company to look to the Dominion government for help. In years past it had received, like all Canadian railways, public aid from several sources and in several ways. Now that it needed more, the government was unwilling to commit itself further without receiving consideration in return. Already this process had begun, for by an act of

1913 (3 & 4 Geo. V, c. 10) subsidies to the Canadian Northern Ontario and Canadian Northern Alberta were granted on condition of the transfer to the government of $7,000,000 (par value) of the stock of the Canadian Northern. The total stock issued at that time was $77,000,000. When further funds were needed in 1914, a new arrangement was made by an act (4 & 5 Geo. V, c. 20) under which the total authorized capital of the Canadian Northern was limited to $100,000,000. At the same time $33,000,00 of stock was transferred to the government as against a guarantee of the capital and interest on $45,000,000 of bonds. In this way the government secured forty out of a total of one hundred millions of the stock of the company. The greater part of the remainder was nominally held by Mackenzie, Mann and Company, but all but a small portion was pledged to the Canadian Bank of Commerce. The ownership of the common stock helps to explain the process of the transfer of the company, and accounts for the parties to the arbitration; it also affected the freedom of action of the company. It was a curious twist of fortune that the concentration of the voting shares in the hands of Mackenzie and Mann, which was intended to give them control over the destinies of the company, made it possible for them to lose control to the government just when they most needed it.

In spite of governmental assistance – or perhaps because of its limitations – bankruptcy began to loom on the horizon. Sir William Mackenzie, who had already secured loans in New York after the closing of the London market, hoped to make some more permanent arrangement there which would tide the company over its financial difficulties. In 1916 a syndicate headed by Bertron, Griscom and Company had under consideration the furnishing of a large amount of capital. To acquaint themselves with the value and character of the property, they appointed Messrs. Loomis and Platten to investigate, and they in turn arranged for the report which has already been described. Unhappily for this plan, however, the royal commission of 1916 intervened and, by raising the possibility of nationalization, prevented any further steps being taken. A second way out of the difficulty was cautiously mentioned by Mann in his evidence before the board of arbitration. He stated that the company had had an opportunity to sell its whole property a year before the act was passed which provided for the arbitration. As the company controlled only sixty per cent of its stock, and the government would not sell its forty per cent, the party refused to buy.[14] Pressed on this point later, he stated that there had been negotiations with "connections of the Canadian Pacific Railway"[15]– which was presumably the "party" he had previously mentioned. It is interesting to speculate on the course of later history had the negotiations with the Canadian Pacific resulted in a sale. It is also interesting to speculate on the reasons for the government's action in blocking the sale. While such reasons can only be guessed at, it is worthy of note that the government, by blocking the sale, might be judged to have undertaken a moral commitment toward the holders of the securities. A third attempt to avoid receivership was made by inviting the provinces to pay the interest on the bonds they had guaranteed. This, according to Mann, was accepted in principle by British Columbia and one other province, but the process was interrupted by the decision of the Dominion government to buy the road.

The government would not dispose of its minority interest, and thus nullified the plans of the company's directors to escape receivership – whether or not these might otherwise have been successful. It decided to buy the majority interest, which stood in the name of a holding company but was actually held by a bank, and, as a final curiosity, provided for arbitration to decide the value of the majority stock, but set a maximum figure which might be paid.

In approaching its task the board of arbitration very naturally turned to the report of the royal commission of 1916. Drayton and Acworth had used three methods of arriving at the value of the Canadian Northern. From the point of view of cash investment they reached a figure of $370,000,000 as the "maximum possible cost of the Canadian Northern system as at present existing." Secondly, by making use of Swain's investigations, they were able to arrive at an estimate of the cost of reproducing the property new, at pre-war prices. Allowing for depreciation, they put the cost of reproduction at $402,749,663. Considering that the outstanding liabilities were about $400,000,000, they would appear to be about equal to the reproduction cost; but because of the minority holdings in some of the Canadian Northern enterprises, the commissioners subtracted $10,000,000 from the assets. Thirdly, the commissioners considered the value of the property for sale as a going concern. On the basis of earning power, they believed that no purchaser would pay a price equal to the total liabilities. By means of these three arguments Drayton and Acworth arrived at the conclusion,

that the shareholders of the company have no equity either on the ground of cash put in, or on the ground of physical reproduction cost, or on the ground of the saleable value of their property as a going concern. If, then, the people of Canada have already found, or assumed responsibility for, the bulk of the capital; if they must needs find what further capital is required; and if they must make up for some years to come considerable deficits in net earnings, it seems logically to follow that the people of Canada should assume control of the property.

The arbitrators, of course, did not accept without question the Drayton-Acworth report. Early in the proceedings both Phippen, as counsel for the Canadian Northern, and Hellmuth, as counsel for the Bank of Commerce, protested against the Drayton-Acworth calculations on the ground that they left out of consideration a number of assets, such as money in banks, and land, involving an error of $52,000,000. Whether or not this was accepted by the arbitrators is not clear. The statement accompanying their award was general in the extreme, and gave little indication of the weight which they put on the mass of evidence that had been submitted. The relevant part of it reads as follows:

As to whether or not there was a surplus of assets over liabilities was naturally a subject which engaged much time and consideration. It is of course not a conclusive test as to the value of the stock but it is an element which cannot be ignored. Its importance was perhaps emphasized by the fact that a Royal Commission had reported the assets and liabilities of the Company to be about equal. This report which was made in a proceeding to which the company and its shareholders were not parties, was admittedly made on a misconception of some of the facts, and there were omissions of both assets and liabilities. It should also be pointed out that the work of the Royal Commission has reference to a date anterior to the first day of October, 1917, and there were changes in the interval.

In arriving at the surplus of assets over liabilities, the report of Professor Swain as to the reproduction cost of the physical property based on pre-war prices, and also his estimate of the depreciation has been adopted and after a careful examination we found the surplus of assets over liabilities of the Company on the first day of October, 1917, on a conservative basis to be not less than twenty-five million dollars after deducting the full amount of depreciation found by Professor Swain and making such reduction in the value of the land grants and other assets as seemed reasonable.

It is to be pointed out that a valuation of the physical property of a railway company by the reproduction new method, less depreciation, is not to be regarded as an ascertainment of the actual value. It is only a means to that end, but as it was the best, and in fact the only estimate available, it has been adopted as a basis for the foregoing calculations.

While the surplus of assets over liabilities is an element for consideration as has been already pointed out, it is not conclusive as to the value of the stock of the company. The prospective earning power is perhaps more important than any other element in ascertaining such value. And in arriving at a conclusion we have given careful consideration to the past history of the company, the location of its lines and their construction, the rate of interest on the funded and other debts of the company, the probable future growth of the population and business of the country, and all other factors which seemed to us to have any bearing upon the question.[16]

The award, which was signed by all three arbitrators, was that the value of the six hundred thousand shares in question was $10,800,000. How this figure was arrived at is not disclosed, nor its relation to the $25,000,000 of surplus assets. The value set on the shares was very close to the sum fixed as a maximum in the agreement ($10,000,000).

The award did not in any way affect the status of the Canadian Northern, which had already passed into the hands of the government. In September 1918 the government appointed a new board of directors, and in November charged it with the management of the Canadian Government Railways in place of the general manager. In December a further order in council authorized the board to use the designation "Canadian National Railways" for the lines which they operated. For the time being, however, the Canadian Northern was preserved as a separate entity: the final organization of the Canadian National awaiting the nationalization of the Grand Trunk and Grand Trunk Pacific.

3. NATIONALIZATION OF THE GRAND TRUNK

When in 1917 parliament was asked to pass a measure to take over the Canadian Northern it was also obliged to recognize that the Grand Trunk Pacific was in difficulties. At that time, however, it was not possible to take steps in regard to the Grand Trunk Pacific parallel to those taken in regard to the Canadian Northern. The government's policy, as explained to the house of commons, was to make temporary provision for the Grand Trunk Pacific pending further negotiations.

. . . the situation is complicated by the fact that the Grand Trunk Railway Company is . . . largely involved by its guarantee of the Grand Trunk Pacific securities. It is, therefore, not possible for us, even if we were disposed to do so, at this time to deal with the Grand Trunk Pacific Railway Company in the same manner that we propose to deal with the Canadian Northern Railway Company, because a long negotiation would be necessary with the Grand Trunk Railway Company, in order that the public interests might be safeguarded before the Grand Trunk was relieved from any or all of its liabilities in connection with the matters which I have mentioned. Our policy with regard to the Grand Trunk Pacific for the time being is this: we propose to make a demand loan, repayable at six per cent, secured by a mortgage to the amount of $7,500,000. We shall take the power to constitute the Board of Directors of the Grand Trunk Pacific as we see fit.[17]

So much for the present necessity. As to the future, the government apparently looked forward to acquiring the Grand

Trunk Pacific, though whether they would go as far as the Drayton-Acworth proposals by adding to it the Grand Trunk was not yet disclosed. White continued:

Personally I would look forward to the Government some day acquiring the Grand Trunk Pacific system, because with the Canadian Northern system belonging to the Government, as we propose, the two systems could usefully co-operate in the West. . . . It is not our intention to release the Grand Trunk Railway Company from their obligations in respect of the Grand Trunk Pacific Railway Company. . . .

The last remark referred to the Grand Trunk's suggestion, first officially made at the end of 1915, that the government should take over the Grand Trunk Pacific and the liabilities of the Grand Trunk to that company. To this suggestion the royal commission was firmly opposed, as the government subsequently proved to be. The government already had the National Transcontinental on its hands and was unwilling to become the owner of any other lines with such distant prospects of financial success. The divergence of opinion served to complicate and prolong the negotiations with the company.

In May 1918 the prime minister told the house of commons that if the Grand Trunk Pacific were taken over, "that practically involves the taking over of the Grand Trunk Railway as well."[18] This he believed desirable in order to give eastern connections to both the Grand Trunk Pacific and the Canadian Northern; because the Grand Trunk might be crippled if it had to meet its obligations to the Grand Trunk Pacific; and, while it had "no bright future prospects" without its western connections, it might do well if amalgamated with the Grand Trunk Pacific and Canadian Northern. Confidential negotiations, he told the house, were being conducted with the Grand Trunk. These had, in fact, been in train for some months. In January the government asked the Grand Trunk on what terms that company and the Grand Trunk Pacific could be acquired by the Dominion. The terms proposed in reply were that the government should assume all the liabilities of the Grand Trunk, pay an annual amount of $5,287,000 for dividends on guaranteed and preferred stock, and an amount sufficient to cover dividends on the common stock at a rate rising annually from one to two and one-half per cent. After refusing this optimistic offer, the government expressed its willingness to take over the assets and liabilities of the Grand Trunk and Grand Trunk Pacific and pay annually to the shareholders $2,500,000 for the first three years, $3,000,000 for the next five, and $3,600,000 thereafter. This met with no more success than the first proposal, and the correspondence continued. In July the government renewed its offer, together with an alternative one that the whole question of remuneration be referred to a board of arbitration. This again was refused, and a further offer made.

In February 1919 the company notified the government that they expected to have to default on March 1 in respect of the interest on securities falling due in London, and indicated that a serious situation would arise if funds were not found to prevent such an unfortunate occurrence. The minister of finance replied that no further sums would be voted as long as negotiations "remained in their present unsatisfactory condition." The interest was paid; but a few days later, "without any previous intimation or discussion at all," notice was received by the government that the Grand Trunk Pacific could not be operated after March 10, on the ground that the freight rates in the west were not high enough to allow operation without loss. This the government regarded as a threat designed to bring the desired loan;[19] but instead of taking that action they appointed the minister of railways and canals as receiver under the authority of the War Measures Act – holding that the exchequer court was not competent to act in such a case. The Grand Trunk Pacific, with its telegraphs, steamships, hotels and other undertakings, was operated under receivership from March 10, 1919 until September 1, 1920, at which date its management was entrusted to the board of directors of the Canadian National.[20]

It still remained to come to an agreement with the Grand Trunk, which continued to be held responsible for its obligations to the Grand Trunk Pacific. At long last that agreement was reached in October 1919. Two acts (10 Geo. V, c. 17, and 10 and 11 Geo. V, c. 13) and an agreement between government and company covered the acquisition of the Grand Trunk and its subsidiaries. All the capital stock was to be taken over with the exception of the issue of four per cent guaranteed stock, and on that the government agreed to pay interest. To determine the value of the stock a board of three arbitrators was to be appointed, and they were limited to a maximum award of $64,166,666.66.

After some delay, the board of arbitration met on February 1, 1921. Sir Walter Cassels, justice of the exchequer court, was chairman; Sir Thomas White represented the government; and Mr. W. H. Taft, formerly president of the United States, represented the company. The proceedings were similar to those adopted for the Canadian Northern, but in this case only the government and company were represented by counsel. For each party there were a number of distinguished lawyers: W. N. Tilley appearing again for the government, and Eugene Lafleur for the company. The arbitrators were asked to determine the value of the first, second, and third preference stock and of the common stock. As in the previous arbitration, the board examined in some detail the physical and financial condition of the railway; but, since the majority of the board refused to accept evidence bearing on reproduction value, less evidence could be adduced on physical condition. Because the arbitrators failed to reach a unanimous decision, each wrote his reasons for coming to certain conclusions; and these three arguments throw light not only on the arbitration but also on the condition of the company.

At the time when the board met, the Grand Trunk system had not taken over the National Transcontinental, and had lost the Grand Trunk Pacific. Nevertheless, for purposes of estimating the value of the stock, the G.T.P. was included in consideration, because of the financial relation between the two companies. This outlet to the Pacific, on which Hays had pinned his hopes, had proved to be a disastrous failure, as was most clearly evident from the efforts of the parent company to get rid of it. As a matter of policy the line to the Pacific had been built to a high standard, and the large capital expenditure inevitably involved was enhanced by the rising prices of labour and materials in the pre-war and war years. The expected traffic never materialized, partly because the west did not develop as had been hoped, partly because the G.T.P. was supplied with an inadequate system of feeders, and partly because of competition from the spreading Canadian Northern lines. The Grand Trunk claimed, with some apparent justice, that the Canadian Northern had been supported by the government after the agreement concerning the G.T.P.; and that this unexpected competition had upset the calculations concerning traffic. An additional reason, which might or might not have changed with time, was that Prince Rupert was a new port, with no established ocean traffic and no facilities. It was more like a dead end than an outlet to the far east.

For purposes of profitable operation, therefore, the Grand Trunk was confined to its old territory in central Canada and the eastern and mid-western states. An interesting analysis on these lines was made by Mr. Taft, whose attitude toward the company was friendly but not uncritical.

The Grand Trunk System has been burdened with a very great number of branch lines, and with some lines parallel to its main trunk line, which it acquired to avoid competition, and which are not a source of profit. Many of the branch lines of course are feeders, but it is quite apparent that they are in some respects a burden. In a degree the same thing has been true of branch lines acquired in Michigan, but the marvellous growth of business in that State in the centres reached by the Grand Trunk is likely to make them very profitable. With much care and wisdom the business of the Grand Trunk System has been nursed into a large through traffic between Chicago and the Atlantic Seaboard. While the amount of business done in the United States by the Western Lines and the New England Lines of the Grand Trunk System is not more than one-third of the Grand Trunk Railway of Canada, the business which has come to the Grand Trunk is perhaps 70 per cent. due to its business from and to the United States, to and from Canada, and to other business from and to points in the United States through Canada to and from other points in the United States.[21]

The Grand Trunk had in reality continued to rely on its original policy of operating as a through road for New England, central Canada, and the middle west. Nevertheless – and in spite of the financial failure of the Grand Trunk Pacific – it need not be assumed that the general idea of expansion into the west was a mistake. One of its prime difficulties was that it missed the profits accruing from long-haul traffic. In 1920 the Grand

Trunk, operating 4,775 miles of rail, moved 33,026,658 actual net tons, for which it was paid $80,686,623. The Canadian Pacific, operating 13,402 miles, moved 29,919,645 tons, and was paid $143,878,185. Thus the Grand Trunk, moving 3,100,000 tons more freight than the Canadian Pacific, was paid $63,191,562 less for services. The Grand Trunk received $2.44 for each ton and the Canadian Pacific $4.81. The difference may largely be attributed to the fact that the Canadian Pacific carried each ton an average of 463 miles and the Grand Trunk an average of only 212 miles.[22]

Mr. Taft paid a high tribute to the efficiency of the local management in Canada, and believed that if policy, as dictated from London, had been equally enlightened, the fate of the railway would have been different. On the physical condition of the property there was, not unnaturally, considerable disagreement.[23] H. G. Kelley, who had been president of the company since 1917, testified that the road was in good operating condition and could carry a fifty per cent increase in its business without heavy expenditure. He can hardly be taken as an impartial witness, more especially as he had, in 1917, when the company was anxious to exhibit poverty, reported that the road was in need of large expenditure for maintenance. Two inspections were made of the Grand Trunk, one on behalf of the company by J. B. Berry, an American railway engineer of considerable experience, and the other for the department of railways and canals by engineers under Colonel Montserrat. Berry prepared a report on reproduction value less depreciation, but it was not allowed as evidence. His report, according to Taft, was that "the railroad does not show deferred maintenance, but on the whole is in excellent condition." Taft attributed to Montserrat "an enthusiasm of condemnation," and criticized him, and the department, for "calculating the cost of producing a perfect road without regard to economical considerations." On the Grand Trunk Pacific, Sullivan, an engineer and witness for the government, and Berry were in general agreement that a number of wooden trestles would soon have to be replaced by permanent structures.

In their statements in explanation of the award Cassels and White laid great emphasis on the financial condition and future financial prospects of the railway. When the decision was reached that reproduction cost was not relevant to the value of the stock of the company, it was also agreed that "the essential fact to be ascertained was the earning power, actual and potential, of the system." The following table, based on the statement of the company's auditor, indicated the results of operations. The Grand Trunk Pacific and Central Vermont are not included.

YEAR	SURPLUS (+) OR DEFICIT (−)	ADD SURPLUS ON OTHER SUBSIDIARY COMPANIES
1910	+$ 3,617,876	$ 83,360
1911	+ 4,188,783	267,865
1912	+ 4,482,448	249,196
1913	+ 2,874,592	484,648
1914	+ 2,014,176	71,132
1915	+ 5,755,730	245,924
1916	+ 11,319,341	732,834
1917	+ 3,402,540	270,540
1918	− 3,872,344	492,588
1919	− 6,488,918	166,932

To obtain a view of the real position of the railway the sums lost by the Grand Trunk by reason of its support of the Grand Trunk Pacific should also be considered. Apart from the sums lent from time to time to the G.T.P., there remained an absolute guarantee of $2,292,760 annually for interest and a further guarantee of $1,395,170 annually, conditional on the parent company having a surplus after paying its own running expenses and interest on funded obligations and guaranteed stock. It is no wonder that the Grand Trunk had made spirited efforts to rid itself of a company which had a deficit of $30,845,828 by January 1, 1920: and equally not surprising that the government persisted in holding that the Grand Trunk's guarantee was still binding.

The Grand Trunk executive had always suffered from the demands of stockholders for dividends, and had very often had to face the problem of whether profits should be used for interest on an over-capitalized system, or to meet obligations to the government, or go back into the road. At the beginning of the explanation of his award, Cassels refers to two points raised by the government's counsel: that the accounts of the railway had been manipulated, and that dividends were paid "when"– to quote Cassels' words –"to the knowledge of the chairman, there were no earnings applicable to the payment of such dividends; and those moneys so paid were diverted from paying claims due to the Government, which should have been paid, leaving the Government claim unpaid to the present time." The latter point is well reinforced by a series of cables between the chairman and the president of the company.

In a case involving the value of any railway, and particularly a railway with such complicated finances as the Grand Trunk, it was not unnatural that there should be differences of opinion. A. W. Atwater, in his argument for the company, took as a fair period the years 1912 to 1916, and showed that during that time there was an average of two and one-half million dollars annually available for dividends on the preferred and common stock, and that the operating ratio was approximately the same as that of the eastern rate group in the United States. In 1920, he said, the Grand Trunk operating ratio was higher than that group, so that if the transportation act of the United States operated, as it was intended, to produce a return, the Grand Trunk would have $2,800,000 available for dividends on preference and common stock.[24]

In September 1921 the official award was made, Cassels and White both holding that there was no value in the shares in question. The latter summed up his conclusions as follows:

(1) The actual earning power of the Grand Trunk Railway Company of Canada before, during, and since the war, and, so far as can be estimated, for the future does not justify the assumption that any profit would, from the date of the acquisition by the Government of the preference and common shares, viz., May, 1920, ever have been available for distribution to the holders thereof, after providing for the contingent liability of the company in respect of the Grand Trunk Pacific securities guaranteed by the company and dividends upon the "guaranteed stock."

(2) Having regard to its own continued heavy deficits, the necessity for making provision for deferred and extraordinary maintenance and capital construction, and its heavy liabilities in respect of securities of the Grand Trunk Pacific Railway Company of Canada bearing its guarantee, the Grand Trunk Railway Company of Canada, but for the financial support of

the Government since May, 1920, must have been forced into a receivership.

Upon these conclusions I find that the preference and common stock of the Grand Trunk Railway Company of Canada has no value. Any question as to compassionate consideration of the shareholders must be for the Government and Parliament of Canada to deal with and not for the Board.

In a dissenting judgment Taft analysed the earnings of the past and estimated earnings for the future, which enabled him to rate the value of the stock at not less than $48,000,000.

In the light of the actual history of the Grand Trunk Railway since 1920, either under separate management or as part of the Canadian National system, one is tempted to believe that the majority of the arbitrators were right in their conclusion. But, taking into consideration all the circumstances, it is not surprising that there was a strong feeling generated in England against the award and against the government's acceptance of it. A parallel was at once drawn with the arbitration on the stock of the Canadian Northern. In the Drayton-Acworth report the stock of the Canadian Northern was held to have no value, but the subsequent board of arbitration found a value of $10,800,000. In the case of the Canadian Northern arbitration a basis of "reproduction new" was allowed as the principal test of value, while no evidence bearing on that point was admitted by the board in the case of the Grand Trunk.[25] Furthermore, the Canadian Northern was a Canadian company, whose stock was largely in the possession of a Canadian bank; while the Grand Trunk was an English company, whose stock was widely distributed throughout England. Neither the appeal to the privy council on a point of law, nor that to the Canadian government for equitable consideration, met with success, and a sense of grievance was left to flourish.

In general, the English point of view was that a great deal of capital had been expended on this pioneer railway in Canada, and that the investment had been jeopardized primarily by the insistence of the Canadian government on its own plan for the Grand Trunk Pacific. It was felt that the attitudes of both government and board of arbitration were biased against the railway, and that they were willing to sacrifice the shareholders because they were not Canadian. On the other hand the point of view held in Canada was that the railway had always been operated too much for the shareholders; that its losses were due in large part to mismanagement from a distance; that it had not been forced to undertake the Grand Trunk Pacific; and that its recent history showed a consistent attempt to trick the government out of a repayment of the sums which had been advanced. A last act of the English directors made a bad impression in Canada. On the date of the ratification by the shareholders of the acquisition agreement, they voted a year's salary to the leading officials (a total of $306,000) out of the company's fire insurance fund, and five years' salary to the directors ($167,800). A royal commission later severely criticized the president and vice-president as responsible for this misplaced generosity.[26] Between the English and Canadian positions it was hard, if not impossible, to build a bridge; and the result was that a railway which had done much for Canadian development passed out of separate existence amidst protests and recriminations.

The Grand Trunk did not at once become part of the Canadian National organization. A temporary arrangement was first made by which a board of management, consisting of C. A. Hayes and S. J. Hungerford, representing the Canadian National, W. D. Robb and Frank Scott, representing the Grand Trunk, and H. G. Kelley as chairman, operated the railway from the end of May 1920. A year later, on the expiration of the legal term of the board of arbitration, a further act was necessary to continue the arbitration; and in this act provision was made for the resignation of the English directorate of the railway and the establishment of the head office in Canada. The new board nominated by the government consisted of Sir Joseph Flavelle, Toronto, chairman, H. G. Kelley, Montreal, A. J. Mitchell, Toronto, E. L. Newcombe, Ottawa, and J. N. Dupuis, Montreal. Kelley remained the president of the company for the time being.

Following the award of the board of arbitration and the dismissal of the appeal to the privy council, the process of consolidating the Grand Trunk and the Canadian National began. By the end of January 1923 the two had been united under a single board, and the act to incorporate the Canadian National

Railway Company brought into effect. The head offices of the company were established at Montreal, and a new president, Sir Henry Thornton, a man with a successful record in American and English railways, was appointed. So ended the long process by which the Dominion became possessed of a great system of state railways.

4. THE CANADIAN NATIONAL RAILWAYS

To those who see in a great railway something more than steel and wood, offices and balance sheets, there must come a moment of sentiment at the loss of its corporate soul and the passing of a name which has stood for the hopes and labours of its servants and a link with the outer world for hundreds of communities. The history of the Grand Trunk and the Canadian Northern railways spans the long years from the first bold attempt to provide railway transportation for what was then settled Canada, through the rush of expansion of the early twentieth century, to the time when it was tacitly acknowledged that optimism unrealized must at last yield place to the harsh facts of deficits. But the mood of the time in which the Canadian National Railways were born was more critical than sentimental; more conscious of the burden that was to be carried than of the ambitions that had been foiled; more censorious of the sins of the fading companies than proud of the achievements they had made. "For half a century on this continent," Sir John Willison reminded an audience, "the clamour against railways after they have been constructed has been almost as vociferous as the clamour for railways before they were constructed."[27] Unemotional painters hurried to erase the names of the old companies, and to write on locomotives and cars the new emblem, "Canadian National."

The name was symbolic of a new era in the history of Canadian railways: a new tradition had to be evolved to replace the old. The people of Canada had not launched into this great expansion of public ownership by design but from the pressure of existing facts. Here and there, in parliament and press, voices were raised in support of public ownership as a principle; but on the whole it was undertaken with no enthusiasm, and from necessity rather than from choice. Alternative proposals were made but not adopted. Lord Shaughnessy proposed in 1921 that the then government lines should be operated by the Canadian Pacific in conjunction with their own lines. Sir Thomas Tait, on the other hand, argued that the whole railway system of Canada should be operated by a new corporation, in which fifty-one per cent of the capital would be subscribed and owned by the Canadian government. His plan provided for guarantees to holders of Canadian Pacific securities. W. F. Tye, an engineer, propounded a similar solution to "the railway problem," with the difference that the government should hold only forty per cent of the stock. The government, however, continued to follow at least the general terms of the Drayton-Acworth report: the Canadian Pacific to be left as it was, and the remaining railways to be owned by the Dominion, but operated by a semi-independent body.

The Canadian National Railway Company was evolved by degrees. When the Canadian Northern was taken over in 1918 a small body of directors, with Mr. D. B. Hanna as president, was appointed to administer it. In the same year the Canadian Government Railways were placed under the same board, and in 1920 the Grand Trunk Pacific was added – the whole being now known as the Canadian National Railways. In October 1922 this board resigned, and its place was taken by a new one, with Sir Henry Thornton as president and chairman. The new board also took the management of the Grand Trunk Railway, the provisional board of that company having also resigned. The formal unification of the Canadian National and the Grand Trunk was made in January 1923 by an order in council, which also brought into effect the act of 1919 (9 & 10 Geo. V, c. 13) incorporating the Canadian National Railway Company. The act provided for a board of not more than fifteen directors, appointed by the governor in council, and empowered the board to issue securities against its mileage, except on the former Government Railways, any deficit on which was to be met out of the consolidated revenue fund.

The first period of reorganization (1918-1922) was faced by Mr. Hanna's board. It found a heavy problem in deferred maintenance, which had to be met at a time when wages and prices were high and freight rates stationary. "If the National

Railways," wrote Hanna, "were to be managed as a business, and not as a makeshift, the Board felt that there should not only be a thorough rehabilitation of the property, but that all possible costs should be charged to revenue so that there could be no mistake about the strictly businesslike character of the whole administration. That meant requests for vast sums of money, and the charging of them against revenue, which in turn meant the declaration of huge, and to the short-sighted, terrifying deficits."[28] Holding that the Canadian National not only could never pay, but that part of it would fall into complete disrepair unless it were put into better condition, the board approached the government, which proved to be ready to provide the money required. Put in the form of figures, the results of this policy seem depressing enough, but in Hanna's view the figures of earnings and expenses justified the policy adopted.

CANADIAN NATIONAL RAILWAYS, 1919-1922[29]

	1919	*1920*	*1921*	*1922*
Gross earnings	$105,036,176	$125,641,753	$126,691,456	$120,135,957
Operating expenses	125,349,797	162,484,723	142,784,358	129,872,275
Operating deficit	20,313,621	36,842,970	16,092,902	9,736,318
Deficit after fixed charges	49,004,545	67,505,060	56,673,934	51,103,297

The new national railway company was rich in physical property, if in nothing else. By 1923 there had come within its management the Canadian Government Railways, including the Intercolonial, Prince Edward Island, National Transcontinental, Saint John and Quebec (leased), and Hudson Bay railways; the Canadian Northern system; the Grand Trunk Pacific; and the Grand Trunk Railway, including the Grand Trunk Western (American) line and the Grand Trunk New England lines. For purposes of operation this great system was divided into four regions: (1) the Atlantic region, comprising all lines in the Maritime Provinces as far west as Rivière du Loup, and Monk on the Transcontinental – a total of 2,760.08 miles. The headquarters were at Moncton. (2) The central region, comprising all lines west of the Atlantic region as far as, but not including, Port Arthur, and Superior Junction on the Transcontinental. It included the Portland line, and amounted to a total of 7,830.91 miles. The headquarters were at Toronto.

(3) Grand Trunk Western lines, comprising Grand Trunk lines west of the Detroit River – a total of 991.69 miles, headquarters being at Detroit. (4) Western region, from Port Arthur and Superior Junction to the Pacific coast, including Vancouver Island – a total of 10,268.21 miles. The headquarters were at Winnipeg.

The executive officers were appointed to the several regions, each of which had a general manager and superintendents. The central office in Montreal was headed by the president and five vice-presidents, the latter being assigned to the following departments: operation, maintenance, and construction; finance; insurance, immigration, development, lands, express, and telegraphs; legal affairs; and traffic. With the exception of the president, the officers of the company were drawn from the component railways of the national system, a policy which called not only for tact in establishing precedence, but also for the creation of an *esprit de corps* amongst men who had formerly belonged to competing organizations.[30]

Even more formidable was the task of bringing some unity out of a number of railways that had been deliberately built to rival each other. Hundreds of miles of parallel tracks, with the corresponding terminals and other equipment, were nothing but a liability to a single company. The company was empowered by the act of 1919 to abandon operation, with the approval of the governor in council and on the recommendation of the board of railway commissioners, on lines on which operation and maintenance had "become unnecessary or inexpedient through duplication, or other economical considerations," and to dismantle or dispose of these lines with the consent of shareholders representing the majority of securities; but, while such drastic measures might make for economy and efficiency in operation, they would leave a dead weight of debt to be carried by operated lines. To parallel lines and a mountainous debt was added the ogre of deferred maintenance. Whatever may have been the exact degree to which the component railways had been allowed to deteriorate, there was no doubt in the minds of Canadian National executives that there was a crying need for expenditure on the road. The Canadian National company was visited with the sins of the private companies, but the railway map was a reflection too of national policies, wise or foolish:

the Intercolonial, the National Transcontinental, the Grand Trunk Pacific.

The calendar year 1923 was the first in the history of the Canadian National system after the addition of the Grand Trunk. By bringing in that railway, with its profitable business in eastern Canada, the general operating ratio was brought down to 92.06 – a figure which, though higher than the agreed danger mark, was lower than had obtained on some portions of the National system. For the year 1923 the revenue was $254,926,456.04 and the expenses $234,689,892.95, leaving net earnings of $20,236,563.09. The latter amount, though it might be regarded as a good start by the management, looks small indeed when set against the whole financial position of the company. An impression of its position may be gained from the headings from the consolidated balance sheet as of December 31, 1923. This covers all parts of the Canadian National except the Central Vermont.

The burden of fixed charges could not be fully met by increased earnings, more especially since the total continued to mount as further loans were made by the government to effect improvements in the property and pay interest on the securities held by the public. A suggestion was made that the capital of the railway should be written down to a point where it bore some real relation to possible earnings, but no action was taken at the time.

ASSETS

Investments	$1,899,407,586.74
Current assets	101,724,097.90
Deferred assets	12,683,832.93
Unadjusted debits	8,400,169.71
	$2,022,215,687.28

LIABILITIES

Stock	$270,230,913.70
Government grants	16,204,520.40
Long term debt	1,937,282,331.65
Current liabilities	59,018,478.92
Deferred liabilities	3,287,585.83
Unadjusted credits	19,582,262.25
Corporate surplus	283,390,450.47 deficit
	$2,022,215,687.28

Since the administrators of the railway could do nothing to modify the capital structure, they devoted their attention to reducing the cost of operation and securing more traffic. Such additional business might come from a general development of the country, based on immigration and prosperity of agriculture and industry; or it might be diverted from the Canadian Pacific. The creation of the national system left the Canadian Pacific as the only important rival and the only large private railway company in Canada. Built on a consistent plan, and ably managed, the company was making a large revenue and paying handsome dividends on its preferred and common stock. At the same time the railway and equipment had not been allowed to depreciate. It appeared, therefore, to the Canadian National executive that they must bring their property at least up to the standard of the Canadian Pacific, if they were to compete successfully with that well-established company. This was exactly the kind of task which Thornton knew, and he threw himself with great energy into it. Before many years had passed the pace was accelerated by the economic prosperity which swept all business forward in a torrent. There thus arose the latest, and perhaps the last great period of railway growth in Canada.

CHAPTER 12

Railways in Sunshine and Shadow

1. A NEW ERA OF EXPANSION AND COMPETITION

The history of Canadian railways in the dozen years since the organization of the Canadian National System is so obscured by a cloud of controversy, by personalities, and by political entanglements that it is difficult to see the whole significance of the period. The experience of public ownership on a large scale and violent fluctuations in national prosperity have bulked so large in the picture that they tend to hide a background that on closer examination proves to have changed little from earlier days.

As long as the frontier continued to be pushed northward the pioneers called for railway connections, and were little impressed by a superabundance of lines in older parts of the Dominion. It meant little to compare the total population with the total number of miles of railway, much as this ratio might signify for the public purse. For those living in regions already served by railways there arose the perennial question of freight rates. It was not that the Canadian railways charged an exorbitant rate per mile, but that the number of miles normally to be covered was large. Whether for internal or for export trade the Canadian producer or manufacturer had ordinarily to count on heavy transportation expenses, which fell unevenly according to geographic position. The alternative means of relief in spreading the burden more equally were to develop shorter routes, especially to tidewater, and to favour certain districts by adjustment of rates.

The solution of these general problems was influenced, in the period with which this chapter is concerned, by the existence of the Canadian National Railways and the operation of the trade cycle. The lines included in the Canadian National were already built: the expenditure was made and the plant ready for use.

The creation of the Canadian National did not aggravate but rather eased the situation in some respects, for it made possible the abandonment of unnecessary track and equipment. Although much duplication still remained, the position was manifestly sounder in this way than it would have been under the two private companies which had expected to operate the lines.

A new element in the situation was the nature of the relations of the Canadian Pacific and Canadian National. The two were very different in composition. One was a private and the other a publicly owned company. One was designed on a unified plan, and the other was a congeries of separate railways, in many places arranged as rivals. One had prestige, ample resources, and was in excellent physical condition; the other was deficient in all these respects. All but a small portion of the railway mileage in Canada was in the control of two companies, and the process of absorption of the smaller companies continued to take place.

Competition there had always been, and competition, said the public, there should still be. But it was to be competition of a type that the Canadian Pacific had not known since it had been harried by the Grand Trunk in the eighties and nineties, for, instead of poor companies skating on the edge of bankruptcy, came this new one that had behind it the long purse of the government. Hanna had done the spadework of reorganization and rehabilitation, but there was a new note struck from the outset of the Thornton régime. It was Sir Henry Thornton's belief that a character had to be created for the Canadian National: it must stand in the public eye not as a monument to the past, but as a vital force of the present. In the years immediately preceding their nationalization no one of the constituent companies had a reputation comparable to that of the Canadian Pacific. Grand Trunk trains were proverbially late; the Canadian Northern was cheaply built; the Intercolonial was part of the cost of confederation; and the National Transcontinental had been spurned by the Grand Trunk Pacific. If there had been a great wave of enthusiasm for public ownership the past might have been buried beneath the tide, but there was no such enthusiasm. The public had been warned over and over again that public ownership was at best a doubtful expedient for meeting an unfortunate situation, and for once was inclined to believe what it was told.

Thornton, who was rather like Van Horne in his flair for building up a decayed property, set about the task of improving lines and equipment, reducing expenses, and offering improved service. Since his competitor was necessarily the Canadian Pacific, that must also be his standard, and because he had to gain prestige for his railway he forced the pace. He would not merely copy the Canadian Pacific; he would show the public that the Canadian National was even better – hence the improved passenger cars and faster schedules. When, in 1924, the National cut the running time to Winnipeg, and the Canadian Pacific had to follow suit, it was evident that the new railway had taken the initiative.

The presidents of both railways became peripatetic, explaining to audiences all over Canada their respective opinions on the railway situation. Mr. (later Sir) Edward Beatty, appointed president of the Canadian Pacific in 1918, necessarily adopted a defensive position. The Canadian Pacific, a private corporation, felt itself menaced by the vigorous opposition of a rival which seemed to have the unlimited resources of the government at its disposal. Leaving in abeyance for the present the question of amalgamation, Beatty adopted a formula which has since become familiar, a legacy – if an unconscious one – from the Grand Trunk.[1]

It is a peculiar anomaly that the less profitable the operations of the National System, the greater the taxes of the C.P.R., while if the National Railways prosper through diversion of traffic from the C.P.R., we lose in revenues more than we gain in taxes. . . . This company has every reason to hope for the success of the National Railways, provided it is accomplished without withdrawing from us traffic which we have taken so many years to build up and secure. The greatest factor which will contribute to the National Railways' progress is the development of Canada. . . .[2]

Thornton made a series of barn-storming expeditions, telling the people of Canada that the National railway was going to be all right, that it was going to pay both its expenses and overhead charges. He, too, stressed the importance of the progress of the country, from which indeed he had as much to hope as had the rival orator. In his first report as president (1922) he made this brief but discerning remark: "The success of the National System . . . is not entirely to be obtained by methods generally applied to Railways which are not producing returns, viz., improving the physical condition and operating methods – it is a matter of building up the country to support the Railways."

Competition in services was inevitable, and the determination of the Canadian National's officers to obtain a good share of the traffic meant that that competition must assume a particularly active character. Its origin, therefore, was not dependent on any tangible signs of better times, but it was given a great impetus by a period of prosperity that was comparable in effect to, if greater in degree than, the rich years at the opening of the century. The depression which followed the war was succeeded in the latter part of 1925 by a "boom" which rapidly began to assume unprecedented proportions. For Canada it meant expanding markets for natural and manufactured products, ample supplies of capital, and a revival of immigration. The following table[3] will indicate the trend.

NET VALUE OF PRODUCTION
(000 omitted)

INDUSTRY	1924	1925	1926	1927	1928
	$	$	$	$	$
Agriculture	1,140,895	1,382,598	1,400,244	1,522,948	1,501,271
Manufactures	1,256,643	1,360,879	1,519,179	1,635,923	1,819,046
Total (including other industries)	3,018,182	3,364,824	3,640,356	3,901,505	4,122,509

Between 1923 and 1929 foreign investments in Canada increased by $1,337,000,000.[4] Owing partly to changed conditions in Europe and partly to the completion of construction work on the Canadian transcontinental railways, immigration never again approximated to the volume it had reached just before the war. It did, however, show a marked increase within this period. The low figure of 67,446 in 1923 was changed to 145,250 in 1924, and reached 167,723 in 1929. Business was what the railways most needed, and the general rise of prosperity was favourable to them.[5]

YEAR	GROSS EARNINGS	RATIO OF EXPENSES TO RECEIPTS
	$	%
1922	440,687,128	89.39
1923	478,338,047	86.52
1924	445,923,877	85.77
1925	455,297,288	81.70
1926	493,599,754	78.91
1927	499,064,207	81.68
1928	563,732,260	78.53
1929	534,106,045	81.08

Once again in Canadian history a forward movement in railways paralleled a general economic advance of the country. The determination of the directors of the Canadian National to secure more traffic led to a considerable movement in the railway world before the dawning of general prosperity. The advance of the railways was then caught up by the national economic expansion, which carried it along on the flood tide of optimism. It is not to be wondered at that the railways should have shared in the epidemic of capital expenditure that was characteristic of the four or five years before the collapse of 1929. Always they had been in the van in periods of expansion, and more was demanded of them as a public service when prosperity seemed to have no bounds. Faster and more frequent passenger trains, new outlets for grain, branch lines into progressing districts – all these were called for by the public, contractors, and the companies themselves. In years when factories were built for an imaginary future demand, when precarious fortunes were based on watered stock, when municipal bodies mortgaged the future, and when hardly a voice was raised against senseless gambling throughout the community – at such a time it was not to be expected that the railways, whose profits depended on a capacity to undertake the business that was offered, should alone have adopted a wise and conservative policy.

Without attempting to describe all the additions made to railway mileage and facilities in these years, some indication may be given of the most significant moves. One was the provision of railways for the steadily broadening belt of settlement. The Peace River country, far to the north of Edmonton, and centering in the river valley, was the frontier area which made most progress in the years just before and after the war. Here was a district of some millions of acres of good agricultural land, with a climate that allowed for the growing of wheat and other field crops; and here was re-enacted the never-ending story of pioneer farming. The fur traders, who had first discovered the Peace River, used their accustomed system of water transport, but for the farmer the birch-bark canoe and snowshoes were not useful; and as he sought to send his crops to a market governed by a world price, the labour and expense of hauling overland was so slow and expensive as to eat up the profits in a most discouraging way. Hence he called, as generations before him had called, for railways.

Three related railway companies, at first under private ownership, built into the Peace River country and eastward of it. From Edmonton, then the nearest point, the Edmonton, Dunvegan and British Columbia Railway took its solitary course north along the Lesser Slave River, and past the south shore of Lesser Slave Lake to McLennan (1915) – a distance of 245 miles. From there it was built another hundred miles westward to Roycroft (1916), on to Hythe, and over the boundary of British Columbia to Pouce Coupé. From this trunk line the second company, the Alberta Great Waterways, branched off near Edmonton, and ran north-easterly for a distance of three hundred miles to Waterways on the Clearwater River (1921). The third company, the Central Canada, built from McLennan to Peace River, and west to Fairview (1928). All three companies were operated together, and in 1920 were leased to the Canadian Pacific. In 1929, after prolonged negotiations with the Alberta government (which had taken over the railways) they were bought by the Canadian Pacific and Canadian National and operated jointly as the Northern Alberta Railways.

Besides requests for further branches in the Peace River country there developed a number of plans for a direct outlet from that area to the Pacific. A joint board of engineers of the Canadian Pacific and Canadian National undertook an examination of the question and made a report in 1925. "The reason this subject is being discussed," they wrote, "is the general opinion of the settlers in the Peace River district, who, without any study or thought as to whether or not their business can afford the cost, believe that if there was constructed a shorter railway to the Pacific coast that they would be entitled to, and would obtain lower freight rates."[6] The board expressed the opinion that it would be "more economical to handle the business, regardless of the rate received, over the existing lines until the traffic was many times the present," but nevertheless reported the results of their study of routes. The one which they regarded as most feasible involved joining the Central Canada to the Canadian National at Obed, east of the Rockies, and so using Canadian National lines to Vancouver or Prince Rupert, the cost being estimated at $80,000,000. An alternative was a line through the Monkman Pass, and to Vancouver over the Canadian National or Pacific Great Eastern or via the Canadian National to Prince Rupert. A second alternative was by the Peace River Pass and direct to the coast at Stewart (north of Prince Rupert), or over existing railways as before.

In spite of the board's disapproval of even the Obed connection, and in spite of a reduction of freight rates from the Peace River to the head of navigation on Lake Superior in 1924 and 1925, the Pacific outlet continued to be urged by local members in the house of commons. Mention of a new railway to a new port on the Pacific gave rise to a project, entertained by a group of English capitalists, for building a railway from Stewart to join the Peace River railway, a plan which had once before been attempted but dropped after a few miles of rail had been laid. Such a northern route, or that by Obed, were held to be unsatisfactory in British Columbia, where much concern was felt for the future of the Pacific Great Eastern Railway. In 1912 a private company was chartered by provincial statute to build from North Vancouver to Prince George, and two years later was further authorized to extend its line to the Peace River block. Securities to the extent of $42,000 per mile were guaranteed by the province over a distance of 480 miles. The purposes in building the railway were twofold: to open up and develop central and northern British Columbia, and to effect a junction with the Grand Trunk Pacific at Prince George. To ensure the latter connection an agreement was made between the two companies the gist of which was that the Grand Trunk Pacific would route its Vancouver traffic over the P.G.E. Construction went forward, and by 1921 the line was in operation from Squamish at the head of Howe Sound to Quesnel, a point on the Fraser River seventy-eight miles from Prince George. Completion of the line was delayed partly because of the difficult nature of the country between Quesnel and Prince George. In the meanwhile fate had been unkind. The Grand Trunk Pacific was taken over by the government of Canada, which already owned the Canadian Northern, and the latter's line to Vancouver was used by the consolidated companies. In 1918 the P.G.E. fell into the hands of the British Columbia government, and proved to be an embarrassing possession. There was, it is true, a not inconsiderable traffic in lumber and from the gold mines of the Cariboo district, but the direct connection with a transcontinental railway had not been made, and there was little hope that the line could be operated without loss on the scanty local traffic of a sparsely settled area. The only hope that seemed to remain for profitable operation was in linking up with the Peace River lines. For a time there appeared to be a possibility that the Pacific Great Eastern could be sold to one of two or three groups of capitalists that considered the property, but in the end none of them went further than preliminary negotiation. The provincial government, therefore, sought to deposit the foundling on the federal doorstep.

If the eyes of British Columbia and Alberta were turned toward the Pacific, those of Manitoba and Saskatchewan were fixed on Hudson Bay. As long as the province of Manitoba had existed there had been talk of a railway to the bay, which would mean a far shorter land journey than to Montreal and even a slightly shorter voyage to Liverpool. Throughout the eighties and nineties there was much interest in this project, stimulated by the hope of offering competition to the Canadian Pacific and thus reducing freight rates to Montreal. Beyond the formation of a company no steps to realize this ambition were taken until Mackenzie and Mann acquired Hugh Sutherland's charter, with its land grant, for their Lake Manitoba Railway and Canal Company and began to build northward on the west shore of Lake Manitoba. This line, however, turned westward to Prince Albert and left the bay project still to be completed. In 1906 it was carried a step further when the Canadian Northern began an extension northward from Hudson Bay Junction to the Pas, the line being put into operation in 1911.

At that point the activity of private companies ended, and it was left to the Dominion government to complete the work. Nothing loath, the government began in 1910 the erection of a bridge over the Saskatchewan River, and, in succeeding years, the laying of track. Progress, however, was slow. Late in 1913 passenger service was opened for fifty-six miles to Scott, but the outbreak of war slowed up and finally stopped further construction. When work was stopped in 1918 track had been laid to within ninety miles of Nelson, but over one hundred miles of this had never been operated. During the period of eight years (1918-1926) in which construction was suspended, maintenance also ceased, so that considerable repairs became necessary. After the war the Hudson Bay Railway was debated vigorously in parliament and in the newspapers. The legislatures of Manitoba and Saskatchewan urged completion of the road, as did a number of newspapers such as the *Manitoba Free Press* and the *Regina Leader*. In 1924 the On-to-the-Bay Association was inaugurated with a mass meeting at Winnipeg, with representatives from the three prairie provinces and from North and South Dakota. In eastern Canada there was less support and even active opposition, particularly in Montreal. For a few years little was done, except to repair a portion of the line earlier constructed, and to run the "Muskeg special" for a part of the way.

Hesitation as to the wisdom of completing the railway was due to a number of considerations. It was questioned whether further outlay would be justified by the volume of traffic, especially in view of the growing importance of Vancouver as an alternative outlet for grain. There was doubt as to the practicability of navigating Hudson Bay and Hudson Strait. The Hudson's Bay Company had done so for some two and a half centuries, but not without difficulty and during a very short season. Expert opinion differed widely as to the length of the season of navigation which could be regarded as assured. Furthermore, there were doubts as to the wisdom of selecting Port Nelson as the terminus, although such a decision had been made in 1912. In spite of the greater distance to Churchill (some eighty-seven miles) it was argued that it would be a better terminus, since it was a better harbour. In 1920 a committee of the senate, to which the question was referred, gave the opinion ". . . that the Government should not make further important expenditures at this Port [Nelson] without first making a new and thorough examination into the relative merits of Churchill and Nelson as a terminus for the railroad." In January 1926 the government announced its intention of providing for the completion of the railway, and a year later Frederick Palmer, an English engineer, was requested to make a report on the two harbours. In October of the same year Palmer expressed strongly his preference for Churchill,[7] and in the meantime government surveys had shown that there were no serious obstacles to the continuation of the railway there. The route of the railway was, therefore, changed to turn north at Amery on the Nelson River, and preparations were made for developing a port at the old Hudson's Bay post. Whatever could be moved of the considerable works already undertaken at Nelson was then transferred to the new terminus. By the summer of 1931 the new part of the railway was completed, and the old, much of which had fallen into disrepair, was restored. A grain elevator, with a capacity of two and one-half million bushels, had in the meantime been built, and in September 1931 two cargoes of wheat were shipped to Europe. From 1920 to 1926 the Hudson Bay Railway was included in the Canadian government railways. In the latter year it was returned to the department of railways and canals until completed, and subsequently was operated with the other government railways on behalf of the government by the Canadian National.

Once more the bay had recovered its old position as an outlet for western Canada, and the ghosts of generations of fur traders looked amazed at the tall elevator, great wharves, and puffing engines. Whether it was a triumph for economic principles of transportation remained to be proved. Completed at a time of depression, the bay route came into operation under unfavourable circumstances. There was the problem of insurance rates, which remained high relative to the St. Lawrence route. In 1931 the insurance rate for the bay route was two per cent and in 1936 it was reduced to one per cent. For the St. Lawrence the rate was almost stationary at a quarter of one per cent. The railway from the Pas to Churchill, together with the facilities at the port, cost some fifty million dollars. The argument that other railways could not handle the through traffic in wheat had ceased to be valid before construction had even begun, but the mining area north of the Pas had already provided some local traffic. The Hudson Bay route, however, has not been open long enough to test its permanent value. In 1934 four million bushels, and in 1935 two and one-half million bushels, of grain were exported from Churchill. For 1935 the operating loss on the railway was $336,000.[8]

Further to the east, too, rails were being laid to James Bay. At the beginning of the century the Ontario government had begun a colonization railway, known as the Temiskaming and Northern Ontario, from North Bay into the clay belt. The discovery of mines added greatly to the business of the road, and this encouragement – combined with the oncoming National Transcontinental – led to an extension as far as Cochrane, where it joined the line of the other new railway. The distance thus covered was 252 miles, and there for a time the railway halted. After the war the legislature decided to carry out a plan which had once been considered for private enterprise, to build on to James Bay, nearly as far again as from North Bay to Cochrane. The object of this adventurous move was apparently more to open up the northern part of the province than to reach tidewater, but when completed in 1932 the T. & N.O. constituted another outlet to the sea. The terminus was at Moosonee at the mouth of the Moose River, and although it could not be used by ocean-going vessels, it gave to Ontario a door on the ocean.

The new railways that have thus far been traced show a development in marked contrast to the policy of earlier years. From force of necessity the first emphasis had to be laid on the provision of railways from coast to coast, serving a relatively narrow belt. This accomplished, branches were thrown out from the trunk lines, intended at once to facilitate settlement and create traffic. By this means the area served was gradually widened. A third phase came with the trunk lines to the north, which modified the east and west conception of railway growth. The Peace River railways, the Hudson Bay Railway, and the James Bay line all made possible development of the country through which they passed; but they did more than this, for they could be combined with other methods of transportation to serve the whole northern area. With the completion of the line to Moosonee, the Hudson's Bay Company supplied the James Bay district by rail. The railway to Churchill gave an entrance to the minerals of the northern pre-cambrian shield, and formed a base for further transport by tractor and aeroplane. In conjunction with steamships on Hudson Bay, the railway also provided a route to the eastern Arctic alternative to that by the Mackenzie River. From Churchill ships can carry goods to Wager Inlet, and tractors have been used to portage the cargo over the neck of land to Cockburn Bay at the mouth of Backs River.[9] In 1937 the Hudson's Bay Company brought the eastern and western Arctic even closer together by way of Bellot Strait. The old problem of the north-west passage is thus in course of being solved by a series of links with the south, and an integration of rail, water, and air transport.

At the same time the transcontinental trunk lines, with their established termini and ports, remained the basis of the Canadian railway system. In this field the governing factors were the general economic expansion, competition between the two large companies, consolidation of the Canadian National lines, and problems of freight rates. On the main lines there were steady improvements, such as ballasting and double-tracking, made necessary by the increasing speed and weight of trains. These sufficed for the Canadian Pacific, but more complex adjustments were required for the Canadian National, which was faced with the problem of unifying as far as possible the lines which it had inherited. One drastic expedient was to tear up one set of rails where two Canadian National lines closely paralleled each other, such as part of the old Canadian Northern line between Toronto and Napanee, at which latter point the lines branched, the Canadian Northern turning north to Ottawa. On a longer stretch from Edmonton to the Yellowhead Pass, the Grand Trunk Pacific and Canadian Northern track had been built side by side, and no difficulty arose in unifying them. A little over a hundred miles of Grand Trunk Pacific track was torn up as early as 1917 and the rails sent to France. Similarly a hundred miles of Canadian Northern track was torn up in other parts of the stretch. At Red Pass Junction, near Mount Robson, the line forked, leaving the former Grand Trunk Pacific line to Prince Rupert and the Canadian Northern to Vancouver. The National Transcontinental was left intact, but an ingenious combination was made between it and the Canadian Northern by the construction of the Longlac cut-off, thirty miles in length, which made it possible to route through trains between Toronto or Montreal and Winnipeg by the Canadian Northern as far as Longlac and thence to Nakina and over the Transcontinental straight to Winnipeg. By avoiding the long loop south to Port Arthur a saving of 102 miles was made.

Nothing more was done – and little more could be done – to unify the Canadian National main lines. In New Brunswick there remained the National Transcontinental and Intercolonial, but to abandon either of these would be to leave a part of the province without railway communication. Similarly the National Transcontinental from Quebec to Winnipeg was a pioneer railway for northern Quebec and Ontario, even if built to the standard of a trunk line. On the other hand the National Transcontinental was too far north to replace the Canadian Northern for regular western trains, except for the portion from Nakina west, which was thus utilized; as was, for a time, the line west of Cochrane, in conjunction with running rights over the Temiskaming and Northern Ontario. In the mountain region, where traffic was light, something had been done to avoid duplication; and the only other possible step was to abandon the Prince Rupert line, a step which would shatter the hopes of any development of the northern part of British Columbia.

A railway depends for profits on its branch or "feeder" lines as well as on its trunk lines: particularly in Canada, where urban centres are few and far between, and where the railways look to agricultural, mining, and lumbering districts for freight. In the ten years from 1924 a programme of expansion of branch lines which was startling in its magnitude was approved by parliament. Including new work on the Hudson Bay Railway, a total of 4,198 miles of branch lines was projected, which, as was pointed out by the deputy minister, was "considerably greater than the transcontinental mileage between Halifax and Vancouver. From this, it is apparent also that new mileage of the two chief railway systems of Canada is being added to at an average rate of more than a mile a day."[10] Not all of this work was actually carried out, but even that it should have been planned, and partially built, shows that the country was prepared to add materially to its railway system. Given two competing railway companies, it was inevitable that in some at least of the branch line projects the motive of building for the needs of an area should be mixed with an element of rivalry. In many places the borders of the territory of one company were not recognized by the other: and, particularly in the prairie provinces where new settlements were constantly being made, there were invasions and counter-invasions that added unnecessarily to the costs of the companies. That such cases existed, however, should not be allowed to conceal those others where new branches were beneficial both to the company concerned and to the public.

Saskatchewan and eastern Alberta were the chief scenes of activity in branch lines. New lines were built both in the northern areas and to those other districts throughout the provinces which were still far from any railway. In the pursuance of their respective programmes for branch lines in the west the Canadian National and the Canadian Pacific became involved in a long dispute. In 1929 the presidents of both railways issued statements decrying wasteful competition, but there was no agreement as to which should give way, or as to the limits of spheres of influence. The bulk of the new mileage in Alberta and Saskatchewan was intended primarily to serve agricultural districts, but elsewhere branches were built to recently developed mines, as, for example, those to the Flin Flon and Sherritt-Gordon mines in northern Saskatchewan and Manitoba, and to the Rouyn mine in Quebec.

	MILES OPENED FOR OPERATION DURING THE YEAR					
PROVINCE	1925	1926	1927	1928	1929	1930
Prince Edward Island		0.06				9.95
Nova Scotia	4.22	0.13	0.04			0.02
New Brunswick		0.26	0.01			0.01
Quebec	22.37	22.88	91.55	52.18	22.99	3.86
Ontario	32.83	2.48	1.48	52.17	20.33	70.27
Manitoba	22.48	47.01	0.04	0.16	1.07	126.16
Saskatchewan	123.94	215.04	94.56	194.71	215.46	406.64
Alberta	154.40	85.90	127.60	171.68	243.84	94.13
British Columbia	145.51	1.89	0.06	11.97	0.36	1.97
Total new mileage	505.75	375.65	315.34	482.82	504.05	713.01
Total miles in operation	40,352	40,352	40,572	41,024	41,382	42,049

The preceding table will indicate the location and extent of new railway mileage. With the exception of the Hudson Bay Railway, the greater part of the new mileage may be attributed to branch lines. The discrepancy between the additional mileage and the totals is explained by the abandonment of certain existing lines, and to other minor factors such as reclassification.

Important developments were made in terminals during the period. After some delay, the Union Station in Toronto was opened in 1927, together with the elevated tracks leading into it from both directions. While both companies made use of this, the Canadian Pacific also rebuilt its North Toronto station on the northern track, which eliminated the gradient from the edge of the lake to the higher ground east of the city. A larger project was the Montreal terminal undertaken by the Canadian National. For some years the Bonaventure (Grand Trunk) station had been considered unsatisfactory because of the level crossings involved, and with the growth of the Canadian National the management of that railway was anxious to secure a central terminal which would both obviate this difficulty and give to the railway a stronger position in Montreal. The plan which was evolved was to build a single passenger station at the site of the Canadian Northern's tunnel station. Before sanctioning this plan the government engaged the English engineer, Mr. Frederick Palmer, to examine its desirability. Mr. Palmer reported favourably, adding, however, the suggestion that the proposed terminal should also be used by the Canadian Pacific.[11] As it proved that that company was unwilling to participate in the scheme, holding that the Windsor Station was capable of expansion, authority was given by parliament in 1929 for its commencement by the Canadian National alone. Work was therefore begun, but a halt was later called on the ground of expense. In Halifax a new hotel was built by the Canadian National, which also inaugurated a steamship service to the West Indies for the carriage principally of passengers and fruit. In 1928 the first of the five "Lady" boats was put into service, and the completion of the others followed.

The conditions of Canadian geography created unequal economic opportunities for the various areas. On the one hand the areas remote from tidewater sought relief from the heavy transportation charges on their exports; and on the other hand the provinces or districts possessing seaports wished to secure the maximum volume of business through those ports. The development of Vancouver, the railway to Churchill, the projected Peace River outlet, improved facilities at Halifax, and the car ferry to Prince Edward Island (with standard gauge on the Island railway) were – together with the improvement of the St. Lawrence–Great Lakes waterway – means of attaining the aims of the two interests. There was, however, a limit to the results that could be achieved in this way, for there must remain sections, like the central prairies, still distant from tidewater. Furthermore, the provision of further outlets as a solution to the problem as a whole involved inherent contradictions. The more the traffic of the centre was drawn to west and north, the more the ports of the far east would suffer. New Brunswick and Nova Scotia had come into the federation with hopes that their ports would carry a large portion of the business of central Canada, and to make this possible the Intercolonial Railway became an integral part of the federation scheme. Bitter experience had shown, however, that Montreal and American ports took the lion's share, and "maritime grievances" were the result. Out of this complexity of factors had long since arisen the device of modifying the charge on freight with lower rates on certain routes.

A great many factors, such as competition from water and highway transport, and from American railways, bear on freight rates; but without attempting to analyse the complicated rate structure of Canada,[12] two aspects of it which affect the point under discussion may be mentioned. The first of these is the most noteworthy attempt to compensate for geographical position by the reduction of freight rates. Complaints in the Maritime Provinces that railway rates were too high to allow trade with the rest of Canada led to the appointment of a royal commission under Sir Andrew Duncan. In its report, presented in 1926, the commission in general accepted the point of view of the Maritime Provinces, and advocated a reduction of twenty per cent on all freight originating on the Atlantic division of the Canadian National (which division was to be enlarged for the purpose), without prejudice to the Canadian Pacific. The proposals were, in the following year, embodied in the Maritime

Freight Rates Act, with the provisoes that the lower rates were to be operative on all railways in the area, and that the loss to the companies was to be made up by the government. In other words, all freight from the Maritime Provinces was subsidized to the extent of twenty per cent at the expense of the taxpayers as a whole. Another case in point was the continuance and expansion of the operation of the Crow's Nest Pass agreement. The lower rates were suspended in 1918 and revived in 1922. In 1925 the Crow's Nest Pass rates on grains and grain products were extended to cover shipments to Vancouver, and subsequently to cover shipments of grain over the Canadian National to Quebec at the request of those interested in that port.

While such reductions were intended to benefit shippers, and in general to compensate for the peculiarities of Canadian geography, they could hardly be viewed with anything but apprehension by the officials of the railway companies. Shortly after his appointment, Thornton indicated the views of his company in regard to the burning question of freight rates:

Railway freight rates in Canada are and have been for many years the lowest in the world. The average freight receipt per ton per mile for Canadian Railways in 1914 was 0.742 cents. War time increases forced this unit of earning up to a point approximately 75 per cent. over the pre-war level. The series of reductions which began on January 1, 1921, have substantially reduced this average so that in 1923 it stood at 0.980 or 32 per cent. above the pre-war level. In contrast to this the average prices of labour, material and supplies prevailing in 1923 were somewhat in excess of 90 per cent. over the pre-war scale. . . . There is no way by which freight and passenger rates can be continually reduced and net earnings at the same time increased; and, moreover, restricted net earnings must inevitably mean additional taxes to provide for annual deficits. . . .[13]

A similar note was struck by the president of the Canadian Pacific Railway:

. . . The Canadian producers suffer from a geographical disability due to the great distance their products have to be hauled. This difficulty has always existed and cannot be entirely eradicated. The remedies which are suggested are for the most part

artificial and of doubtful soundness. A general lower scale of rates is not possible without grave unfairness to the transportation companies. . . . In public discussions of the subject the value of the work of the transportation companies . . . is frankly recognized, but the fact that their work can only be carried on successfully under a fair scale of rates is overlooked. . . . [14]

It will be obvious that the public and the private companies were in somewhat different positions, but both had an eye to profitable operation. The simple economic facts to which the presidents referred set natural limits to the use of rate changes for the solution of the problem of shippers.

2. THE DEPRESSION AND THE RAILWAYS

In the autumn of 1929 feverish selling and tobogganing prices on the New York stock exchange heralded the end of the hectic period of prosperity and the beginning of a severe depression. The resultant contraction of general business had an almost immediate effect on the railways. The following table[15] shows the rapid decline from the maximum figures of 1928.

YEAR	TOTAL TRAIN MILES	PASSENGERS CARRIED	FREIGHT CARRIED (TONS)	GROSS EARNINGS
1928	125,034,253	40,592,792	141,230,026	$563,732,260
1929	117,645,670	39,070,843	137,855,151	534,106,045
1930	107,620,076	34,698,767	115,229,511	454,231,650
1931	93,443,731	26,396,812	85,993,206	358,549,382
1932	81,291,028	21,099,582	67,722,105	293,390,415
1933	73,938,707	19,172,193	63,634,893	270,278,276

Both passenger and freight traffic were cut in half, as were the gross earnings. The number of passengers carried in 1932 was less than for any other year since 1902, at which time the railway mileage was about forty-four per cent and the population about half of the 1932 figures. In the case of passengers, and to a lesser extent of freight, the decrease was due partly to the competition of motor vehicles, which, however, increased only slightly in numbers during the same years. Export of wheat, a principal source of income for the railways, was exceedingly high in 1929, low in 1930, fair in 1931 and 1932, and better in 1933. It is not possible, therefore, to attempt to establish an exact correlation between the decline of traffic for the railways and any single factor: rather it would be more accurate to say that the railways suffered from the general shrinkage in business, in both export and internal trade.

The railways thus were caught – as were most industrial and financial organizations – by a severe and unexpected depression at a time when they were in the process of expanding their services in both quantity and quality. Their losses were alarming when the national income was declining and an era of extravagance was giving way to one of retrenchment. Individuals suffered from a reduction of dividends on the stock of the Canadian Pacific Railway, but the greater part of the stock was held outside Canada, and in any case there was no direct charge on the public funds. The Canadian National had been steadily showing a better net revenue and there was hope that this would soon meet a fair proportion of the fixed capital charges, but the depression changed the surplus into a loss, and the fears, scarcely stilled, that the national railway would be a greater financial burden than could be borne, quickly revived.

The loss to the public on the Canadian National, because it could be expressed in figures, was a reality in a way that watered stock, overbuilt factories, and personal extravagance could never be. Viewed in a depression atmosphere, the mounting debt and declining revenues of the company took on the role of a national bogey, and the railway problem once more was dominated by its financial aspect. E. W. Beatty decided that "the time would be opportune for an enquiry into the whole question of transportation in Canada by an independent tribunal,"[16] and suggested to Thornton that he make the proposal. Thornton accordingly, on June 25, 1931, put forward the idea of a royal commission to the select standing committee on railways and shipping, which in turn recommended it in their report. In November the royal commission was appointed. Instead of three commissioners, as in the commission of 1916, there were now seven. The Right Honourable L. P. Duff, justice of the supreme court of Canada, was chairman, and the other members were Lord Ashfield, chairman of the London Underground Railway; L. F. Loree, president of the Delaware and Hudson Railroad;

Sir Joseph Flavelle, a financier, of Toronto; Beaudry Leman, general manager of the Banque Canadienne Nationale; W. C. Murray, president of the University of Saskatchewan; and Dr. J. C. Webster of Shediac, New Brunswick. Each area in Canada was thus represented, while there were also experts from England and the United States.

The commissioners were empowered to "inquire into the whole problem of transportation in Canada, particularly in relation to railways, shipping and communication facilities therein, having regard to present conditions and the probable future development of the country, and report their conclusions and make such recommendations as they think proper." The usual procedure of taking evidence from officials of the two principal railways and from other persons in different parts of the country was followed. In spite of the broad implications of their terms of reference, the commissioners seem to have concentrated on two points: the seriousness of the existing financial situation in the railways, and the cure of this disease. While undoubtedly these were the aspects of the problem that required most immediate consideration, they might have taken a somewhat different colour if placed against a background of the fundamental geographical, economic, and political problems of the Dominion in respect of transportation. Such phenomena as over-building, light traffic, and even competition have significance only in relation to past, present, and future conditions. All forms of transportation in Canada have always involved public subsidies of some kind, whether in land, money, or guarantees. Periodically there came a day of reckoning in which an attempt was made to balance the national services of transport against its cost. Such a time was 1931. It is perhaps only a question of emphasis, but one is led to wonder whether the approach in the report of the royal commission gives a true impression of the full meaning of a problem which came not only from the mistakes of man, but also from the basic conditions of Canada and the vicissitudes of the business cycle.

The position of the capital securities of the two railways in the period 1923-1931 shows that both companies had materially added to their fixed charges.[17] These figures do not give the full picture of the increase in the C.N.R. debt, for there were also added during the period government loans of $132,468,521 and accrued interest on government loans of $287,663,169.

C.N.R. CAPITAL SECURITIES

	INCREASE, 1923-1931	TOTAL, DECEMBER 31, 1931
Capital stock	$650	$270,220,963
Funded debt	$471,954,063	$1,276,457,206

Of the funded debt part was guaranteed by the Dominion or provinces and part was not so guaranteed. The proportions were:

Guaranteed	$1,042,746,777
Unguaranteed	233,710,429

The fixed charges of the Canadian Pacific were also raised during the same period by additions to the debt, due to increased expenditure. The bonded indebtedness remained low compared with the Canadian National, but the C.P.R. to some extent departed from its traditional policy by floating large issues of bonds.

C.P.R. CAPITAL SECURITIES

	INCREASE, 1923-1931	TOTAL, DECEMBER 31, 1931
Capital stock	$131,575,000	$472,256,921
Funded debt	151,824,772	475,374,638

The following tables[18] show the figures for the operating accounts of the two companies over the period 1923-1931.

C.N.R. OPERATIONS

YEAR	GROSS EARNINGS FROM OPERATION	OPERATING EXPENSES	NET OPERATING REVENUES
1923	$216,578,175	$204,921,713	$11,656,462
1924	201,224,493	189,460,403	11,764,089
1925	208,218,920	184,373,201	23,845,719
1926	225,547,852	190,173,271	35,374,581
1927*	227,560,927	198,646,705	28,914,221
1928*	260,418,924	217,780,172	42,638,751
1929*	248,222,476	217,223,886	30,998,589
1930*	213,446,581	196,502,057	16,944,523
1931*	171,675,445	171,673,132	2,313

*including Eastern Lines.

C.P.R. OPERATIONS

YEAR	GROSS EARNINGS FROM OPERATION	OPERATING EXPENSES	NET OPERATING REVENUES
1923	$192,827,930	$155,040,207	$37,787,722
1924	180,796,044	143,258,643	37,537,400
1925	182,610,791	140,663,058	41,917,733
1926	197,636,215	149,713,398	47,922,817
1927	201,805,486	159,060,224	42,745,262
1928	230,406,354	173,871,972	56,534,381
1929	211,635,660	164,304,606	47,331,054
1930	180,022,386	138,523,657	41,498,729
1931	141,999,359	112,692,927	29,306,432

The reports of the Canadian National Railway showed, for 1930, a net income deficit, including interest due to the public, of $61,228,621, and, for 1931, $84,262,718. Whatever might be the explanation of such large deficits, it was clear that the burden on the public was becoming heavy.

Believing that "drastic measures of economy" were "imperative," the commissioners were faced with the necessity of making a most important decision – whether or not to recommend any form of amalgamation. It is probably a reasonable inference that it was just because that decision had to be faced that the commission had been made so large and, geographically at least, so representative. The evidence[19] which the commissioners took gave them a number of opinions which bore directly on the future of the two railways in relation to each other. In Calgary representatives of the United Farmers of Alberta asked for amalgamation under national ownership with a view to lowering the cost of transportation. In Edmonton Premier Brownlee spoke of the "premature development of railway facilities to the far north of the province" by private companies, but expressed himself as satisfied with the joint operation of those northern lines by the Canadian National and Canadian Pacific. He felt strongly that the solution of the railway problem should not be based only on the existing depression, but also on the future of the country. As to amalgamation, he believed that it would be acceptable to the west if it were under public ownership. Representatives of the trade union movement in Alberta demanded that there should be no interference with the principle of public ownership. In Regina the attorney general and the counsel for the Saskatchewan wheat pool both spoke of a strong feeling against amalgamation under private ownership. In Winnipeg the attorney general stated explicitly that "the government of Manitoba is opposed to any form of amalgamation of the railway systems. It is unqualifiedly opposed to any monopoly that is not entirely controlled by the government. In the present circumstances it does not favour a government monopoly of the railways."

In so far, then, as the evidence given indicates western opinion, it was clear that the west was as hostile as ever to a Canadian Pacific monopoly and lukewarm about a governmental monopoly. In the east there was a much less clear expression of opinion. The premier of Nova Scotia thought that his province would not fear a monopoly so long as it brought economic advantages. The premier of New Brunswick preferred co-operation to amalgamation, but was evidently more concerned about the port of Saint John than either of these alternatives. In Toronto the representative of the Canadian Brotherhood of Railway Employees startled the commissioners by a speech on planned economy, and strongly defended public ownership.

In the intervals of these hearings the commissioners spent long hours on the train in consultation with officers of the two companies, one of whom, S. W. Fairweather, director of the bureau of economics of the Canadian National, sought to show that the savings from amalgamation would not justify a monopoly. How far the commissioners had been affected by the expression of opinion in the west it is, of course, impossible to say, but it was perhaps a new factor to some of them. In Ottawa came the important sessions with the presidents of the two companies. As to the line that Mr. Beatty would take there can have been little question. The Canadian Pacific had never attempted to conceal its alarm at the course of events, either from its own point of view or from that of the country as a whole. Since 1921 it had urged the desirability of some type of amalgamation. The president expressed the view that co-operation, while it would result in saving – estimated at $6,348,000 – would not be sufficient. "Under existing conditions in Canada," he told the commissioners, "the only solution which will stand the test of the country's necessities is a consolidation through a lease on a profit-sharing basis of the government railways and the Canadian Pacific." Abandonment of line on a large scale would be possible, to the extent of about 5,000 miles. Particular instances of this were the National Transcontinental between Winnipeg and Nakina, Canadian Northern between Longlac and Ottawa, Canadian Pacific between Glen Tay and Whitby, Woodstock and Windsor, Saskatoon and Unity, Kamloops and Hope. In passenger traffic his officers estimated that 7,500,000 train miles or 16.2 per cent, and in freight traffic, 5,300,000 train miles or 9.2 per cent, could be saved. On the total, $64,267,000 could be saved on operating expenses. Asked how he would divide the earnings, Beatty answered: "I would take the gross earnings of the combined system, and what is left over I would divide in agreed proportions between the owners of the C.P.R. and the Government of Canada. The agreed proportions would be ascertained by taking, for example, the percentage of each company's earnings to the total over a period of years, net." He stated, in answer to another question, that he was not afraid of the size of the undertaking from an operating point of view. As to the objection against the plan of joint operation that it would result in a monopoly, he argued that the public would be protected by the railway commission or some similar body.

If the Canadian Pacific policy was, in general, known beforehand, there was much uncertainty as to whether Thornton would follow suit or would defend the independent existence of the Canadian National. It has been suggested that he had accepted some form of unification, and only changed his mind at the last moment. Be that as it may, it is certain that he took a clear stand before the commission. Amalgamation, he said, "would be definitely repugnant to the people of the Dominion." Unification under the state would entail some degree of political interference, while under private enterprise it would arouse public apprehension. A further objection would be the removal of competition. Some other solution, then, must be devised. He sketched a plan which would allow for the "development of that form of direction and administration which will, as near as may be, approach that of a prudently and efficiently organized private enterprise, which would necessarily involve the reduction of political interference to a minimum"; and secondly, "the development of an intensive degree of co-operation between the two companies in order that waste in whatever form it is found may be eliminated." The first object, he suggested, would be secured by the appointment of a board of ten directors for the Canadian National, two of whom should be the president and legal vice-president of the company, and the remainder, appointed by the government, to include two Conservatives, two Liberals, two Progressives, one representative of labour, and one representative of the minister of railways and canals.

The practical measures which Thornton suggested for co-operation were pooling of competitive passenger services, elimination of competitive city ticket offices, co-ordination of competitive fast freight services, elimination of dual trackage where possible, consolidation of telegraph and hotel systems, joint use of local facilities wherever possible, and interchange of trackage rights. He contemplated the abandonment of 2,434 miles of track and a total saving of $30,000,000 for both systems. Thornton denied the suggestion made by Ashfield that his plan meant "a complete fusion of the interests of the two railways," but admitted that if freight also were pooled it would mean the end of competition. To enforce co-operation, he suggested the retention of all or part of the royal commission, which would also pass on the annual budget of the Canadian National.

A scheme which was a compromise between those advanced by Beatty and Thornton, and one which revived an older idea, was presented by Gerard Ruel, legal vice-president of the Canadian National. It called for the creation of a single managing company, called the Canadian Railways Company. Five of the ten directors would be nominated by the government and five by the Canadian Pacific. To the company would be entrusted for management all the companies in the Canadian National and all those in the Canadian Pacific which were willing to co-operate. Profits would be divided amongst the owning companies on an agreed basis. It would admittedly put an end to competition, in which Ruel did not believe.

After hearing these and various other opinions on the question of amalgamation, it remained for the commissioners, who, unlike the witnesses had no special interest in the matter, to come to a judicial decision. In their report they declared for the continuance of competition, fearing the power of a monopoly of such magnitude, and distrusting the perpetual lease of one company to the other as equally resulting in monopoly. Seeing, too, a possible growth of population and of railway mileage in the future, they hesitated "to commit . . . future generations, and even the present one, to a policy adopted under the stress of difficult circumstances, which may not be best adapted to a new set of conditions difficult to forecast." As positive aims they set up economy, co-operation, and that the "management of the National Railways should be emancipated from political interference and community pressure."

In pursuit of these aims the commission proposed that the board of directors of the Canadian National should be replaced by three trustees, appointed by the governor in council, of whom the chairman should give the whole of his time to the duties of his office. The trustees would control the annual budget and submit an annual report to parliament. They would also appoint a president as chief operating officer. To provide for co-operation it was recommended that the trustees should meet at regular intervals with an equal number of directors of the Canadian Pacific, and that the united body should discuss "such co-operative measures, plans and arrangements as shall, consistent with the proper handling of traffic, be best adapted to the removal of unnecessary or wasteful services or practices, to the avoidance of unwarranted duplication in services or facilities, and to the joint use and operation of all such properties as may conveniently and without undue detriment to either party, be so used." A statutory duty should lie on the trustees and directors to plan and adopt measures of co-operation, but in case the two failed to agree in the suggested joint committee, the issue was to be settled by a new body, the "arbitral tribunal," consisting of the chief commissioner of the board of railway commissioners and one representative from each of the two railways.

A bill "intended to be a statutory incorporation of the report of the Duff Commission" was introduced into the senate in October 1932 and finally received the royal assent in May 1933. Revised and elaborated by the railway committee of the senate, it was debated at great length both there and in the house of commons. As finally passed, the act (23 & 24 Geo V, c. 33) ended with a statement that "nothing in this Act shall be deemed to authorize the amalgamation of any railway company which is comprised in National Railways with any railway company which is comprised in Pacific Railways nor to authorize the unified management and control of the railway system which forms part of National Railways with the railway system which forms part of Pacific Railways." Such a warning, though regarded by some members as superfluous, well expressed the basic view of the great majority of members of both houses. Here and there, in both houses, were found those who cast longing glances at an amalgamation of some type, but that aspect of the act was never an issue. In the upper house Senator Meighen spoke of the great size of the existing railways and added:

Unite them and you will have a power which, in the hands of competent, shrewd, far-seeing men, could be made an almost insuperable factor in the political life of this Dominion. Some attach to that spectre more sinister and more terrible consequences than do others. That it is undesirable I admit — that it is very undesirable I admit; and I say most emphatically that the great mass of the Canadian people consider it so undesirable that so long as the democracy that reigns in Canada is the democracy of mind that now reigns, there is no possibility of bringing about such a condition of affairs. Those who say that this is so only in regard to political matters — that we are being political when we ought to be businesslike — are really indicting democracy. It is not at all a political party that is being challenged, but democracy itself; and I do not know that democracy is altogether foolish in seeking to guard itself against what conceivably, because of its immensity, might become domination.[20]

The act was divided into three parts. The first empowered the governor in council to replace the existing board of directors of the Canadian National with three trustees, as advocated in the report of the royal commission. The chairman of the trustees was cast for a part rather like Napoleon as first consul: the difference being that in the latter case the part was written for the actor. In the commons the powers and methods of appointment of the trustees and their relation to the government were discussed at some length. Mackenzie King raised the question as to whether their position would be in accord with the retention of ministerial responsibility. "A ministry," he said, "cannot divest itself of all responsibility. If government ownership and operation means that it cannot be carried on without the ministry divesting itself of all responsibility therefor, then we had better pass a resolution to that effect, and get rid of government ownership altogether."[21]

Part two of the act directed the two railways to endeavour to agree on, and bring into force, measures of co-operation such as pooling of services and joint trackage and running rights. Part three provided for an arbitral tribunal, consisting of three persons, as sketched by the royal commission. Its powers might be invoked by either company, and were to be very comprehensive. No appeal could be made, except to the supreme court of Canada on a question of jurisdiction. The section dealing with the tribunal was subjected to a good deal of criticism in both houses. It was said by various members to infringe the rights of the Canadian Pacific as a private corporation, and by one member of the commons to be nothing less than amalgamation of operation.

But the fierce lion of co-operation, whose early roars so alarmed the officers of the Canadian Pacific Railway, proved to be a very mild beast when let out of its cage. Little of the act of 1933 was ever put into effect. In December 1933 the directors of the Canadian National were replaced by a board of trustees consisting of C. P. Fullerton (chairman), F. K. Morrow of Toronto, and J. E. Labelle of Montreal, and in the following January they appointed S. J. Hungerford, who had been acting president since the retirement of Sir Henry Thornton, as president. As a move toward co-operation a joint executive committee of the two railways was organized, which in turn appointed a joint technical committee. After investigation, passenger service between Montreal and Toronto, and Ottawa and Toronto was pooled, and some other works, such as switching, car-cleaning, and freight shed operations, were undertaken in common. But such co-operation as was actually put into practice was slight indeed as compared with the intentions of the royal commission and of the act. It is significant that the arbitral tribunal was never called into being: significant because it was regarded by both its defenders and its critics as the sanction behind co-operation. Because so small a degree of co-operation was attempted, it is not possible to say whether or not the new policy was capable of being made a success.

Certain it is that the relief which was obtained from 1933 on was negligible. In 1933 the joint annual saving of measures already put into effect was estimated at one million dollars.[22] A detailed list of savings by co-operative measures practised during 1934 showed that this estimate was only slightly below the actual figure.[23] Of the items in the list, that referring to pooled services between Quebec, Montreal, Ottawa, and Toronto accounted for all but a few thousands of dollars. Both companies made efforts, and with some success, to reduce expenditures within their own control. Abandonment of line did not play a major part in this programme, although in 1935 the Canadian National applied to the board of railway commissioners to abandon operation on branch lines with a total of 560 miles. Consent was given in respect to about one-third of the total; a third was refused; and the balance not decided within the year. The various efforts of the companies to make economies, however, whether by co-operative measures or internal changes, enabled them to save themselves from further net losses on operations.[24]

YEAR	RAILWAY	GROSS EARNINGS FROM OPERATIONS	OPERATING EXPENSES	NET OPERATING REVENUES
1933	C.P.R.	$113,998,657	$ 89,251,849	$27,746,808
1933	C.N.R.	126,701,228	122,572,229	4,128,998
1934	C.P.R.	125,642,229	97,081,831	28,560,398
1934	C.N.R.	140,824,360	130,296,562	10,527,798

Experience of co-operation, such as it was, led the trustees of the Canadian National to believe that it could be carried further and to express the hope that arbitral tribunals would either be eliminated or little used.[25] On the other hand the president of the Canadian Pacific told his shareholders that

Experience with co-operation strengthens the view that unification alone offers an adequate solution to the Canadian railway problem. No other plan can eliminate the tremendous waste caused by maintaining duplicate services in a country which can

no longer afford to pay for the duplication. Unification would also offer a solution to the unfair and dangerous anomaly of a Government-owned enterprise engaging in direct competition with private capital. The solution of the railway problem on fair and sound lines will produce benefits to Canada far in excess of mere operating savings. The Canadian Pacific, in complete co-operation with the Canadian Government – for that is what unification means – can achieve infinitely more for the future welfare of Canada than can the two railway systems separately within the present working limits of their statutory authority.[26]

Just what the last sentence means is not quite clear, but for the rest it was the gospel which the C.P.R. had long been preaching – and was preaching with added sincerity, now that the company could no longer pay interest on its capital stock.

Such was the state of the railways in the years of depression, that is, under conditions which touched the railway structure at its weakest point. The Canadian Pacific adopted a perfectly logical policy, and one that could be defended from the point of view of either the company or the country. But logic is never a fixed commodity, and the public as a whole was more ready to face deficits than monopoly. It was hard to startle a people who had already contributed a billion and a quarter dollars in cash, a like amount in guarantees, and an empire in land, so that railways might run throughout the Dominion.

3. THE PRACTICE OF PUBLIC OWNERSHIP

Opinion in Canada has always favoured the construction and operation of railways by private enterprise, and where the Dominion or the provinces have undertaken the responsibility themselves it has been because of the failure of private capital either to undertake or to maintain particular railways. Cases of one or other which have been mentioned are the Intercolonial, Prince Edward Island, Temiskaming and Northern Ontario, Hudson Bay, Pacific Great Eastern, and National Transcontinental railways. The dominating principle, therefore, has not been an insistence on private enterprise, but rather a belief that certain lines of railway were essential to the economic and political life of the country. When capitalists could be interested they were given financial assistance by the state, and when they could not be interested direct action was taken by the governments. The establishment of the Canadian National Railways does not run counter to the general rule, but that railway had special characteristics which caused it to be viewed in a somewhat different light from the other government lines. Besides the federal government railways it included three great companies (Canadian Northern, Grand Trunk, and Grand Trunk Pacific) which were built in the expectation of profitable operation, and together comprised two transcontinental roads. The Canadian National, then, was bound to be judged on standards similar to those applied to any other transcontinental line, rather than with the tolerance allowed to a pioneer railway undertaken without hope of profit by a government. Hence public ownership was felt to be on trial in a sense that it had not been before.

Two main issues have emerged, both fundamental to a consideration of the success or failure of this great experiment in public ownership. The first of these is the degree of efficiency with which the railway has been managed – interpreting efficiency as meaning a satisfactory relation between expenditure and results. Here a series of difficulties is immediately encountered. By what standard should the Canadian National be judged? The tendency has been to use the Canadian Pacific as that standard, which is very natural since it is the only other important railway in Canada, and happens also to be a private corporation. Obviously, however, such a comparison is very unsatisfactory because of the utterly different character of the railways. The Canadian National inherited, for operation and management, all the Canadian government railways, and to these were added the insolvent private systems. Both groups were grossly over-capitalized, and, when brought together, the units jostled each other in the same territory. The Canadian Pacific, on the other hand, suffered from none of these handicaps.

The royal commission of 1931, while pointing out that such differences affected any comparison between the two railways, conveyed the general impression that the Canadian National had been more extravagant and less efficiently managed than the Canadian Pacific. Their sharpest reproofs are aimed at the Canadian National, while the Canadian Pacific – though manifestly equally extravagant in certain respects – escapes with mild reproof. Probably this attitude on the part of the commissioners may be explained by a sense of responsibility for a public company whose losses were an undoubted burden on the taxpayer. The report, however, does appear to portray a degree of difference in extravagance and efficiency between the two companies which did not, in fact, exist.

Neither the commissioners nor subsequent investigators have been able to find a satisfactory measure to apply to the relative operating efficiency of the companies, though a good deal of light has been thrown on the problem.[27] A comparison of the operating ratios reflects the consistently stronger position of the Canadian Pacific.[28]

YEAR	C.N.R.	C.P.R.
	%	%
1923	91.8	81.0
1924	92.5	80.5
1925	86.7	77.3
1926	82.5	75.8
1927	84.9	78.5
1928	82.0	75.4
1929	85.6	77.3
1930	91.4	78.4
1931	99.8	80.3

That the ratio of the Canadian National was steadily higher than the Canadian Pacific is due largely to historical causes: the point of interest in the table is that the Canadian National fared worse at the height of the depression than the other company. But the operating ratio is not a satisfactory means of judging the position of a railway. A detailed examination would have to proceed through the various fields of operation. Such an examination has been made by one student of the subject, who arrives at the conclusion that the record of the C.P.R. was markedly better than that of the C.N.R.[29]

Assuming, as the weight of opinion seems to reveal, that the Canadian National had a less creditable record over the nine-year period than the Canadian Pacific, what deductions may be made? There is first the question of the relative density of traffic. Again there is the possibility that the Canadian National lacked an organization comparable to that of the Canadian Pacific, owing, perhaps, to the consistent way in which the latter had maintained an able personnel and directed its work to a steadily increasing task. If such a weakness were to be found the cure would lie in reformed organization and improved personnel: a process familiar to public and private bodies in all periods of history. The alternative deduction is that the Canadian National was weak because it was a public body. This is hinted at in the report of the royal commission.

Running through its administrative practices, however, has been the red thread of extravagance. The disciplinary check upon undue expenditure, inherent in private corporations because of their limited financial resources, has not been in evidence. Requisitions of the management have been endorsed by governments, and successive parliaments have voted money freely, if not lavishly.

Such a problem is of the very essence of public ownership, and as such has been debated from every angle. If it be true that extravagance is a necessary corollary of public ownership, then the whole railway question in Canada must be viewed in that light. Now the experience in connection with the Canadian National is the best test case for Canadian purposes, for, although there have been important experiments in state railways in other countries, it is the Canadian political scene which has to be considered.

The majority report of the royal commission of 1917 vibrates with alarm lest politics should interfere with railways. Both Hanna and Thornton issued grave warnings. The royal commission of 1931 stated as a main consideration that " the management of the National Railways should be emancipated from political interference and community pressure." Indeed, almost every public man and every railway official who has spoken or written on the subject has expressed the same sentiments. The possible dangers are many: the simplest is corruption for the benefit of a party or an official of the railway; another lies in concessions to the railway for the purpose of winning votes; a third is concessions by the railway to a community at the behest of local members of parliament; and a fourth – of a somewhat different character – is governmental extravagance or parsimony intended to aid or hamper a railway for political ends.

The cure for these ills which has been most frequently

suggested is to remove the railway from politics. The effect of this would be to approximate the status of a private company, substituting parliament for the shareholders. But the relations between private railway companies and politics have not, in Canada, been idyllic. A number of cases have already been cited in this history in which railways and political parties have gone hand in hand toward their respective goals. That such an unholy alliance is still thought to be possible is evidenced by the fear of the royal commission of 1931 that a monopolistic railway might exercise influence prejudicial to the interests of the Dominion. Less detached observers have painted this picture in more vivid colours. Lobbying and votes on the one hand, and concessions on the other might be written into a *chronique scandaleuse* of Canadian history.[30] Railways and politics have, in fact, never been completely dissociated in Canada, and it is a question whether they will ever be. At best, the hope has been to protect the public railway from the more obvious kinds of political interference, and to leave the government and parliament to protect themselves.

Up to 1933 the control of the Canadian National was in the hands of a board of directors appointed by the government, which also designated its chairman and appointed the president. Such a policy was contrary to that proposed by the royal commission of 1917, whose advice was to utilize a self-perpetuating board of trustees. Inasmuch as the railway was dependent on public money, parliament retained a final control over its budget. In 1924 a select standing committee on railways and shipping owned, operated, or controlled by the government was first set up, and continued to be appointed in each succeeding session. The committee provided a useful bridge between parliament and the railway officials who appeared before it to give evidence and express their own opinions. The pages of Hansard show that parliament was at least active, if not always wise, in its attention to railway matters. The senate showed more resistance to expenditure than did the house of commons, though such resistance has been sometimes explained by motives other than those of public interest.

The report of the royal commission advanced the view that,

the directors' functions have been in practice nothing more than advisory. It would seem that they generally gave a formal approval to programmes of expenditures which they appeared to regard as the main concern of the president and the Government. This left the railway open to political influence and to public pressure exerted by communities and by associations of business and labour interests.

Given the consent of the government, the president could exercise almost unlimited authority, while his financial needs could be met by the government majorities in parliament. The Canadian National was guided neither by an active board of directors whose policies would reflect the limited resources of a company, nor by a government department which would assume the same responsibility. In effect the chief operating officer of the railway was allowed almost unlimited funds for objects which he saw to be, from an operating point of view, desirable. From 1926 to 1930 the Liberal government, with an adequate majority and in years of plenty, gave a free hand to Thornton, whose immediate object was to improve the railway rather than to reduce the fixed charges. In 1929 the business cycle went through another change, and the Conservative administration which came into office in 1930 was faced with the very different problem of financing the Canadian National in time of depression. A policy of retrenchment was immediately needed, and with the change in policy came a change in management. Whether Sir Henry Thornton fell because of a Conservative plot,[31] as the ally of the defeated government, or as the scapegoat for the extravagance of parliament, it was certain that in any case a drastic change was almost certain to be made.

In January 1934 three trustees were appointed in place of the old board of directors. Three months after the appointment of the trustees, the chairman, the Honourable C. P. Fullerton, addressed a message to the employees, in which he spoke of an "agitation" for the amalgamation of the two railways which might have "a very serious effect upon the morale of the workers." The first argument for amalgamation, that it would effect large savings, he countered by advocating economy by co-operation. The second argument, he said, was to relieve the management from the evils of political influences. On this he made the comment:

Everyone will admit that political interference can work great harm, and that it is highly desirable that those who are directing any great enterprise should be free to bring to the performance of their task whatever abilities they may have, untrammelled by a consideration of party politics. Let me say once for all that to-day the Canadian National Railways are just as free from having to consider matters from a political angle as is any railway in Canada, and it is the intention of myself and my fellow-trustees that this shall remain so.[32]

An interesting criticism of the machinery for the management of the Canadian National was made by a newspaper, a staunch supporter of the public railway, when the act of 1933 had just been passed.

The chief advantage claimed for the system thus set up, that it will "take the C.N.R. out of politics," must be in one sense illusory. The C.N.R. is a utility owned by the Canadian people, and the trustees, in managing it, will be performing a public or political function. What the bill does is not to remove the C.N.R. from politics but to divest parliament, the organ of public opinion, of its power to direct C.N.R. policy. Whether this was wisely done remains to be seen. The trustees, no doubt, will be beyond the reach of politicians seeking local favours. But they will also be beyond the reach of parliament's will to maintain the C.N.R. as a going concern, and to resist influences hostile to C.N.R. success and growth as a National property.[33]

The system of trustees lasted no longer than the tenure of office of the Conservative government. In 1936 the new minister of railways (C. D. Howe) introduced into the house of commons a bill, the effect of which was to abolish the system of trustees and replace it with a board of directors of seven persons.[34] The trustees, he said, had failed either to improve the position of the company or to introduce co-operative measures. Furthermore, the board was not representative enough, and "is responsible to no one." It had been the intention of the act under which the trustees were appointed that they should confine themselves to policy, but in practice the chairman had taken over part of the operation.

Under the new arrangement the offices of chairman and president might be held by the same individual, and there were other similarities to the system used before 1933. Howe claimed, however, that his bill did not "change the intent and purpose of the 1933 measure other than to the extent necessary to provide for the substitution of a board of seven directors for the present board of three trustees." He further attempted to disarm criticism by stating that the effect of the bill would not be to return the Canadian National "to the same form of direction that obtained under the late Sir Henry Thornton," the difference being that the new chairman and board would have a greater measure of autonomy.

The minister's speech had been a mixture of criticisms of the personnel of the board of trustees and of the system as such. The way was left open for the opposition to suggest that the whole bill was nothing more than a means of replacing one group of men with another; and they bitterly prophesied that in future the tenure of the board of directors of the Canadian National would be no longer than the life of a government. "I say to the minister," retorted the leader of the opposition, "that he has not made out a case. The only case he has made this afternoon is that in his opinion the chairman has not done his duty and is unfit for his position. . . . What is the sense of saying that they [the directors] are appointed for five years or three or any other term? Why not simply say that they are to remain in office until such time as another government puts someone else in their place?" In spite of this obvious objection to the new measure – whatever may prove to be its merits – the bill passed through parliament, and the Canadian National once more had a board of directors.

The conflicting objects of the supporters of public ownership of railways have not as yet been fully reconciled. There appears to be agreement that the normal operation should be left to men unconnected with politics, and that such executive officers should be free from political interference. But what is meant by "political interference"? Presumably pressure on the railway officers to take action intended to bring advantage to a party or individuals. That, of course, is undesirable. But, if it be recognized that government and parliament must have some control, how are they to exercise it? One can juggle with the word "politics," but the fact is that parliament is a political body, operating by means of a system of organized parties. The risk must be taken one way or the other. If the administration of the railway is insulated from political control, the risk envisaged by the *Free Press* must be faced; if parliament is to retain a supreme function of directing policy, then the dangers of what is loosely called "politics" will be the problem. There seem to be three ways of managing a publicly owned railway: by a government department; by an independent body appointed by the government or parliament; or by a dependent body, appointed by and constantly responsible to the government or parliament. The advantages and disadvantages of each are immediately obvious. Can the advantages of all be combined into one system? A search has earnestly been made for a passage between the Scylla of political control and the Charybdis of an irresponsible executive. If, after the necessary years of experiment, Canadian democracy cannot trust its representatives either to direct, or to appoint those who should direct, a public enterprise, the future of public ownership is doubtful indeed.

Modern Waterways

1. ENLARGEMENT OF CANALS

During the period after confederation when railways were planned and built, waterways continued to be developed too, as complementary to them in the system of Canadian transportation. Scant attention was given to further development of the waterways during the discussions and negotiations in connection with the federation of the provinces, yet shortly after the Dominion of Canada was born a royal commission was appointed to consider the adequacy of the existing canals and the desirability of constructing certain new ones. It was appointed in 1870 and issued a majority report in 1871.[1] Since the burst of energy in the forties little had been done either to deepen existing canals or cut additional ones. The St. Lawrence canals still had a depth of only nine feet, with the Welland a foot better. No steps had been taken toward either the proposed canal across the Isthmus of Chignecto, or that to Georgian Bay via the Ottawa River. The commission had wide terms of reference which covered all these, as well as some minor canals or proposed canals. Their approach to the question is enlightening if it may be taken — as seems reasonable — as not untypical of informed opinion of the day. In a careful examination of the "commercial aspect of the question" the commission found two main uses for canals: for transport to and from the "west," and as a channel of interprovincial trade.

By the "west" they meant not primarily, as in the discussion of railways, the newly-acquired provinces of Manitoba and British Columbia or the North West Territories, but the country bordering on the upper lakes. The "west" was Ontario and such states as Illinois, Michigan and Minnesota, with only a passing thought for the Canadian north-west. This report of 1871 was written in the atmosphere which, for railways, had been dissipated in the sixties – an atmosphere in which there flourished dreams of a system of waterways that would bring the trade of half a continent through Canada. The old battle was fought out again on paper.

The commerce of this fertile and progressive country . . . depends on several routes of communication. Nature has intended the St. Lawrence to be the great commercial highway of the West, and if it has not fulfilled its destiny to the extent it should have done, It is because the enterprise of man has endeavoured to divert its trade into other and artificial channels.

The most important of these artificial channels was, of course, the Erie Canal; while the New York railways were gradually draining business from it as well as from the Canadian waterways. The division of traffic may be indicated by the following figures.[2]

TONNAGE OF VEGETABLE FOOD, 1869

Total on New York canals	1,302,613
Total on Welland canal	503,860
Total on New York Central and Erie railways	1,087,809
Charged at Buffalo and Tonawanda by Erie canal	786,436
Cleared at Oswego by canal	267,815
Through Welland canal in transit between U.S. ports	337,530

The obvious way to checkmate the route by Buffalo and the Erie Canal was to encourage the use of the Welland Canal, which, as the commissioners pointed out, had nearly trebled its business in the previous twenty years. Wheat, lumber, copper, and iron from the upper lakes would pass through the Welland Canal in ever-increasing quantities were it not for the fact that the larger boats of this period could not go through. It was stated that three-quarters of the tonnage on the lakes could not use the canal.

The first step, therefore, in the improvement of the Inland Navigation of the Dominion is the enlargement of the Welland Canal, the great link of commercial intercourse, not only with the prosperous Western Country of the United States . . . but with that vast territory belonging to the Dominion, which must ere long be peopled by thousands. . . . On improving the Welland we take the step pointed out to us by the unerring finger of Progress.

Descending unwillingly from these dizzy and poetical heights, the commissioners turned to the further problem, which was to divert the traffic, once past the Welland Canal, safely down the St. Lawrence, rather than to allow it to break off to New York at Oswego. They found that there had been a steady increase in the amount of flour and wheat going down to Montreal in the previous few years, and they believed that improvement of the St. Lawrence canals would greatly accelerate this increase. The fears of Americans interested in the Erie Canal were quoted as showing the natural advantages of the St. Lawrence route, and the deduction drawn that it only remained for Canadians to exploit that advantage. The commissioners' arguments were largely based on the relative distances, number of locks, and cost of transport, without taking into consideration the advantages of New York over Montreal as a port attracting the shipping of the world. They emphasized in their recommendations the importance of the trunk line to the upper lakes, for which they considered necessary enlargement of the Welland and St. Lawrence canals to twelve feet depth, with locks two hundred and seventy feet long, and the construction of a canal on the Canadian side at Sault Ste. Marie.

The second object to which the commissioners devoted their attention was to facilitate trade between the Maritime and central provinces. The goods exchanged would be bulky, such as coal and grains, and therefore demanded cheap and direct water transport. Part of the route – the upper St. Lawrence – would in any case be enlarged sufficiently, and the only new work required would be a short canal across the Isthmus of Chignecto. This was the Baie Verte Canal, an old and natural idea for allowing direct water connection between the Gulf of St. Lawrence and the Bay of Fundy. The commission was satisfied that, if this direct route were opened, a considerable trade in fish, coal, grain, and manufactured goods would develop. In connection, therefore, with communication between the provinces, the commissioners were more concerned with national boundaries than they were in the case of western trade. The St. Lawrence – Baie Verte route was in most ways a companion in purpose to the Intercolonial Railway; though no such parallel existed between the Pacific railway and the western canals.

Besides these two primary routes, the commission considered

a number of other canals to which they attached less importance. They advocated deepening the canals on the Ottawa from six to nine feet. The Georgian Bay Canal they regarded as a more remote possibility. They recommended that the Chambly Canal be deepened to nine feet, so that it – together with the Ottawa – might be used for the carriage of lumber to the American market. Finally, they advised that the channel in the St. Lawrence between Montreal and Quebec be deepened to twenty-two feet at low water.

In sum, therefore, the commission had in mind a channel of twelve-foot depth from Lake Superior to Montreal, which they believed was as much as the resources of the country and the needs of lake vessels justified. This route would on the one hand act as a trunk line from the ports of the upper lakes to Montreal and Quebec; and on the other serve interprovincial trade, which would follow through to the Baie Verte Canal and Maritime ports. In addition they planned the nine-foot channel across country from Ottawa to Lake Champlain. It remains to be seen how the programme was carried out in succeeding years.

The enlargement of the St. Lawrence canals was undertaken not long after the presentation of the commission's report. The recommendations of the commission were accepted, but before the plan of enlargement had been carried out it was decided to adopt fourteen feet instead of twelve feet as the standard depth. Around the Lachine Rapids a new canal was built to give an immediate depth of twelve, and an ultimate depth of fourteen feet. (The old canal also remained in operation for some years.) The Beauharnois was replaced by the Soulanges Canal, on the north side of the river, although, again, the old canal was retained for the use of a few small boats. The Soulanges was not begun until 1891, and was completed in 1899, with a depth of fifteen feet. Work on the Cornwall Canal was begun in 1876, but the whole was not ready for use until 1900. In this case the old channel was widened, deepened, and straightened, and the new locks put in to allow the regulation depth of fourteen feet and length of two hundred and seventy feet. The three Williamsburg canals (Farran's Point, Rapide Plat, and Galops) formed the last link in the St. Lawrence navigation. The enlargement of these canals to the new standard dimensions was not completed until 1903.

From Prescott through to the Niagara River there was no interruption in navigation, but at the latter point was the old Welland Canal, the enlargement of which had been so much stressed by the commission of 1870. It was decided to deepen the western section of the canal and to install locks of the same size as those adopted for the St. Lawrence. The eastern section, however, from Allanburg to Port Dalhousie, was replaced by a new work following a slightly different course. Fourteen-foot navigation was available by 1887.

For over forty years Canadian shipping depended for an entrance into Lake Superior on the American canal at Sault Ste. Marie, which was in operation from 1855. Although the number of Canadian ships passing through was not large – in 1890 they carried only 3.5 per cent of the total freight – the view was strongly held that the increase of wheat production in the Canadian west necessitated the early construction of a canal on the Canadian side of the straits. The representations of shipowners induced the government to build a lock considerably larger than any other then in Canada, it being 900 feet long and 60 feet wide, with a depth of 18 feet, 3 inches. This canal was opened in 1895.

The proposed Baie Verte Canal was never dug. An alternative scheme for a marine railway across the isthmus was undertaken by a private company subsidized by the government, and a considerable amount of work was actually done. The company, however, got into financial difficulties and the railway was never completed.

On the north and south route the Chambly Canal was left unchanged, but the three canals on the lower Ottawa were enlarged to the dimensions of the old St. Lawrence canals, that is, locks of 200 by 45 feet, with a depth of 9 feet. The extension of the Ottawa system, known as the Georgian Bay Canal, was an attractive scheme. The Ottawa River above the capital, together with Lake Nipissing and the French River, were to be made into a water route to Georgian Bay, and thence to Lake Superior. By this means western grain could be brought to the port of Montreal by the same direct line as that which the North West Company had used for the carriage of furs. While the roundabout passage by Lake Erie could be avoided, the old difficulty which the fur traders had encountered in the portages on the

Ottawa route would be eliminated by the use of locks. The Georgian Bay route would be entirely on Canadian territory, whereas the Welland Canal was available to American vessels which might be *en route* to Oswego. The Georgian Bay Canal was proposed as an alternative to the Welland, and continued to be advocated even after the latter had been deepened. Before confederation, engineers appointed by the province of Canada brought in reports in 1858 and in 1860. Again in 1904 a board of engineers was asked to examine the question, and their report, delivered in 1909, showed plans for a waterway with a depth of twenty-two feet, twenty-eight miles of canal excavation, and sixty-six miles of channel-dredging at a cost of $100,000,000 (later estimated at $125,000,000). In the spring of 1914 a royal commission (the favourite device for transportation problems) was appointed, with wide terms of reference, to consider the matter further. The commission showed great energy in issuing interim reports containing factual material concerning the conditions of transportation, existing and potential traffic, and so on. For some reason, perhaps because the Georgian Bay Canal had by that time ceased to be an issue, the commission never made any specific recommendations as to whether the canal should or should not be built, and the inquiry was suspended.

The Ottawa – Lake Nipissing – French River route was but one, though probably the most convincing, of the plans put forward for a short cut from Montreal to the upper lakes. A second proposal was for a waterway from Lake Ontario, at Toronto, to a point on Georgian Bay. The Huron and Ontario Ship Canal Company was incorporated to build it, but not a shovel of earth was ever dug. The commission of 1870 reported that "the cost of carrying out such a project would be so great as to render it commercially worthless," and nothing more seems to have been heard of it. A third proposal, the Trent Valley Canal, when first advocated, would have been a boon to settlers by providing a water route from the Kawartha Lakes to Lake Ontario. A modest start was made in 1833, but the work was then abandoned. Railways were built to take care of local traffic, while the Canadian Pacific Railway and the enlarged St. Lawrence canals were designed to carry traffic to and from the west. In 1907 parliament, obsessed by the unfortunate belief that any form of transportation would pay, decided to proceed with the project. Not content with the initial error, the government ensured the uselessness of the canal for through traffic by making some of the locks 134 by 33 feet, with a minimum depth of 6 feet. It followed a circuitous course of 240 miles from Trenton on the Bay of Quinte, through a series of rivers and lakes to Lakes Simcoe and Couchiching, and thence along the Severn River. It never was completed to Georgian Bay, and only vessels of fifteen tons can be carried on the two marine railways which took the place of locks on the lower reaches of the Severn River.

The royal commission found that the Rideau Canal was adequate for the traffic which offered, and no change was made.

2. SHIPS AND CARGOES

Improved by canals, the inland waters of North America give unique opportunities for transport. Marked changes in the character and position of shipping accompanied improvements in canals. Sailing vessels began to be forced out by their steam-driven rivals. Passenger traffic by water especially suffered from alternative methods of transport – first the railway and then the motor car – but it did not disappear. St. Lawrence steamers continued to operate from Montreal to Quebec and on to the Saguenay. Above Montreal passenger vessels were operated to Kingston, Toronto, and Hamilton. For a time a combined water and rail route served passengers to the west. After completion of the Northern Railway to Collingwood (1855) the normal way through Canada to the prairies was over that railway, and by boat to Fort William. With the completion of the Canadian Pacific Railway the Northern ceased to be used, but both the C.P.R. and G.T.R. placed ships on the upper lakes as an alternative route for passengers from the west. On the smaller lakes the vessels which were once essential have disappeared, or, as on the Muskoka Lakes in Ontario, wage an unequal battle with the motor car.

Freight vessels, on the other hand, have been able to maintain and improve their positions by virtue of their cheaper transport of bulky articles. The types of vessels have been governed by the size of the locks and their kinds of cargo. As the locks have increased in size, larger vessels have been built.

Between 1899 and 1913 the number of Canadian freight and passenger vessels engaged on the Great Lakes, upper St. Lawrence, Ottawa River, and Rideau Canal rose only from 242 to 265, but the tonnage increased from 90,924 to 310,176.[3] Small vessels were found to be less economical, and larger ones were introduced as the canals were enlarged. In 1931 the steel bulk freighters accounted for eighty-five per cent of the total gross tonnage.

The movement toward large freighters was, however, strictly limited. For carriage to Montreal the depth of the St. Lawrence canals (14 feet) was the controlling factor. The vessels used to Montreal were known as "canallers" or "lower lakers," and those through the Sault Ste. Marie and Welland canals as "upper lakers." While upper and lower lakers were similar in build, the former were most striking in appearance because of their greater length. "The Great Lakes bulk freighter is literally a huge, self-propelling barge with machinery aft, navigating bridge right up forward, and a long, clear parallel almost box-shaped cargo hold between. The machinery portion aft and the forward end are the only ship-shaped parts of the hull."[4] The largest vessel in the Canadian service, and on the Great Lakes, the *Lemoyne* (a bulk freighter of a type for carrying grain, coal, or ore), has a length of 633 feet, beam of 70 feet, and 25 hatches. "Package" freighters carrying assorted cargoes are of the same general design as the bulk freighters, but rather smaller, and fitted with booms and winches with which to unload. Oil tankers have become common in recent years. The "whaleback," with rounded hull and long, spoon-shaped bow, is disappearing.

The general trend toward large-scale enterprises accompanied the increasing size of ships. A number of companies were organized to operate fleets of various sizes, and these in turn were amalgamated, as in the case of the Canada Steamship Lines, which in 1936 operated 101 vessels ranging from 2,000 to 7,000 tons.

The success of Canadian inland shipping has depended primarily on the transport of bulk freight from west to east. The lake carriers have had the advantage of being able to offer low rates for the long distances covered, while the steady improvements in loading mechanism have reduced labour costs and the time spent in harbour. In 1929, for example, the *Lemoyne* loaded her cargo of 555,069 bushels of wheat at the rate of 1,746 bushels a minute. In maintaining their position the lake carriers were obliged to contend with the seasonal character of the business, caused not only by the freezing of the narrow waters, but also by the peak load coming in the short period between the first shipment of the new crop of western wheat and the close of the season of navigation. The latter handicap, however, has been mitigated by vessels being able to transport in the spring the wheat stored in elevators throughout the winter. The depth of water available is affected not only by the standard dimensions of the canals, but also by the level of water in any given season; and "when it is realized that a lake steamer will lose from 35 to 80 tons in carrying capacity, according to size, for each inch of loss of draught of water at minimum load-line, it is not difficult to understand that the water level makes a great difference in the matter of economical operation."[5]

While some departments of lake shipping have suffered from the competition of railways, such loss was more than compensated by the service which the railways rendered in acting as feeders of grain, ores, and coal at ports on the upper lakes. Since both the Great Lakes and the St. Lawrence either form the boundary or run near to it, the shipowners of the United States and Canada would appear to have an equal chance of gaining from the traffic of two countries. The laws of both countries, however, set limits to the participation of foreign vessels in the coasting trade. The United States forbade Canadian vessels from carrying between two American ports, and for many years Canada had a similar regulation. In the early twenties, however, there was a shortage of Canadian tonnage; and to remedy this, and at the same time to tempt American ships down the St. Lawrence, a royal commission of 1923 recommended a change.[6] The Canada Shipping Act was consequently amended in the same year (13 & 14 Geo. V, c.36), giving to the governor in council power to suspend the operation of the act so as to allow foreign ships to trade between two Canadian ports. As the new arrangement did not prove to be successful in its second object, and as there was then ample Canadian tonnage, the Canada Shipping Act of 1934 (24 & 25 Geo. V, c.44) restored the position as it had been before 1923.

The Canadian aims were two: to secure as much traffic as possible for Canadian vessels, and to secure as much business as possible for Canadian ports. The following table[7] shows the United States and Canadian bulk freight tonnage on the Great Lakes and canals in 1922, the year before power was given to admit American vessels to trade between Canadian ports.

DESCRIPTION	U.S. GROSS TONNAGE	CANADIAN GROSS TONNAGE	U.S. AND CAN. GROSS TONNAGE	CANADIAN PERCENTAGE
Steel bulk freighters in ore, coal, grain and stone trades	1,956,189	231,962	2,188,151	10.6
Steel bulk freight barges in ore and coal trades	88,075	3,265	91,340	3.5
Composite bulk freighters in ore, coal and grain trades	6,704	6,765	13,409	50.0
Composite bulk freight barges in grain, pulp and coal trades	673	3,741	4,414	84.7
Wooden bulk freighters in ore, coal and grain trades	43,917	51,299	95,216	54.0
Wooden barges engaged in all trades	34,840	36,253	71,093	51.0
Total freighters and barges	2,130,398	333,225	2,463,623	13.5
Package freighters	100,462	27,968	128,430	21.8
Passenger and freight steamers	69,541	24,853	94,394	26.3
Grand total	2,300,401	386,046	2,686,447	14.4

In the dozen years after 1922 the proportion between United States and Canadian tonnage changed; the former had only increased by about ten per cent in 1935, while the latter doubled in the same period. The Welland Canal was a strategic point in the route to the sea, since it had to compete with the railways and the Erie Canal from Buffalo. The following table shows the traffic through it.[8]

	CANADIAN VESSELS		U.S. VESSELS	
YEAR	NUMBER	TONNAGE	NUMBER	TONNAGE
1900	1,765	575,381	634	437,431
1910	1,852	1,461,499	692	687,018
1920	2,430	2,013,817	694	514,439
1934	3,854	6,216,866	1,296	2,407,577
1935	3,931	6,300,820	1,161	1,896,732

An examination of the figures for 1935 shows that the largest two items in the total tonnage were the down traffic in Canadian vessels from Canadian to Canadian ports, and the down traffic in Canadian vessels from United States to Canadian ports. The opening of the Welland Ship Canal in 1930 attracted more United States vessels, but the advantages of the enlarged canal were to some extent counterbalanced by the increasing use of the Panama Canal. The traffic on the St. Lawrence canals, as the next table indicates,[9] has been overwhelmingly Canadian as to vessels.

| | CANADIAN VESSELS | | U.S. VESSELS | |
YEAR	NUMBER	TONNAGE	NUMBER	TONNAGE
1900	8,737	2,033,206	921	105,151
1910	8,834	2,910,395	1,392	482,144
1920	6,145	3,233,029	813	442,250
1934	9,006	5,602,426	339	238,208
1935	10,009	5,847,341	317	209,798

American tonnage has failed to come to Canadian seaports, partly because of the relative disadvantage of those ports as compared with the rival American ones. Neither Montreal nor Quebec is a winter port, while Halifax and Saint John are far removed from the points of origin of the principal exports. The rates of ocean shipping are necessarily dictated in part by the ease and safety of navigation, and in part by the prospect of return cargoes; and the lower St. Lawrence, though steadily improved, could never be other than a difficult passage.

Iron ore has been the basic cargo for the large American bulk freighters, less than five per cent being available for Canadian vessels in 1922.[10] From the time the Canadian west became a wheat-growing area the Canadian bulk freighters found most of their cargoes in wheat from Fort William, though they were also able – as they had been before – to participate in the carriage of American wheat to Canadian ports. In 1922 Canadian vessels carried forty-five million bushels of wheat from Duluth, Chicago, Milwaukee, and Buffalo to Canadian ports.[11] The largest part of their business, however, has consisted in the transport of wheat from the Canadian west. In 1913 east-bound wheat travelled over routes as follows.[12]

DISTRIBUTION TO INTERIOR PORTS

	BUSHELS
From Fort William and Port Arthur via Great Lakes	130,181,954
From Duluth via Great Lakes	7,830,740
Total	138,012,694

TO CANADIAN PORTS (BY WATER)	BUSHELS	AMERICAN PORTS (BY WATER)	BUSHELS
Depot Harbor	2,963,915	Chicago	374,967
Port McNicoll	7,774,110	Port Huron	3,992,437
Tiffin	11,639,728	Detroit	15,000
Midland	630,000	Toledo	950,525
Collingwood	337,869	Fairport	5,198,205
Meaford	110,000	Erie	7,628,824
Goderich	6,608,085	Buffalo	54,643,639
Point Edward	386,142		
Port Stanley	340,302		
Port Colborne	20,806,527		
Kingston	1,972,473		
Prescott	80,059		
Montreal	11,559,887		
Total	65,209,097	Total	72,803,597

It is apparent that a large number of Canadian ports received some portion of the wheat. Port McNicoll and Tiffin were Canadian Pacific and Grand Trunk ports respectively. Port Colborne, at the western end of the Welland Canal, did the largest business, while only eleven and a half million bushels passed through the St. Lawrence canals to Montreal. Buffalo, on the other hand, took so much Canadian wheat (for rail and water transport to American ports) that the total amount passing through American lake ports was larger than that passing through Canadian. In addition to the wheat passing by all-water route to seaboard (that is, the portion which went to Montreal), and that which went by combined water and rail (that is, all the amounts shown against the other ports, except the small portion that passed through the Erie Canal), 1,030,000 bushels went by an all-rail route over the Canadian Pacific Railway – the only transcontinental line which was complete in 1913. The next table[13] shows the distribution of Canadian wheat to the different ocean ports for export in the same year.

CANADIAN PORTS		U.S. PORTS	
	BUSHELS		BUSHELS
Montreal	26,834,373	Portland	8,223,463
St. John	7,666,998	Boston	14,334,932
Halifax	554,712	New York	22,616,905
		Philadelphia	12,797,843
		Baltimore	12,690,009
Total	35,056,083	Total	70,663,152

The balance then began to change. In 1933 lake shipments of wheat from Fort William and Port Arthur to Canadian ports amounted to 100,677,537 bushels and to American ports 45,240,497 bushels. Meanwhile other factors had begun to affect the position of Canadian shipping on the Great Lakes. Vancouver first began to export considerable quantities of wheat to Europe, by way of the Panama Canal, in 1921, and sent 31,868,187 bushels to the United Kingdom and 63,130,254 bushels to other countries (excluding the United States) in 1928.[14] Prince Rupert and Victoria also entered the picture to a small extent. Possibly significant for the future was the completion of the railway to Churchill, and the beginning of export through Hudson Bay — amounting to 4,049,871 bushels in 1934-1935.[15] Canadian lake boats had secured a larger proportion of the wheat to be carried to ocean ports, but the movement of wheat by rail to the ports of the west and north was a new threat. High prices of wheat, increased acreage, and rising freight rates had led to a great increase in tonnage — from 240,000 to 575,000 tons in the years 1921 to 1931.[16] The demand for tonnage then decreased; freight rates dropped heavily; and the shipping companies ran into difficulties.

Freight rates on the lake grain carriers have fluctuated widely. In 1915 the rate per bushel of wheat from the head of the lakes to Montreal was 4.99 cents. In 1920 it reached a high mark of 11.64 cents and by 1932 was down again to 5.09. Not only in different years, but even as between different parts of the same year, the rates fluctuate. They are not based on standard maxima set by a governmental body, as is the case of railway rates, but on individual contracts. Space in vessels is purchased by individuals, in general before the grain itself is bought, and when the time comes for shipment there may be other cargoes moving at a different rate.[17]

Apart from the relation of existing tonnage to the freight offering, rates on lake vessels are controlled by rival transportation services. The character of the goods carried enables the vessels to compete successfully with Canadian railways for through traffic, but they must maintain their lower rates in order to preserve that position. A further source of control lies in the rates on United States routes to the sea. The maintenance of Canadian shipping and of the St. Lawrence route to the sea are twin problems of long standing. How can more traffic be attracted to the "natural" route by the St. Lawrence? The answer that has been given by Canadians for over a century is to improve the Great Lakes – St. Lawrence navigation. The depth of the canals was increased first to nine and then to fourteen feet as a means to attain this end. Still another improvement has been advocated in a plan known as the St. Lawrence seaway.

With the possible exception of the Rideau, the canals of Canada were designed and first built for normal commercial purposes in an age when railways were in their infancy. The St. Lawrence canals were opened as a through route just as the first period of active railway construction was beginning. The completion of the pre-confederation railways – in particular the Great Western and the Grand Trunk – deprived the water routes of a portion of their passenger traffic, and of their freight traffic in certain goods. With the opening of the west the railways aided the canals. They delivered wheat to the freighters at Fort William and Port Arthur, some of which was carried through to the St. Lawrence, some to Buffalo, and some to a number of ports on Lake Huron and Georgian Bay. From these latter ports the railways again picked up the wheat and carried it to tidewater.

Has the expenditure on the improvement of inland navigation – canals, harbours, and lighthouses – been justified? The money spent on canals by provincial and federal governments amounted in 1935 to a total of $339,583,604, including the cost of maintenance and staff. Against this was a total income over the whole period of $31,689,570. The income did not cover carrying charges and depreciation. When tolls were abolished on Canadian canals in 1903, following similar action in European countries and in the United States, the principle was admitted that the returns from governmental expenditures were, apart from the income from rentals for power purposes, to be totally indirect. This point of view generally applied to forms of transportation. In Canada the aid given by government to transportation has been based on the assumption that adequate facilities had to be provided, that the country could not progress without them. Rates on the Intercolonial Railway (which correspond to tolls) were not based on the capital and operating costs of the railway. Assistance given to other railways, amounting to very large figures, was thought to be well spent, whether or not it returned in cash to the government. So it was with canals. Without them, it was believed, the trade of the Canadian, as well as of the American, west would in large part cease to flow through Canada.

3. THE ST. LAWRENCE DEEP WATERWAY

With such considerations in mind, it may seem anomalous that the most ambitious design ever made for the development of the Great Lakes – St. Lawrence navigation should be a joint project of Canada and the United States, more especially when it is realized that the origins of the scheme are as much American as Canadian, and that it is not a plan foisted on a gullible United States by a persuasive Canada. On the other hand, participation of the United States did not affect the fact that, from the Canadian point of view, the St. Lawrence scheme was a possible means of saving the water-borne traffic of the lakes from escaping south before it reached the St. Lawrence. The United States shares the Great Lakes with Canada, and owns the southern shore of the St. Lawrence from its source at Lake Ontario to a point almost opposite Cornwall. From the early years of the existence of the United States there was a desire to make use of the navigation of the Canadian part of the river – that is, from Cornwall to the sea. This right was granted by the Reciprocity Treaty of 1954; and on the abrogation of the treaty, the same right was conceded by the treaty of 1871. Since 1854, too, American vessels have been allowed to use Canadian canals, which, since 1903, have been free of tolls of American and Canadian vessels alike.

For the United States, however, there are two alternative approaches by water to the interior of the continent, by the Mississippi and the Hudson rivers. The former, because of its shallow water, has never been available for vessels of deep draught; and even the artificial connection between the Mississippi and the Great Lakes via the Chicago drainage canal has not threatened serious competition with the St. Lawrence. The Hudson has been a continuous rival. Early in the present century it was decided to improve the old Erie Canal, long the bugbear of Canadian transportation interests, and by 1918 the new Erie Barge Canal was opened for traffic after it had been deepened to twelve feet and a partial change of route made. The canal might also, as before, be entered from Oswego instead of Buffalo. But, although the barge canal has carried some grain which might otherwise have moved through the St. Lawrence, it cannot be regarded as the major threat to Canada. There have been a number of proposals for deep waterways through American territory, but none has as yet received general support. The foremost rivals to the St. Lawrence route have been the various American railways from Buffalo to New York.

Such support as the St. Lawrence deepening plan has received in the United States has been based on a belief that lower transportation costs could be achieved, and – for a time – that existing facilities were not adequate for the traffic at its peak.[18] Both these views have been shared by Canadians, with the additional interest in routing the heavy traffic of the west through the Canadian section of the St. Lawrence to Montreal. Thus the deepening plan has been to Americans purely a problem in transportation, and to Canadians, that, plus a more general economic interest.

The first official move toward a common improvement of the St. Lawrence came from the United States.[19] In 1913 the senate unanimously adopted the following resolution, moved by a senator from Michigan.

Requesting the President to enter into negotiations with Great Britain with the view to securing an international agreement for the concurrent or co-operative improvement of navigation in the boundary waters of the United States and Canada, for the advancement of the commerce of the two countries.

Some months later the American government suggested that the International Joint Commission be asked to explore the question, with reference to navigation, power, and fisheries. The outbreak of war put a temporary end to discussion, but shortly after 1918 the pressure of both power and navigation interests brought the matter to a head. Early in 1920 the Canadian and American governments requested the International Joint Commission to examine the possible improvement of the St. Lawrence for navigation and power, and each appointed an engineer to co-operate with the commission in the investigation. In 1921 the two engineers reported to the commission that the development of the river for both purposes was feasible. They advised a channel of twenty-five feet for the present, with structures designed to allow an eventual depth of thirty feet. They reported that nearly all the potential power in the river – some 4,100,000 horsepower – might be developed in connection with the deepening plan, but pointed out that this should not all be developed at once since it could not all be sold in the present or near future. They estimated the cost of a twenty-five-foot channel from Montreal to Lake Ontario, with the development of 1,464,000 horsepower in the international section, at $252,728,200.

After receiving the report of the engineers and conducting public hearings, the Joint Commission recommended that a treaty be entered into between the United States and Canada to carry the plan into effect, and that the new Welland Canal be embodied in the scheme. They recommended that the cost of navigation works be apportioned between the two countries on the basis of benefits received, and that additional construction required for power be divided equally. While accepting the report of the engineers as the basis of work between Montreal and Lake Ontario, they recommended that further investigation be made by an enlarged board of engineers. The proposed board was actually set up in 1924. Shortly before this was done, the government of each country appointed a non-technical advisory committee, that of the United States having Herbert Hoover as chairman, and that of Canada, G. P. Graham (minister of railways and canals), and, after his resignation, W. E. Foster.

Both advisory committees reported in favour of the St. Lawrence scheme and the continuation of negotiations, the

American committee reporting in 1926 and the Canadian in 1928. In the meantime the joint board of engineers proceeded with a detailed study of the technical aspects of the question, after which it made its report toward the end of 1926. The plans of the board were "prepared in accordance with the recognized principle that the interests of navigation of the St. Lawrence are paramount." They pointed out, however, that the generation of electric power would not conflict with this principle. Their general plan for the improvement of navigation was to flood out the rapids by dams, rather than to make use of side canals as had formerly been the practice. On the placing of dams, the route of the channel, and the depth to be attained the board was not unanimous. All members were agreed that permanent structures should be designed to permit an eventual depth of thirty feet, but for immediate use the majority of the Canadians were in favour of twenty-seven feet (the depth of the new Welland Canal), and the majority of the Americans preferred twenty-five feet. To secure through navigation to Lake Superior it would be necessary to deepen the channels in the Detroit River and the St. Clair River, and possibly to build a new canal at Sault Ste. Marie. The Welland Canal, the remaining link, was already provided for. No single figure can be given as the estimate of cost, since the amounts varied in relation to the various modifications proposed; but for a twenty-five-foot channel between Lake Ontario and Montreal, with the development of five million horse-power, the joint board put the cost at from $620,000,000 to $650,000,000.[20]

From the time of the various reports which have been mentioned the St. Lawrence project moved steadily toward the point at which it could be submitted to the legislatures of the two countries. In July 1932 the treaty embodying the agreement which had been reached by the governments was signed at Washington. Its specific concern was with the international section of the St. Lawrence, where a twenty-seven-foot channel was to be established, the cost to be divided between the two countries, Canada receiving credit for $128,000,000 of the expenditure on the Welland Canal. The remainder of the works necessary to complete twenty-seven-foot navigation from Montreal to the upper lakes were to be undertaken by the two governments independently. The treaty also provided for the development of electrical power.

In March 1934 the treaty was rejected by the senate of the United States, in spite of its acceptance being urged by the president. Although a few comic interludes, such as the suggestion that the British government was really seeking a naval base on Lake Michigan, may have pleased the more ignorant constituents, the real opposition to the treaty came from the rival power and transportation interests of certain sections and groups. In any case the senate had exercised its constitutional right, and the treaty was – for some years at least – a dead letter. There was no question, in spite of early suggestions to that effect, that Canada would continue the deep waterway scheme single-handed. All that remained of the seaway route was the Welland Ship Canal, which was opened for some traffic in 1930, and for the largest upper lake vessels in 1932. The dimensions of the locks of the new canal were 859 feet in length, 80 feet in width, and 30 feet in depth. For the time being the depth between locks was only 25 feet, but this was sufficient for the largest upper lakers. The new canal followed in part the route of the old one, but some changes were made. The Lake Ontario entrance was moved from Port Dalhousie to Port Weller, and at other points the course was changed with a view to obtaining a straighter line. The general position, then, was that navigation through Canadian waters to the sea was controlled by the Sault lock (18.2 feet), the Welland Ship Canal (25 feet), and the St. Lawrence canals (14 feet). By making use of the American locks at the Sault (24.5 feet) the largest lake freighters could be navigated between Lake Superior and Lake Ontario, but the St. Lawrence remained closed to upper lakers from the west or large seagoing vessels from the east.

Leaving aside the development of power[21] (which must, however, be taken into consideration in estimating the final cost of the work), it appears that the scheme was one to obliterate the rapids and low water as hindrances to navigation, and to provide an inland waterway from the Gulf of St. Lawrence to the head of Lake Superior – a waterway such as did not, and could not, exist in any other part of the world. On the merits of this grand design experts have always disagreed, both as to its economic value, and its probable use by large vessels. The second point may be disposed of first. There is general agreement that the present type of upper lakers could not be used on the ocean, inasmuch as their design makes them unsuitable for anything but inland navigation. There is even doubt whether they could be economically and safely worked through the St. Lawrence canals. Similarly it seems clear that ocean vessels working on a fixed schedule ("liners") would not proceed above Montreal; and uncertain whether tramp steamers would use the canals in any large numbers.

The economic value of the deep waterway plan depends on more complicated considerations. In general there must be taken into account on the one hand the total cost, including new construction, deepening, improved harbours, and compensating works – such as for flooded lands; and on the other hand the returns in electrical power, lower freight rates, and added transportation facilities. The advantages of the waterway must also be considered from two points of view: as benefiting the communities of the middle west of the United States and Canada, and as directing a larger amount of traffic through Canadian channels.

The whole economic question hinges on whether such added facilities are required, and whether they would result in freight rates sufficiently lower to justify the cost to the country. Canada has already three outlets to the sea: on the Atlantic, on the Pacific, and on Hudson Bay. The enthusiasm for the deep waterway plan was born in an age when the economic trend was actively upward: is the waterway required for the traffic of the present or immediate future? Clearly the only valid argument in favour of the waterway is that it would bring a net advantage to the people of Canada; that is to say, result in cheaper transportation without an equal loss to the existing facilities.

Many estimates have been made as to the probable saving in cost of transportation. Probably the most optimistic was that of two American writers who argued that,

The saving on grain will amount to from 8 to 10 cents a bushel, and this saving will affect not only the grain which actually moves for export, but practically all that produced within the area tributary to the Great Lakes. This saving will amount

annually to approximately the entire cost of the improvement required to admit ocean vessels into the Lakes.[22]

A more cautious advocate of the waterway scheme has estimated the probable saving at 3.7 cents a bushel.[23]

Whatever the fate of the deepening scheme, water transport continues and will continue to play a vital part in Canadian life. No railway, no road has destroyed its value. And the men who have since the days of the *voyageurs* of New France carried the country's goods will still follow their lawful occasions.

CHAPTER 14

Transportation By Electricity and Gasoline

1. ELECTRIC RAILWAYS

Just as the discovery of the force of steam led gradually to its application as motive power on both land and water, so the discovery of the similar qualities of electricity suggested a new, and possibly more satisfactory, form of energy. It was one, however, which could be utilized only under certain conditions. Experiments were made with electrically-driven boats, but it was found that even the smaller ones could not be satisfactorily operated by storage batteries. Only slightly more success was obtained with electric automobiles. Electricity is most efficiently supplied in a continuous flow, and its indirect provision, by means of batteries, is expensive and inadequate for such purposes. The use of electricity in transportation, therefore, was confined to railways operating under conditions where electric power could be supplied through overhead wires or a third rail.

The essential feature of electric traction is the removal of power generation from the train to a stationary power unit, and this fact is responsible for most of its economies and advantages. This same fact also gives rise to the great drawback of electrification, since a large amount of capital has to be expended in providing the overhead or third-rail equipment, together with the necessary feeders, transmission cables, and sub-stations. This capital once expended is definitely tied to the route and cannot be moved if the scheme does not prove a financial success.[1]

The first need of electric railways is, obviously, an adequate supply of power, which may be obtained either from natural water power, or by artificial generation. The most favourable conditions for electric railways are where water power is plentiful and coal scarce, as in Switzerland where thirty-two per cent of the railway mileage had been electrified by 1930. Austria, also mountainous and without coal, has followed the same course.

Electric locomotives can be run in either direction without turning; require less labour; can be kept in use more continuously than steam locomotives; have better acceleration and more reserve power; and, not only have greater braking capacity, but can regenerate power through braking. On the other hand, electric railways have not proved profitable over great distances or where traffic it light, for under such conditions the overhead charges are relatively too high. The steam locomotive is in itself a travelling power unit involving a relatively low capital outlay; but the electric locomotive depends on elaborate equipment for power production, which is only economical when in full use. Electric railways are particularly suitable for passenger traffic in well-populated areas. By the elimination of smoke and noise, by ease in starting and stopping, and the small space which it occupies, the electric engine can be used in and near cities. The steam locomotive, on the other hand, is not only an unwelcome visitor to city streets, but cannot be operated economically. It requires a larger train unit and is both clumsy and expensive in starting and stopping.

It will be apparent that the electric railway has had a limited use in Canada. Electric power could not be economically used for long distances in either passenger or freight business, even in those parts of the country where water power existed in large quantities, for the traffic was not sufficient to justify the capital outlay. On the other hand, electric railways were admirably suited for suburban transport. As village grew to towns and towns to cities, horse-drawn omnibuses appeared on the streets, but were hampered by bad roads. In 1861 the first street railway was opened in Toronto with every sign of enthusiasm, but while rails were used to advantage, the motive power supplied by horses was inadequate, particularly as the city grew in size. Electric railways in Canada date from 1887 when a line was opened at St. Catharines, Ontario. Three years later a second company began operations in Vancouver, and in the next few years the street railways of Ottawa, Montreal, Toronto, and other eastern cities were electrified.

Electric railways were also extended beyond the cities to

their suburban areas, or for short runs between cities or towns where the steam railway service was inadequate. Tracks were laid expressly for the purpose, rather than by the electrification of existing railways as has been widely done in England. These "radials" were built in all provinces, and the mileage increased from 256 (including street railways) in 1893 to the maximum figure of 1,737 in 1925. The most far-reaching plan for radials was that put forward by the Hydro-Electric Power Commission of Ontario to operate some 325 miles for rapid transport. Of this total about 150 miles were already in operation, though requiring to be improved for fast trains. There were to be the following lines: from Toronto, through Hamilton, to St. Catharines; from Toronto east to Bowmanville; from Toronto to Guelph; from Hamilton to Kitchener and Guelph; and from St. Catharines to Niagara. The commission had the support of a number of municipalities and believed that there was a great future for electric railways. A new government in Ontario, however, was sceptical of the merits of the plan, and, since financial support from the provincial government was needed, appointed a royal commission to investigate. In 1921 this commission, under the chairmanship of Mr. Justice Sutherland, issued a majority report[2] which was wholly unfavourable to the project. It was argued that "the financial condition of electric railways in Ontario and the United States in and prior to 1920, has been so precarious and unsatisfactory, and the outlook for improvement so dubious and discouraging, that the proposed system of electric railways should not, in our judgment, be entered upon unless the evidence of competent operating experts justifies the conclusion that they will be self-supporting." In the opinion of the commissioners all the evidence indicated that they would not be self-supporting. The commissioners also considered the relation of electric railways to other forms of transport, and came to the conclusion that there would be an uneconomic competition. The business of the Canadian National, they felt, might well be affected by new electric lines, and the Canadian National must be given consideration. Moreover the province had just undertaken a plan for the construction of highways at great cost, and the commissioners believed that the effect of this additional provision for transportation should be observed before the province also committed itself to expenditure on electric railways, which might prove to compete with its roads. The scheme as a whole was dropped; and, while some new lines were built, no such sweeping programme for electric railways was ever again brought forward. After 1925 a steady decline in mileage was evident to 1,293 in 1934.

Electric railways, whether in town or country, were dependent on a sufficient supply of electricity at a cost low enough to justify operation. Most of the early street railways used electricity made by steam, but in the nineties, at the time when more ambitious lines were being built, hydro-electric power was introduced as an alternative. There was plenty of water power to be developed, and as the machinery was improved power could be transmitted over considerable distances; for example, the power developed at Niagara Falls was used in the cities of western Ontario.

Especially outside the towns, electric railways were designed in a period when the roads were in general so bad as to make travel by them difficult, and when there was an absence of effective motive power on the roads. Even when the motor car was introduced, it was at first too expensive and too primitive for general use, and the state of the roads forbade easy travel by that means. In the early years of the twentieth century the electric railway was regarded in many communities as the most hopeful means of travel for short runs, such as would connect the towns between Toronto and Hamilton with those cities. The bulk of the business of electric railways was in the carriage of passengers. In 1933 the total number of passenger cars owned by all the electric railways was 3,773, while their freight cars numbered only 300. In the same year they carried 585,385,094 passengers as against 1,547,202 tons of freight. The character of the traffic of the electric railways was notably different from that of the steam railways. The former catered to the short haul and the latter to the long; the former used, for the most part, single-car trains, while on the latter the size of trains was constantly increased. Neither of the large steam railway companies had made considerable use of electricity.

Electric and steam railways have both met a loss of traffic from the competition of motor vehicles. Both the urban and suburban electric railways have suffered, but the latter have been particularly vulnerable. Within large cities the street railways have still an important role to play, which has been reduced by motor cars but not in most cases by buses, whereas outside the cities lines have felt the full force of the competition from both motor cars and buses. The companies have recognized the effectiveness of competition by themselves operating buses. In many cases the tracks of the radials have been pulled up, and from 1926 to 1934 thirteen interurban and ten urban electric railways ceased operations.

The situation which the radials had been designed to meet – a situation in which there were few good roads and no means of rapid transit by road – had disappeared. For freight and passenger traffic the public turns to that mode of transport which offers the most attractive combination of convenience and economy. The railway was hampered by the inelasticity of its route in that field where its rival was most effective, in the short haul. From its eclipse of many years the road had found a new weapon with which to belabour its old enemy the rail. The internal combustion engine had once again rearranged the balance in methods of transportation.

2. ROADS AND MOTOR VEHICLES

The construction and maintenance of roads was, in the nineties, still entirely under the direction of the provinces, with the actual work delegated to the local authorities. Perhaps because of the emphasis laid on railways, little progress had been made in the improvement of roads. In Ontario the sorry condition of the roads led in 1894 to the organization of the Ontario Good Roads Association, which began a campaign, in the newspapers and through public meetings, to interest the public in the need for improvement. At the request of the association, the provincial government appointed a provincial road instructor, whose first report bore out the need for reform. He wrote that roads in many municipalities were worse than they had been ten years before, and that neglect and evasion of statute labour were more general than ever.[3] A report issued two years later continued to paint a gloomy picture, and one that was probably true of all provinces.

It is doubtful if there is a mile of true macadam road in Ontario outside a few towns or cities. There are miles of roads which are covered with dirty gravel or rough, broken stone, and are popularly supposed to be macadamized. To-day the majority are little better than trails. From the middle of October until the end of December, and from the first of March to the end of May, a period of five months, by far the greatest part of the mileage of the province is mud, ruts and pitch-holes. There are at least two months when the roads are practically impassable.[4]

Up to the beginning of the new century there was little change in the administration. Roads were built and maintained either by the townships or by toll companies. Statute labour was still the rule, although some of the townships began to abolish it at about this time. The cost of construction, over and above the statute labour, was met by provincial grants. The provincial governments, however, now began to take more responsibility. The first important step was the Highway Improvement Act passed by the legislature of Ontario in 1901, which provided for the sum of one million dollars a year (later increased to two million) as government subsidy toward improvement of roads in the organized counties, to be granted as one-third of the cost of such works. The novel part of the act was that grants would be made only on roads built according to government standards. It was hoped that the weaknesses of the old system, in which there had been evident a lack of expert knowledge, might be avoided.

The federal government first undertook the building of roads in pioneer areas, such as the Dawson road between Port Arthur and Fort Garry. After the gold discoveries in 1896 the Dominion government undertook a programme of road-building in the Yukon Territory, and by 1913 there were some five hundred miles of good waggon roads radiating from Dawson and Whitehorse, together with main roads such as that between those two towns, a distance of 330 miles.

Toward the end of the nineteenth century a vehicle was being developed that could move under its own power, and which would be to roads what the steam locomotive was to rails. The motor car, driven by an internal combustion engine and using gasoline as fuel, came as the result of years of experiment in England and France, and began to be effective in the nineties. At this time it was first introduced into Canada, but it was some years before it became a common mode of transport. In 1907, a little more than ten years after the introduction of the first motor car, the total number registered was only 2,130. Compared with the modern car, they were expensive, clumsy, and undependable. The existing roads were unsuited to mechanical vehicles and made driving uncomfortable and hazardous. The first relief to owners came from the manufacturers of cars rather than from road-builders. Continuous attention to the mechanical side led to steady improvement both in safety and dependability. The first low-priced cars in North America were put on the market by Henry Ford, and the number of owners increased rapidly. By 1912 there were over fifty thousand motor vehicles registered in Canada.

Early motor cars were for the carriage of passengers rather than freight, but motor trucks began to be common in the years immediately before the war. The privately owned passenger car is the successor to the horse and carriage of the previous period, and has the advantage that it can be used to suit the owner's convenience, and can be driven when and where he may choose, provided that adequate roads are available. It has, however, characteristics that the horse and carriage cannot have – speed and endurance. A car may (and frequently did) break down, but it does not become exhausted. Thus the old system of travel by stages could be replaced by an uninterrupted journey, limited by the endurance of the driver and the state of the roads.

With the increasing use of the automobile there came an additional and powerful argument for better roads, and the provinces were compelled to take a more active part. As the result of the findings of a commission appointed in 1913 a highway department was established in Ontario, with a minister and deputy minister. Further provision was made for subsidies of twenty per cent of the cost of county roads and forty per cent of trunk roads, the government retaining in both cases the right of approval of the plans. An act of 1917 empowered the government to take over any highway, and to assume sole responsibility for construction and maintenance. By virtue of this arrangement the modern arterial roads began to come into existence. Much the same process was followed in the other provinces. In Quebec the provincial government made grants for county roads and began to take over toll roads from the various companies which held them. The roads branch of the department of agriculture was made into a separate department and a deputy minister put in charge. In each province the steps were the same: grants to local authorities, partial control of construction, and provincial highways.

The Dominion government, too, increased its participation by degrees in road-building. In 1911 the Conservative party adopted as part of its platform federal aid to municipal authorities for the construction of roads, and, when returned to power, introduced a bill to that effect. It also allowed for construction of highways by the Dominion government, but the bill failed to pass the senate, and eight years elapsed before the project was revived. The Canada Highways Act of 1919 authorized the expenditure of $20,000,000 on the construction and improvement of highways over a period of five years. A minimum grant of $80,000 was to be made annually to each province, and the remainder to be allotted in proportion to population. At the same time a separate highways branch was established in the department of railways and canals. Finally the federal government entered directly into road construction in 1931 by undertaking the Trans-Canada Highway as a step to alleviate unemployment and to allow travel by road from coast to coast on Canadian soil. The constitutional position of the Dominion in regard to highways involves some nice problems, but it seems unlikely that federal expenditure on roads will be resisted by the provinces.

Before 1914 almost no hard-surfaced highways were to be found in Canada, and motor traffic was severely handicapped. It was no uncommon experience for motorists, as late as 1915, to be stuck in mud holes on the principal highways of Ontario. Motoring was still a series of adventures in which the driver pitted his skill and his luck against mechanical imperfections and the hazards of the road. As the number of motor cars and trucks increased (there were nearly 200,000 in 1917) serious attention began to be given to the roads, and during the war the first highways adequate for motor vehicles, such as the Toronto-Hamilton highway, were begun. The change consisted not so much in cutting new roads as in improving old ones, by straightening, widening, re-surfacing, and lowering the grades. Provincial and federal authorities studied various types of roads and made use of the experiments conducted in other countries. The resulting roads, of course, differed greatly in character, according to the purposes for which they were intended. Only those receiving the heaviest traffic were required to be of cement or other hard surfaces, while in many parts of Canada gravel or earth was the rule. The result over a period of years has been to produce a number of main highways that can be used by motor vehicles at all times of the year, together with many roads that are still difficult in the spring. There remain a number of country roads of unimproved dirt, some of which are impassable when the frost is coming out of the ground. There are still many sections in the northern parts of the central and western provinces that are without good roads, but these are for the most part sparsely, if at all, settled. Recently attention has been given to colonization and tourist routes that cut into the forests of northern Ontario. The Trans-Canada Highway, when completed, will pass through some territory in which there are few inhabitants and little local traffic. The partly completed road through the Rockies is an engineering feat comparable to the railways through those mountains, and will necessarily depend largely on tourist traffic.

The growth of roads in modern Canada lacks some of the romance of the earlier period, when the typical problem was to cut a road through virgin forest; yet the importance attached to good roads, especially in the years since the war, indicates a similar value to the community. The following table[5] shows the character of roads in the various provinces at the end of 1934. For the whole Dominion the total mileage of roads was: provincial roads, 87,496; other roads, 321,773; grand total, 409,269.

Nova Scotia and New Brunswick have, until very recently, pinned their faith to gravel. Saskatchewan, with much the greatest mileage, has only a small proportion of gravel and few hard-surfaced roads. Of the central provinces, Ontario shows nearly twice the mileage of Quebec, with a fair proportion of macadam and cement surfaces. The different types of roads in use depended on the extent, wealth, population, density of traffic, physical conditions, and financial policy of each province.

PROVINCE

Prince Edward Island
Nova Scotia
New Brunswick
Quebec
Ontario
Manitoba
Saskatchewan
Alberta
British Columbia

The city dweller has an exaggerated idea of the extent to which the horse has been replaced by the motor vehicle: a mistake which may readily be rectified by a visit to a typical country district, especially in the winter when rows of sleighs will be seen in any village or small town. In some districts, oxen are still in general use for heavy hauling. Nevertheless, the test of a modern road, and especially of any main highway, is its suitability for motor vehicles. The motor car has long since ceased to be regarded as a luxury, or the rich man's perquisite; while its less flashy brothers, the motor truck and the motor bus, play a vital part in transportation. Motor vehicles of all kinds have increased in numbers at a startling rate in recent years. By 1934 the registrations for Canada were as follows: passenger cars (including taxicabs), 952,427; commercial cars, buses, and trucks, 166,799; motorcycles, 10,306 – a total of 1,129,532.

The most obvious effect of the combination of motor vehicles and improved roads is to reduce distances and to alleviate the remoteness of even the most sparsely settled areas. The railway had gone far toward performing this service, but there was a limit to what the railway could accomplish. On the one hand, the towns, villages, and farms have been brought into touch with the cities, and are thus enabled to buy and sell in a larger market. Such products as fruit, vegetables and dairy **products may readily be carried in trucks or even passenger**

UNIMPROVED MILES	IMPROVED EARTH MILES	GRAVEL MILES	WATER-BOUND MACADAM MILES	BITUMENIZED MACADAM MILES	BITUMENIZED CONCRETE MILES	CEMENT CONCRETE MILES	TOTAL MILES
1,789	1,651	195			12	1	3,651
7,081	3,722	3,903	30	10	37		14,783
2,567	2,228	6,791		13	15		11,614
	18,394	14,394	1,396	186	637	142	35,149
3,331	18,217	42,112	188	2,312	803	1,687	68,675
28,502	1,307	4,377			177	26	34,389
56,696	96,573	2,363			68		155,700
40,109	20,190	2,455		80			62,834
2,906	10,364	8,358	41	613	72	47	22,474

cars, and sold with or without the aid of a middleman. At the same time the farmer or villager has a wider choice as a buyer, and in many instances may have goods delivered at his door. The rural delivery of mail and newspapers has also been accelerated by the use of motors. On the other side of the medal is the further destruction of the independent life of villages and small towns, already reduced by the coming of railways. The old self-sufficiency, the local trades, and even the consciousness of local pride and corporate existence have to some extent disappeared.

The principal uses of motor vehicles may be divided into those of the truck, omnibus, and passenger car. The truck may be operated by the company whose business it does, or it may be a common carrier, or a contract carrier. Trucks are commonly used for the delivery of almost all classes of goods in cities and in the areas immediately surrounding them, and many manufacturers and large-scale retailers use them both in the delivery of their products and acquisition of materials. A use of trucks that illustrates their peculiar value is in the moving of household furniture, where the necessity of crating and the inevitable delay attendant on its transport by rail are avoided. The milk supply for the large cities is for the most part carried by truck, a method which allows for the collection of cans at the gate of each farm and their delivery to the dairy with the least possible delay. The produce of market gardens is usually carried to urban centres by truck; livestock are transported to market in trucks designed and licensed for that purpose; and in many cases grain is carried to the elevators by truck, a fact which is significant to the farmer in the saving of time at a busy season. In 1924 the highways branch of the department of railways and canals conducted an interesting investigation into the haulage of farm crops by waggon or truck over rural roads. By means of a questionnaire, it was ascertained tht 7.2 per cent of the produce of the farmers who replied was carried by motor truck. At that time only 12,500 trucks were owned by farmers. Transport either by waggon or truck was appreciably cheaper on improved roads. The comparatively small number of trucks used by farmers was in part due to the poor condition of the average market roads, especially in western Canada. By 1931, for 728,623 farms listed there were 48,402 motor trucks, or about one truck for every fifteen farms. At the same time about one-fifth of the farms of Canada were located on unimproved earth roads, while a very small portion were on macadam, asphalt, or concrete highways.[6]

The motor bus has developed rapidly following the construction of first-class highways. It has been of great convenience in suburban and interurban runs particularly. While buses are operated over considerable distances, the bulk of their work is in trips not exceeding one hundred miles. To some extent the motor bus has taken over the traffic formerly carried by electric railways, and to a much lesser extent that carried by steam railways. Like the truck, it can be driven wherever adequate roads are to be found; but, because it necessarily carries a large number of passengers at once, it can hardly offer the door-to-door service which makes transport by truck so popular. Of a total of 2,255 buses registered in 1929 less than one-half operated outside the limits of cities. Figures prepared for the same year, 1929, show that buses obtained only 1.7 per cent of the total passenger miles.

In contrast, passenger cars were responsible for 78.5 per cent of passenger miles. Private cars rather than buses have brought a revolutionary change in passenger traffic. Nine hundred and fifty thousand passenger cars registered in 1934 stand against one thousand, seven hundred buses of the same year. Besides its obvious use as the private transportation service of countless families, the car is widely employed by persons travelling on business. A commercial traveller can cover more territory in a given time with the aid of a motor car than he can by train, except where his stopping points are far apart; and with a modern car, good highways, and a radio as companion, he can roll up a heavy mileage without too much discomfort. Cars, too, have reduced the isolation under which farmers have traditionally lived in Canada.

Tourist traffic has existed since the early days of Canadian history, and all methods of transportation have profited by it, but the characteristic modern tourist traffic is that by motor car. For Canada there are two main sources of motor tourists: from within the country, and from the United States. It is not possible even to guess at the numbers in the first of these classes, for no records are or could be kept. It can only be said that observation shows a large number of Canadian cars on tour during the summer, for periods varying from one day to several weeks. Because of immigration regulations, fairly accurate statistics are available for foreign cars, which in effect means cars from the United States. In 1928, when the tourist traffic had reached important dimensions, the number of foreign cars entering Canada was 3,645,455 – fifteen times greater than the figure for ten years earlier. By 1930 the total had increased to 5,409,458. Of these cars 4,110,100 entered on twenty-four-hour permits, 1,297,030 on sixty-day permits, and 2,328 on permits good for six months. Of those entered on the shortest permits, probably the majority went no great distance from the border and cannot be considered as serious users of Canadian roads. But even the 1,300,000 cars admitted for the longer periods, carrying as they did, an average of 3.5 persons per car, represented a migration of important dimensions.[7] For 1934, when the number of cars entering had decreased to 2,373,648, the total expenditure by American tourists is officially estimated at $86,259,000. Tourist traffic has, in fact, become a major industry of Canada. The attraction of touring by motor, whether by Canadians or visitors, depends on a number of factors. Scenery, summer resorts, and sport may be said to form one group, and in all of these Canada is well supplied. A second requirement is in hotels and their more recent counterparts – camps, cabins, and lodging houses.

The provision of accommodation has required rapid development, but apparently the supply has kept pace with the demand for the main highways are studded with all these forms of hospitality. Finally the coming of tourists depends to a large extent on the existence of adequate roads. This has meant the improvement of existing highways and the construction of new ones.

Improvement of highways involves heavy expenditures. Much of this may be balanced against the income from visiting tourists, for although they may enter the country without charge, the money spent indirectly helps to support the roads. No complete figures are available, except in recent years, for the income and expenditure on roads in Canada, but reference may be made to current figures. Income is derived from licences for cars and drivers, mileage tax on motor trucks and buses, and gasoline tax, and in each instance is controlled and receivable by the province. For the year 1934 the revenue from all sources and in all provinces was $50,622,683. The whole problem of costs has been actively raised in recent years not so much from the point of view of whether improvement of roads was justified by the returns, as from that of the competition between road and rail traffic. No amount of energy in gathering statistics will make possible a mathematical comparison between road and rail costs. The railways, built in modern times, have a known cost. Capital outlay, maintenance, equipment, and operating expenses are exactly known. A detailed record is kept of all the traffic which moves over them, and there is no possibility of persons using their lines without permission. In none of these instances are corresponding data available for roads. Except in the case of completely new highways the capital cost has been built up over such a long period, and in such a variety of ways (including, for example, statute labour) that it is manifestly impossible to attempt even a guess at their cost. No complete record is or can be kept of the persons who use the roads. Pedestrians, troops, horse-drawn vehicles, agricultural machines and cattle may at any time take advantage of roads for their various purposes, but no system could be evolved which would relate these uses to the upkeep or capital cost of the road.

Any correlation which may be attempted, therefore, between the cost of roads and the use of them by motor vehicles can be only an approximate one, and will derive its real significance from two considerations: that motor vehicles both require better roads and are the chief agent in their deterioration; and that commercial motor vehicles should be prevented from unfair competition with railways. The conference on rail and road transport organized by the English ministry of transport reached the conclusion that the criterion of allocation of cost should be a combination of ton-mileage and petrol consumption.[8] The royal commission on transportation in Canada, making its report within a few months of that of the English conference, recognized the importance of motor vehicles as a form of transport and urged that steps should be taken to investigate the question further.[9] The situation in Canada, however, is complicated by the control of the provinces over roads and taxation of vehicles, and there has not yet existed any pressure sufficient to induce the provincial governments to attempt a joint solution.

Besides making a higher payment for use of the roads, it has been urged that buses and trucks should be subjected – as railways are – to control of rates and working conditions, and these latter suggestions appear to be just and wise. Viewing the question broadly, however, it seems necessary to think of road transport in terms of its social and national value. It is not sufficient to adopt the negative attitude that the country's investment in the railways must, above all things, be protected. As was suggested in reference to canals, emphasis on different forms of transport changes from time to time, and it is neither wise nor possible to attempt to stop the hands of the clock. It is not in the public interest that the economic operation of the railways should be rendered impossible by the subsidization of road transport: on the other hand it must be recognized that road transport has a special service to render which the railways cannot provide. Commercial motor vehicles should be carefully regulated so as to ensure safety and to avoid unlimited competition in rates (which may lead to dangerous operation). An attempt should be made to charge them with the lion's share of the interest charges and maintenance of the roads. If it should then become clear that railways could not compete in rates with buses and trucks quite a different problem would have to be faced. It would then become necessary to decide how far it was socially desirable to maintain the railways by means of rate fixing. But there is no reason to believe that such a question will arise. The problem for the immediate future is to adjust the railways and motor vehicles into their respective spheres, and to produce complementary services which will result in the maximum of convenience and economy for the public.

3. AIR TRANSPORT

The gasoline (or, later, oil) engine made possible a revolutionary change in air transport, just as, a few years earlier, it had done in road transport. The necessity of motive power and the selection of the gasoline engine apply equally to heavier-than-air and lighter-than-air machines. Before 1914 aviation was in a purely experimental stage, and while some of the tests of the effectiveness of early machines took place on Canadian territory, the latest mode of travel was then only of potential consequence for transportation. It was the pressure of the needs of war that changed the aeroplane from a *rara avis* to a recognized and tried machine. When the war came to an end in 1918 Canada found herself possessed of a large number of military aeroplanes, pilots, and technicians. It was only natural that this new sword should be beaten into a plowshare, that the aeroplane should be fitted into the scheme of civil transportation.

From its very character it was inevitable that the aeroplane should, in Canada, be the complement rather than the competitor of roads, railways, and ships. Manifestly it could not take the place of the passenger motor car, do the unromantic work of the truck, or carry heavy freight in place of ship or railway train. Its special value was to carry passengers and light goods at high speed; and to carry passengers and goods to areas where no other means of transportation existed. It is conceivable that at some future date the aeroplane may compete with railways or road transport, but so far it has not been a serious consideration in Canada. It is possible, too, that other types of work could be done by lighter-than-air machines, although these have not yet been used for either military or civil purposes in Canada.

Natural conditions in Canada are peculiarly suited to the aeroplane as an additional mode of transportation. With a large **area** and scattered population the distances to be covered are necessarily great. An obvious role for the aeroplane, therefore, is to provide a more rapid means of transport than trains or motor cars. The transcontinental railways afford adequate facilities for all normal purposes, but in Canada, as in other countries, there is a small proportion of passenger, mail, and express traffic which requires greater speed, even at the higher rates which air travel involves. In addition, the aeroplane is needed for those northern areas in which neither railways nor roads have been built. In comparison with the width of its territory, the population of Canada is spread along a narrow belt. North of that belt lies a lonely land, still only partly mapped, whose mineral resources have only begun to be exploited. For journeys of hundreds of miles the aeroplane has offered the only alternative to travel by canoe and dog team. Even where single lines of railway have been run far to the north, there remain districts on each side which have not, and for a long time cannot have, the network of branch lines and roads that serve the people further south. Air transport, therefore, whether of passengers or freight, has served more as a feeder than a competitor to railways.

In 1919 an act (9-10 Geo. V, c.11) was passed providing for an air board of five to seven members, appointed by the governor in council for three years and eligible for reappointment. One member was to be a representative of the department of militia and defence (re-named department of national defence), and one of the department of naval service. It was given wide powers to supervise all matters connected with aeronautics and was to study the development of aeronautics, conduct or co-operate in researches, control licenses, government air stations, and so on. Under the terms of the act an order in council was passed at the end of the year providing a detailed set of rules for civil aviation. After 1923 the powers and duties of the air board were exercised by the minister of national defence. In 1927 four administrative divisions were created in the department of national defence to deal with different aspects of aviation. One of these was concerned only with military operations; the second, under the director of civil government air operations, administered governmental but non-military aviation; the third, under the controller of civil aviation, was responsible for the control of commercial and private flying, the location and equipment of airways, and construction of airship bases; while the fourth division, that of aeronautical engineering, was intended to give advice on technical questions to both military and civil branches. After the first establishment of a federal organization to supervise aviation, the question was raised as to whether this matter came properly under federal jurisdiction. The point was argued in the Canadian courts and carried to the privy council in 1931, where it was held that the Dominion had exclusive jurisdiction.

The first civil use to which aeroplanes were put in Canada was for transport in the northern areas. The machines built during the war were unsuited to inter-city traffic either for passengers or goods; on the other hand, the flying boats and seaplanes designed for military purposes were well adapted both to the conditions and needs of aviation in the north country. Again, there was as yet no public demand for inter-city service, but a real need for air transport in the north. Valuable work has been accomplished by aeroplanes in exploration, photography, and forest patrol, superseding the canoe. To illustrate the use of aeroplanes in fire-fighting one story may be borrowed from a recent monograph.

A pilot of the Ontario Air Service detects a fire. He at once heads for the nearest forest ranger station. Thirty-five minutes after sighting the fire, he sees a canoe on a small lake. He immediately alights and tells the canoeist, who happens to be the Chief ranger, about the fire. Continuing his journey, two hours later he is back at the fire with the Deputy Ranger and his equipment. That day and the next and the next – for 10 consecutive days – he makes in all 35 flights before the fire is out and the men are back at their posts. In all the fire burned 3,200 acres and demanded the services of 27 men and 12½ tons of fire-fighting and camping equipment and food, and not a single piece of transport except the D.H. Moth was employed.[10]

The use of aeroplanes for forest patrols has been extended throughout Canada by the provincial governments. The aeroplane has rendered an unique service in the location of mines, and – what is more important in relation to transportation – the conveyance of passengers, supplies, and minerals to and from those mines. The Eldorado radium mine at Great Bear

Lake is some 800 miles (by air) from railhead, a distance which can be covered by aeroplane in one to one and one-half days as opposed to two or three weeks by water.[11] In 1932 thirty-two planes were used at Bear Lake. Sioux Lookout in northern Ontario became such an important air base that in 1930 it is said to have handled as much passenger and freight traffic as any American airport.[12] From this base the Red Lake mining area was served by air from 1927.

Doctors, nurses, police, clergy, surveyors, traders, and trappers have all been carried by air in the north country for distances which by any other means would take weeks or months. The Hudson's Bay Company has made use of air transport both for packs of furs and its officers. For a land of many lakes the seaplane was particularly useful, for, by using water as a landing place, the necessity for artificial flying fields was obviated. In winter use has been made of aeroplanes equipped with skis.

During the first decade after the war, a remarkable development of air services had taken place in Europe, and Europe's example was being followed in the United States. With the aid of governmental subsidies, companies had been established and maintained regular routes between the leading centres; and air transport – for passengers, mail, and express – was taken for granted as an alternative to that by road or rail. The experience that could thus be drawn upon, together with the probability that American airways would tap Canadian traffic, led the government to begin the encouragement of Canadian lines. Air mail services were inaugurated about Christmas 1927 and were rapidly extended. By the end of 1929 a new route between Fort McMurray, Alberta and Aklavik, near the mouth of the Mackenzie River, was opened. The distance was 1,676 miles, and mail was thus carried three hundred miles within the Arctic Circle. In 1931 the following routes were regularly operated:

All Year – Montreal-Toronto-Detroit, Montreal-Albany, Sioux Lookout–Red Lake, Toronto-Buffalo, Winnipeg, Edmonton, Fort McMurray–Aklavik, Peace River–North Vermilion, Amos-Chibougamau, Amos-Sisco, Montreal–Moncton–Saint John, Winnipeg-Pembina.

Summer: – Rimouski-Montreal, Montreal-Ottawa, Lac du Bonnet–Bisset–Wadhope, Montreal-Quebec.

Winter: – Leamington–Pelee Island, Quebec–Seven Islands, Seven Islands–Anticosti Island, Moncton–Magdalen Islands, Moncton–Charlottetown.[13]

A service was also operated, under special arrangement, between Whitehorse and Dawson, Yukon Territory. The other routes listed above were flown by commercial firms under contract from the post office. The total route-mileage was 5,038 miles. If these routes are followed on a map it will be seen that they cover an enormous area, include every province and the terroritories, and run from the southern boundary to the far north, and from the Atlantic to the Rocky mountains. They fulfilled the dual purpose of effecting faster mail delivery between points already served by railways and of carrying the mail far beyond the range of railways.

Mail service was, however, but one of the many objects for which regular air routes were designed. There remained the whole field of carriage of passengers and express. For all these purposes there was needed, in addition to machines and pilots, an elaborate equipment on the ground. In providing this equipment the federal government aided commercial aviation. The terminal airports are either at cities or at the end of the route. Between these, which have been partly built by municipalities and commercial interests, there have to be emergency aerodromes at intervals of twenty-five miles, lights as guides for night-flying, radio direction beams for darkness and bad weather, radio communication between the airports and the aeroplanes, and meteorological service.

Along these airways, as they were developed, an increasing number of commercial companies began to operate as passenger and freight traffic proved to be available. In 1930 came a merger between Western Canada Airways and a number of companies in eastern Canada, the new organization being known as Canadian Airways Limited. The president of the company was J. A. Richardson of Winnipeg, and it was significant that the presidents of both the Canadian National and Canadian Pacific became vice-presidents of Canadian Airways.

The records[14] of Canadian Airways show a great variety of activities. Freight of all kinds has been carried, from gold to live oxen. Their aeroplanes are flown on regular or special services from the Atlantic to the Pacific, from the Arctic to the American border. Into Labrador, on both sides of Hudson Bay, through the Yukon, and over the mountains of British Columbia, mail, passengers and freight are carried. The time-table of the company reads like that of a railway, except that an examination of the names of the stations shows many places far beyond the reach of railways. Could the most enterprising of the Nor'Westers be brought back to life, it would be interesting to show them that planes leave once a week from Fort McMurray for Fort Resolution, and once a month for Fort Norman (on the Mackenzie River). The fathers of confederation might be intrigued to see that a daily service takes passengers from Moncton to Charlottetown in an hour at a cost of $9.00, and express for the same distance for four cents per pound.

The operations of Canadian Airways Limited and Quebec Airways Limited may be seen in a table published in the Company's periodical.[15]

YEAR	HOURS	MILES	EXPRESS LBS.	MAIL LBS.	PASSENGERS
1931	19,143	1,832,794	764,449	459,458	8,047
1932	13,775	1,294,207	1,870,136	299,066	8,963
1933	12,744	1,165,434	2,522,233	328,618	16,942
1934	16,993	1,591,765	5,766,691	472,308	16,594
1935	17,869	1,674,018	5,275,745	817,678	14,542
1936	21,789	2,068,678	7,749,926	955,214	20,948

The growth of civil aviation in Canada in general may be readily seen in a table.[16]

ITEM	1925	1930	1934	1935
Firms manufacturing aircraft	2	7	6	10
Firms chiefly operating aircraft	8	100	125	123
Aircraft hours flown	4,091	92,993	75,871	88,451
Total aircraft mileage	255,826	7,547,420	6,497,637	7,522,102
Number of passengers and crew	4,897	124,875	105,306	177,472
Freight and express carried (lbs.)	592,220	1,759,259	14,441,179	26,439,224
Mail carried (lbs.)	1,080	474,199	625,040	1,126,084
Air harbours	34	77	101	96
Aircraft (all types)	39	527	368	380
Licensed personnel	91	780	997	—

In all the items listed above there is a marked increase between 1925 and 1930, that is, in the period in which commercial aviation was actively encouraged by the Dominion government, and in which general prosperity allowed expenditure on aircraft and air travel by both public and private bodies. On the other hand, a decrease will be observed in some items between 1930 and 1934. In 1935, when more prosperous times returned, the business done by the commercial firms once more increased.

The slackened pace halted the achievement of a trans-Canada airway, the darling project of those most interested in Canadian aviation. There are striking parallels between the first trans-Canada airway and the first trans-Canada railway. Two of the purposes of the latter were to provide transcontinental transportation of the most modern type on Canadian soil, and so prevent the American systems from tapping Canadian traffic; and to form an "all-red" route from Europe to the far east. Both these motives have been strong in an attempt to construct a trans-Canada airway. Though later than Europe, the United States was earlier than Canada in creating through airways. Since the American air routes touched Canada at a number of points, mail, passengers, and express could – in the absence of a Canadian transcontinental line – be shipped over the American system. A letter from Toronto to Vancouver, for example, could, by the arrangement between the American and Canadian postal authorities, be sent by American air mail. While such facilities were an immediate advantage to Canadians, the continuance of a dependent position might well prevent the construction of a Canadian airway in the future.

The enthusiasts for a Canadian railway linked with it their plans for lines of steamships on the Atlantic and Pacific oceans, to form one complete system of transport. The advocates of a transcontinental airway also envisaged such a through route, Their plan, however, in some ways made a stronger appeal to the imagination; for not only would the time taken be only a fraction of that by rail and steamship, but one mode of transport could be used throughout.

The appeal for a trans-Canada airway rested on two grounds: the desirablility of having an airway on Canadian soil that would retain through air traffic in Canada and serve intermediate points;

and the desirability of making Canada a link in an east-west airway. On the first point little need be said. If it is safe to use other means of transportation as a test, then it will be evident that trunk lines are essential to the prosperity of any transportation system. If Canadian airways should prove to be no more than branches of an American trunk line, they would have a dependent and uncertain existence, besides losing the profit that accrues from through traffic. The argument in favour of a trans-Canada airway as a part of a route between Europe and Asia hinges not only on the desirability of an all-British route (with its potential military advantages) but also on the ground that the northern passage is the shortest.

The construction of the trans-Canada airway also bears a resemblance to the history of the Pacific railway. Owing to financial stringency it was thought to be unwise to embark on a through route at once, and in the meantime the intention was to fill in the gaps not covered by available Canadian and American services. The prairie section was attacked first, partly for this reason, and partly because flying conditions were favourable and aerodromes could easily be built. By the spring of 1930 construction in the section was far enough advanced to allow a regular air service from Winnipeg to Calgary and Edmonton. The two sections which had proved most difficult for the trans-continental railway – around Lake Superior and across the mountains of British Columbia – were left for the future, and in the meantime the American airway from Detroit to Pembina was used. In the summer of 1933 construction was recommenced as a measure to reduce unemployment, and by 1934 some 6,000 men were at work in British Columbia, Ontario, Quebec, and the Maritime Provinces.

In November 1935 a meeting was held at Ottawa between representatives of the United Kingdom, Canada, the Irish Free State, and Newfoundland to consider the establishment of a transatlantic air service. Arrangements were there made which were intended to lead to trial flights in 1936, to be followed by mail and passenger services on a minimum schedule of two flights a week in each direction. In December a further meeting was held at Washington, after which the following statement was released to the press by the assistant secretary of state.

As a result of the conferences which have been in progress since Thursday, December 5, between representatives of the United Kingdom, the Irish Free State, Canada and the United States, understandings have been reached which it is confidently hoped will bring about the early establishment of trans-Atlantic air transport service connecting these several countries. These understandings are based upon the principle of full reciprocity between the United States and other countries.

The Department of Commerce has given its approval to the establishment of trans-Atlantic airways by way of Canada, Newfoundland, and the Irish Free State to England, and by way of Bermuda to England, and from Bermuda to Puerto Rico, the latter route to be extended by mutual consent. The Atlantic Sea Board ports in contemplation as termini are New York City; Baltimore, Maryland; Cape Charles or Norfolk, Virginia, and Charleston, South Carolina, any one of which may be designated as ports of entry but no final determination with reference to places has yet been made.

It is recognized that the northern route is much shorter than the southern route and therefore will have the advantage of more economical operation, but this fact does not preclude the possibility of considerable use being made of the southern route. It is expected that experimental flights will be begun early in the summer of 1936 and it is hoped that scheduled services will begin by the summer of 1937. When the full regular service is inaugurated, it is provided that there will be four round trips per week.

The matter of the carriage of mails is necessarily postponed for future consideration.

Further negotiations brought the project within sight of realization in the summer of 1937. The Canadian parliament, in 1937, passed the Trans-Canada Air Lines Act by which a corporation was created known as the Trans-Canada Air Lines, and which was to operate an air service across Canada as part of the route from Europe to the far east. Such a route would make a reality, under new methods, of the dreams of a century ago; a new chapter in the never-ending story of the development of transportation.

Manuscript Sources. There is a wealth of material on the history of transportation in the Public Archives of Canada. The state papers of Nova Scotia (series A), of New France (series C11 A), and of Canada after 1763 (series Q, also known as CO 42) form the basis of study. There are also a number of other collections of importance, such as the papers of Lord Durham, Joseph Howe, Sir John Macdonald, Sandford Fleming, and Alexander Mackenzie. The Baring papers are also of value.

The Archives of the Hudson's Bay Company are indispensable for the history of transportation in the west over a long period. Some of the most important series for this subject are: the minutes of the committee, correspondence with His Majesty's government, correspondence between London and Rupert's Land, letter books, journals of posts, and the reports of Sir George Simpson.

Government publications. There are an immense number of such publications. The statutes of the provinces and the Dominion, the debates of the Dominion parliament, and the journals of the provincial legislatures are all helpful. The sessional papers form a mine of information, particularly in the reports of the department of railways and canals and the various royal commissions.

The Dominion bureau of statistics issues periodically material on steam railways, electric railways, canals, and highways.

Other contemporary material. Newspapers, of which a large number have been preserved, give both factual material and opinion. Various companies connected with transportation have issued publications. The pamphlet material is considerable, the largest collection being in the Canadian Archives.

Reference Works. Detailed bibliographies will be found in the *Review of historical publications relating to Canada* (1897-1918), the *Canadian historical review* (1920-   ), *Contributions to Canadian economics* (1928-34), and the *Canadian journal of economics and political science* (1935-   ).

The *Canada Year Book,* published by the Dominion bureau of statistics, is a most valuable reference book. For the dates of origin, mileage, and subsequent status of Canadian railways consult M. L. Bladen, "Construction of railways in Canada" (*Contributions to Canadian economics,* v and vii). *Poor's Manual of railroads* also contains useful factual information about Canadian as well as American railways, and has a number of maps. A standard authority which should be used, particularly on recent or contemporary conditions, is W. T. Jackman, *Economic principles of transportation* (Toronto, 1935). *Canada and its provinces,* edited by A. Shortt and A. G. Doughty and published in 1914, has a number of sections on different aspects of transportation. In particular, Volume X will be found helpful.

NOTES

CHAPTER 6

From Continental to National Economy
(pp. 1-25)

1. E. W. Watkin, *Canada and the States* (London, 1887), p. 451. In 1864 a Montreal newspaper described this project as "an absolute certainty."
2. Canadian Archives, Baring Papers, Grand Trunk Railway, Watkin to Baring, November 8, 1862.
3. Watkin, *op. cit.*, p. 457.
4. *The International Financial Society Limited: prospectus.*
5. *Parliamentary debates on the subject of the confederation of the British North American provinces, third session, eighth provincial parliament of Canada.*
6. A. G. Doughty (ed.), "Notes on the Quebec conference, 1864" (*Canadian Historical Review*, i, 1).
7. Canadian Archives, Macdonald Papers, "Confederation," vi, C. J. Brydges to Lord Monck, September 19, 1866.
8. S. J. McLean, "The Tariff history of Canada" (*Toronto University studies in political science*, Toronto, 1895).
9. Canadian Archives, Macdonald Papers, "Confederation," vi, Mitchell to Macdonald, May 27, 1867.
10. *Ibid.*, Macdonald to Mitchell, June 1, 1867.
11. *Ibid.*, Mitchell to Macdonald, June 6, 1867.
12. Macdonald Papers, "Railways," ii, Fleming to Macdonald, March 3, 1868.
13. Canadian Archives, Fleming Papers, cxvii.
14. Macdonald Papers, Letter book 14, Macdonald to C. J. Brydges, October 31, 1870.
15. Macdonald Papers, "Railways," ii, Brydges to Macdonald, November 2, 1870.
16. H. A. Innis, *Problems of staple production in Canada* (Toronto, 1933), p. 35.

CHAPTER 7

The Project of a Pacific Railway
(pp. 26-59)

1. Archives of the Hudson's Bay Company, General letter books, February 27, 1822.
2. *Ibid.*, Simpson's reports, July 31, 1822.
3. *Ibid.*, August 1, 1823.
4. *Ibid.*, August 20, 1826.

5. Sir Charles Piers, *The Hudson's Bay Company's transportation system, 1670-1880* (address before British Columbia Historical Association, January 17, 1930).

6. Archives of the Hudson's Bay Company, Simpson's reports, October 16, 1826.

7. Archives of the Hudson's Bay Company, Simpson's reports, August 10, 1832.

8. *Ibid.*, Locked letter books, Simpson to Berens, July 30 and September 25, 1858.

9. *Ibid.*, General letter books, August 9, 1859.

10. *Ibid.*, A. G. Dallas correspondence, N. W. Kittson to Dallas, November 23, 1863.

11. Another party of Canadians passed through the Rockies by the same route in the same year. See Margaret McNaughton, *Overland to Cariboo* (Toronto, 1896). This account is much less full. Cheadle's original diary has also been published as *Cheadle's Journal of Trip Across Canada, 1862-1863*, edited by A. G. Doughty and G. Lanctot (Ottawa, 1931).

12. W. Smith, *History of the Post Office in British North America* (London, 1920), pp. 318-319.

13. Canadian Archives, Governor general's secretary, Fleming to Monck, May 23, 1863.

14. Archives of the Hudson's Bay Company, Locked letter books, Ellice to Labouchere, September 30, 1856.

15. *Ibid.*, Correspondence with His Majesty's Government, Baring and others to Newcastle, July 5, 1862.

16. *Ibid.*, Berens to Newcastle, August 11, 1862.

17. Canadian Archives, Baring Papers, Grand Trunk Railway, Watkin to Baring, November 4, 1862.

18. Archives of the Hudson's Bay Company, Minutes of the committee, June 15, 1863.

19. *Ibid.*, Locked letter books, Berens to Dallas, February 5, 1863.

20. *Ibid.*, Berens to McTavish, February 7, 1863.

21. *Ibid.*, Berens to Dallas, March 20, 1863.

22. *Ibid.*, London inward correspondence, J. Maynard to Sir Edmund Head, August 5, 1863.

23. *Ibid.*, Minutes of the committee, June 15, 1863.

24. *Ibid.*, Telegraph survey of Dr. John Rae.

25. Sir John Smyth, *Railroad communication. A west proposed line of steam communication from London, in England, to China and the East Indies, etc., etc.* (Toronto, 1845).

26. *A letter from Major Robert Carmichael-Smyth to his friend, the author of "The Clockmaker"; The employment of the people and capital of Great Britain in her own colonies . . .* (London, 1849).

27. Allan Macdonell, *The North-West transportation, navigation and railway company. Its objects.* (Toronto, 1858).

28. H. A. Innis, *History of the Canadian Pacific Railway* (Toronto, 1922), p. 44.

29. Canadian Archives, Macdonald Papers, "Railways," ii. Potter to Macdonald, December 14, 1870.

30. *Ibid.*, iv, Brydges to D. L. Macpherson, March 11, 1872.

31. *Ibid.*, Letter book xviii, Macdonald to John Rose, October 18, 1872.

32. *Report of the Canadian Pacific Railway royal commission* (1882), evidence of Sir Hugh Allan.

33. *Ibid.*, Evidence of D. L. Macpherson.

34. Canadian Archives, Macdonald Papers, "Railways," iv, Macpherson to Macdonald, July 27, 1872.
35. *Ibid.*, Allan to Macdonald, October 4, 1872.
36. Blake Papers, Holton to Blake, June 24, 1873.
37. *Ibid.*, Blake to Macdonald, July 3, 1873.
38. *Ibid.*, Cartwright to Blake, July 16, 1873.
39. Canadian Archives, Macdonald Papers, "Railways," vi.
40. *Ibid.* Letter book xx, Macdonald to Lord Dufferin, July 4, 1873.
41. *Ibid.*, Letter book xix, Macdonald to Rose, February 13, 1873.
42. *Ibid.*, "Railways," vi, Allan to Macdonald, April 5, 1873.
43. *Ibid.*, Memo. of June 17, 1873.
44. *Ibid.*, Bellefeuille to Macdonald, July 6, 1873.
45. *Ibid.*, Macdonald to Bellefeuille, August 20, 1873.

CHAPTER 8

The Building of the Pacific Railway
(pp. 60-90)

1. Canadian Archives, Fleming Papers, cxc, Fleming to W. B. Smellie, May 24, 1878.
2. *Ibid.*, Alexander Mackenzie Papers, Mackenzie to Lord Dufferin, May 20, 1876.
3. *Ibid.*, Mackenzie to Edgar, February 19, 1874.
4. J. A. Maxwell, "Lord Dufferin and the difficulties with British Columbia, 1874-1877" (*Canadian Historical Review*, xii, 4).
5. Blake Papers, lxxi, Report of a committee of the privy council, September 20, 1875.
6. Fleming's annual reports are contained in the following volumes: *Report on surveys and preliminary operations on the Canadian Pacific Railway up to January 1877*, and *Report and documents in reference to the Canadian Pacific Railway* (1880).
7. Canadian Archives, Fleming Papers, Smith to Fleming, December 7, 1877.
8. *Report of the Canadian Pacific Railway royal commission* (Ottawa, 1882).
9. Canadian Archives, Fleming Papers, Fleming to Tupper, February 9, 1880.
10. *Ibid.*, Same to same, June 7, 1880.
11. *Ibid.*, Macdonald Papers, "Tupper," Tupper to Macdonald, January 29, 1876.
12. *Ibid.*, "Railways," vii, McIntyre to Macdonald, June 21, 1880.
13. *Ibid.*, Dunsmore to Macdonald, June 30, 1880.
14. E. M. Saunders, *Life and letters of Rt. Hon. Sir Charles Tupper* (London, 1916), i, 286.
15. Canadian Archives, Macdonald Papers, "Railways," vii, Puleston, Brown & Co., to Macdonald, August 16, 1880.
16. *Ibid.*, McIntyre to Macdonald, August 12, 1880.
17. *Ibid.*, "Stephen," i, Stephen to Macdonald, July 9, 1880.
18. J. M. Gibbon, *Steel of empire* (Toronto, 1935), p. 201.
19. *Debates of the house of commons of the Dominion of Canada, 1880-1881*, i.

20. J. B. Hedges, *The federal railway land subsidy policy of Canada* (Cambridge, Mass., 1934), pp. 4 et seq.
21. See, e.g., R. G. MacBeth, *The Romance of the Canadian Pacific Railway* (Toronto, 1924); J. H. E. Secretan, *Canada's great highway* (Ottawa, 1924); J. M. Gibbon's recent work, *Steel of empire*, contains, *inter alia*, good accounts of construction and operation.
22. W. Vaughan, *The Life and work of Sir William Van Horne* (New York, 1920), p. 78. It should be added that Hill further objected to the southern route on the prairies.
23. Canadian Archives, Macdonald Papers, "Railways," viii, McIntyre, Angus and Abbott to Macdonald, January 2, 1881.
24. *Ibid.*, "Stephen," i, January 23, 1881.
25. *Ibid.*, Stephen to Macdonald, August 27, 1882.
26. *Ibid.*, Same to same, August 27, 1882.
27. Vaughan, *op. cit.*, p. 87.
28. Canadian Archives, Macdonald Papers, "J. H. Pope," Schreiber to Pope, July 22, 1888.
29. *Ibid.*, "Van Horne," Van Horne to Stephen, July 24, 1888.
30. *Ibid.*, "Stephen," Stephen to Macdonald, September 3, 1889.
31. T. G. Shaughnessy had been general storekeeper of the Chicago, Milwaukee and St. Paul Railway. At Van Horne's suggestion, he became general purchasing agent of the C.P.R.
32. Canadian Archives, Macdonald Papers, "Stephen," i, Stephen to Macdonald, February 26, 1882.
33. *Ibid.*, Same to same, January 4, 1883.
34. *Ibid.*, Same to same, December 15, 1883.
35. E. M. Saunders, *op. cit.*, i, 45.
36. Canadian Archives, Macdonald Papers, "Stephen," Stephen to Macdonald, December 24, 1883.
37. *Ibid.*, "Railways," ix, Tupper to Tilley, November 28, 1884.
38. *Ibid.*, Rose to Macdonald, December 2, 1884.
39. *Ibid.*, "Stephen," Stephen to Macdonald, January 14 and February 3, 1885.
40. *Ibid.*, Same to same, October 3, 1885.

CHAPTER 9

Consequences of the Pacific Railway
(pp. 91-118)

1. O. D. Skelton, *The Railway builders* (Toronto, 1920), p. 171.
2. Canadian Archives, Mackenzie Papers, Blake to Dufferin, January 6, 1876.
3. H. A. Lovett, *Canada and the Grand Trunk* (Montreal, 1924), p. 83.
4. *Ibid.*, 89.
5. Joseph Nelson, *The very latest Grand Trunk scheme* (London, 1873).
6. M. B. Hewson, *The Grand Trunk Railway of Canada* (Toronto, 1876).
7. Anon., *Canadian Pacific Railway: correspondence and papers shewing the efforts the company has made to secure Portland for its winter port* (Montreal, 1884).

8. Canadian Archives, Macdonald Papers, "Stephen," Van Horne to Tupper, July 30, 1888.
9. *Ibid.*, Stephen to Macdonald, September 3, 1889.
10. Joseph Pope, *Correspondence of Sir John Macdonald* (Toronto, 1921), pp. 454-457.
11. Canadian Archives, Macdonald Papers, "Stephen," Stephen to Macdonald, January 4, 1883.
12. *Ibid.*, "Railways," viii, Hickson to Macdonald, August 17, 1882.
13. *Ibid.*, Rose to Macdonald, August 31, 1882.
14. *Ibid.*, "Railways," ix, Hickson to Macdonald, February 7, 1884.
15. *Ibid.*, "Van Horne," Van Horne to Macdonald, September 26, 1890.
16. *Grand Trunk Railway versus Canadian Pacific Railway* (Toronto, 1884).
17. Canadian Archives, Macdonald Papers, Letter book xxvi, Macdonald to Stephen, September 17, 1889.
18. *Ibid.*, Same to same, June 3, 1890.
19. *Ibid.*, "Van Horne," Van Horne to Macdonald, February 28, 1891.
20. *Ibid.*, "Stephen," Stephen to Macdonald, January 29, 1888.
21. *Ibid.*
22. *Ibid.*, Same to same, October 18, 1880.
23. Sessional Papers, 1888, No. 58B; house of commons debates, 1887, pp. 543 et seq.
24. Macdonald Papers, "Pope," Pope to Macdonald, August 24, 1882.
25. *Ibid.*, "Stephen," Stephen to Macdonald, August 27, 1881.
26. *Ibid.*, Letter book xxiv, Macdonald to Rose, June 25, 1887.
27. *Ibid.*, "Stephen," White to Stephen, May 18, 1887.
28. *Ibid.*, Stephen to Macdonald, November 11, 1887.
29. D. A. MacGibbon, *Railway rates and the Canadian railway commission* (Boston, 1917), pp. 80 et seq.
30. H. A. Innis, *History of the Canadian Pacific Railway* (Toronto, 1923), pp. 183-184.
31. *Reports upon railway commissions, railway rate grievances and regulative legislation* (Sessional Paper No. 20A, 1902).
32. W. Vaughan, *Life and work of Sir William Van Horne* (New York, 1920), p. 229.

CHAPTER 10

The Later Transcontinental Railways
(pp. 119-146)

1. See R. Wilson, "Migration movements in Canada, 1868-1925" (*Canadian Historical Review*, xiii, 2).
2. J. Viner, *Canada's balance of international indebtedness, 1900-1913* (Cambridge, Mass., 1924), p. 139.
3. *Canada Year Book*, 1934-1935.
4. W. A. Mackintosh, *Prairie settlement: the geographical setting* (Toronto, 1934), p. 46. See also the valuable series of maps in this work showing the relation of railways to the distribution of rural population in the prairie provinces (pp. 48-52), and the spread of settlement (pp. 60-73). It is equally true that settlers were vital to railways. One estimate sets the annual potential revenue to the rail-

way of each farm as $282.56 (Robert England, *The colonization of western Canada* [London, 1936], p. 316).

5. Mackintosh, *op. cit.*, p. 55.
6. For more detailed accounts of the Grand Trunk and Canadian Northern see sections 3 and 4 (pp. 135-146).
7. H. A. Lovett, *Canada and the Grand Trunk* (Montreal, 1924), p. 129; L. T. Fournier, *Railway nationalization in Canada* (Toronto, 1935), p. 13.
8. *Canadian Northern Railway Arbitration* (1918: mimeographed), Evidence, p. 2683.
9. *Report of the royal commission to inquire into railways and transportation in Canada (1917)*, xxviii.
10. J. W. Dafoe, *Clifford Sifton in relation to his times* (Toronto, 1931), pp. 265-271.
11. *House of commons debates*, 1903, pp. 6735, et seq.
12. O. D. Skelton, *Life and Letters of Sir Wilfrid Laurier* (Toronto, 1921), ii, 189.
13. As first used, the phrase "National Transcontinental" applied to the whole line from Moncton to Prince Rupert, but to avoid confusion it will hereafter be used in its later connotation, i.e., the government section (Moncton to Winnipeg).
14. *House of commons debates*, 1903, pp. 7658, et seq.
15. *Grand Trunk Railway System, 1896-1907.*
16. W. McNab, *Historical narrative of the inception and development of the Grand Trunk Railway of Canada* (Montreal, 1923, typed), pp. 54, 61.
17. For accounts of the surveys and construction on the National Transcontinental and Grand Trunk Pacific see F. A. M. Talbot, *The making of a great Canadian railway* (London, 1912), and N. Thompson and J. H. Edgar, *Canadian railway development* (Toronto, 1933).
18. *House of commons debates*, 1909-1910, pp. 2335 et seq.
19. Fournier, *op, cit.*, p. 21.
20. *Canadian Northern Railway Arbitration*, Evidence, 395.
21. For an interesting account of this and other early Canadian Northern lines see D. B. Hanna, *Trains of recollection* (Toronto, 1924). Details of lines built or acquired will be found in E. W. Oliver, "History of construction" (C. Price-Green [ed.], *Encyclopaedia, Canadian Northern Railway* [1918]).
22. *Canadian Northern Railway Arbitration*, Evidence, p. 2603.
23. *Ibid.*, 2684.

CHAPTER 11

Nationalization of Railways
(pp. 147-181)

1. *Canada Year Book, 1922-1923*, p. 733. It covers building trades, metal trades, coal mining, printing trades, electric and steam railways.
2. *Canada Year Book, 1934-1935*, p. 861.
3. *Canada Year Book, 1922-1923*, p. 627.
4. D. B. Hanna, *Trains of recollection* (Toronto, 1924), p. 240.
5. *House of commons debates*, 1916, p. 3564.

6. *Report of the royal commission to inquire into railways and transportation in Canada, 1917.*

7. *House of commons debates,* 1917, pp. 4015 et seq.

8. On this question see also the pamphlet, *Railway question in Canada: Liberal legislation from 1896-1911* (Publication No. 30, 1915); W. S. Wallace, *The memoirs of the Rt. Hon. Sir George Foster* (Toronto, 1933), pp. 155-161.

9. Sir Clifford Sifton's comment on this is quoted in J. W. Dafoe, *Clifford Sifton in relation to his times* (Toronto, 1931), p. 434

10. *Canadian Northern Railway Arbitration,* Evidence, p. 3347.

11. "General passenger business" (C. Price-Green [ed.], *Encyclopaedia, Canadian Northern Railway,* [1918]).

12. *Canadian Northern Railway Arbitration,* Evidence, p. 6306.

13. *Ibid.,* 435.

14. *Ibid.,* 2708.

15. *Ibid.,* 2812.

16. The award and explanatory statement were not printed. The above extract is taken from a copy in the records of the department of railways and canals.

17. *House of commons debates,* 1917, p. 4017.

18. *Ibid.,* 1918, p. 2004.

19. *Ibid.,* 1919, p. 664.

20. The receivership was not technically terminated until 1926.

21. *Grand Trunk Arbitration: the award and reasons for the award* (Ottawa, 1921), p. 39.

22. Sir Joseph Flavelle, *The Canadian National Railway System: letter addressed to the Rt. Hon. Arthur Meighen* (Toronto, 1921).

23. The opinions which follow are taken from the Grand Trunk *Award.*

24. *Grand Trunk Arbitration* (1921), Evidence, p. 7260.

25. There was some justification in making this distinction on the ground that the Canadian Northern was well located, but had had no opportunity of demonstrating its earning power; while on the other hand the Grand Trunk had shown that its earning power was insufficient.

26. *Canadian Annual Review, 1923,* p. 366.

27. Sir John Willison, *The railway question in Canada* (speech to the Canadian Club of Montreal, 1921).

28. Hanna, *op. cit.,* p. 278, and chaps. xv and xvi *passim.*

29. L. T. Fournier, *Railway nationalization in Canada* (Toronto, 1935), p. 77. Fixed charges do not include the Canadian Government Railways. See the whole chapter (vi) on the Canadian National from 1919 to 1922.

30. *Report of the department of railways and canals, 1923-1924,* p. 5.

CHAPTER 12

Railways in Sunshine and Shadow
(pp. 182-219)

1. Cf. pp. 105-106.

2. Speech of January 10, 1925, quoted in *Canadian Annual Review, 1924-1925,* p. 114.

3. *Canada Year Book, 1931.*

4. H. A. Innis and A. F. W. Plumptre (eds.), *The Canadian economy and its problems* (Toronto, 1934), p. 226.

5. *Canada Year Book, 1934-1935,* p. 704. All Canadian railways are included.

6. *Report on various proposed railway routes for a western outlet to the Pacific from the Peace River district, by a joint board of engineers of the Canadian National and Canadian Pacific Railways* (Ottawa, 1929).

7. F. Palmer, *Report on the selection of a terminal port for the Hudson Bay Railway* (London, 1927).

8. *House of commons debates,* 1936, pp. 465 et seq.

9. H. A. Innis, "The Hudson Bay Railway" (*The Geographical Review,* xx, 1); H. A. Innis, *Problems of staple production in Canada* (Toronto, 1933), pp. 82 et seq.

10. *Report of the department of railways and canals,* 1928-1929, p. xxii.

11. F. Palmer, *Report on railway terminal facilities at Montreal* (Ottawa, 1929).

12. On this subject see W. T. Jackman, *Economic principles of transportation* (Toronto, 1935).

13. *Report of the department of railways and canals,* 1923-1924, p. 17.

14. *Annual report of the Canadian Pacific Railway,* 1924.

15. *Canada Year Book, 1934-1935,* p. 704.

16. E. W. Beatty, *Canada's railway problem and its solution,* (Speech before the Canadian Club, Toronto, 1933).

17. *Report of the royal commission to inquire into railways and transportation in Canada,* 1931-1932.

18. *Steam railway statistics* (Dominion bureau of statistics).

19. *Royal commission on railways and transportation: report of procedings.*

20. *Senate debates,* 1932-1933, p. 297.

21. *House of commons debates,* 1932-1933, p. 2851.

22. *Canadian Pacific Railway: report of the shareholders' meeting, 1934.*

23. *Canadian National Railways: annual report, 1934.*

24. *Steam railway statistics.*

25. *Canadian National Railways: annual report, 1934.*

26. *Canadian Pacific Railway: report of the shareholders' meeting, 1935.*

27. See L. T. Fournier, *Railway nationalization in Canada* (Toronto, 1935); W. T. Jackman, *op. cit.*; J. L. McDougall, "The report of the Duff Commission" (*Canadian journal of economics and political science,* i, 1).

28. *Report of the royal commission to inquire into railways and transportation in Canada,* 1931-1932, p. 50.

29. Fournier, *op. cit.,* chap. viii.

30. See e.g., G Myers, *History of Canadian wealth* (Chicago, 1914).

31. As argued in D'Arcy Marsh, *The tragedy of Henry Thornton* (Toronto, 1935).

32. *Canadian National Railways Magazine,* xx, 4.

33. *Winnipeg Free Press,* March 17, 1933.

34. *House of commons debates,* 1936, pp. 2365 et seq.

CHAPTER 13
Modern Waterways
(pp. 220-240)

1. *Canada sessional papers*, 1871, No. 54.
2. *Report of the department of railways and canals*, 1903-1904, pt. v, p. 38.
3. *Interim report of the Georgian Bay Canal (Sessional paper*, No. 19B, 1916).
4. A. C. Hardy, *American ship types* (New York, 1927), p. 201.
5. W. T. Jackman, *Economic principles of transportation* (Toronto, 1935), p. 760.
6. *Report of the royal commission on lake grain rates (Sessional paper* No. 211, 1923).
7. *Ibid.*, p. 10.
8. *Canal statistics* (Dominion bureau of statistics).
9. *Ibid.*
10. *Report of the royal commission on lake grain rates*, 1923, p. 8.
11. *Ibid.*, p. 11.
12. *Interim report on the Georgian Bay Canal*, 1916, p. 63.
13. *Ibid.*
14. On the effects of the Panama Canal on Canadian traffic and rates see W. Sandford Evans, "Canadian traffic through the Panama" (*Queen's Quarterly*, xxxvi, 2); H. A. Innis, "Canada and the Panama Canal" (H. A. Innis and A. F. W. Plumptre, *The Canadian economy and its problems* [Toronto, 1934]).
15. *Canal statistics.*
16. F. H. Brown, "Canadian lake shipping" (Innis and Plumptre, *op. cit.*).
17. On the question of rates see *Report of the royal commission on lake grain rates*, 1923.
18. R. S. MacElwee and A. H. Ritter, *Economic aspects of the Great Lakes-St. Lawrence ship canal* (New York, 1921), chaps. iii and iv.
19. For the history of the deep waterway project see G. W. Stephens, *The St. Lawrence waterway project* (Montreal, 1930); C. P. Wright, *The St. Lawrence deep waterway* (Toronto, 1935); G. W. Brown, "The deepening of the St. Lawrence" (*Round Table*, No. 72).
20. *Report of the joint board of engineers on the St. Lawrence waterway project* (Ottawa, 1927).
21. For a detailed examination of the treaty and the economic aspects of the waterway *see* Wright, *op. cit.*, pp. 281, et seq.
22. MacElwee and Ritter, *op. cit.*, p. 290.
23. L. R. Thomson, "The St. Lawrence problem" (*Engineering Journal*, April, 1929).

CHAPTER 14
Transportation by Electricity and Gasoline
(pp. 241-264)

1. K. G. Fenelon, *Railway economics* (London, 1932), p. 176.
2. *Reports of commission to inquire into hydro-electric railways* (Toronto, 1921).

3. *Report of the provincial instructor in road-making, Ontario, 1896.*

4. Quoted in E. C. Guillet, *Early life in Upper Canada* (Toronto, 1933), p. 544.

5. *The Highway and motor vehicle in Canada, 1934* (Dominion bureau of statistics). In the case of Ontario 25, and of British Columbia 73, miles of unclassified roads are included in the totals for those provinces.

6. *Bulletin,* No. 7, 1925 (Highways branch, department of railways and canals).

7. *The Highway and motor vehicle in Canada;* also, "The tourist traffic" (*Round Table,* No. 76).

8. *Report of the conference on rail and road transport* (1932).

9. *Report of the royal commission to inquire into railways and transportation in Canada, 1931-1932.*

10. A. E. W. Salt, *Imperial air routes* (London, 1930), p. 197.

11. W. R. Finlayson, *Aviation and its place in Canada's transportation system* (M.A. thesis, Toronto, 1933), p. 84.

12. Salt, *op. cit.,* p. 196.

13. *Report of the department of national defence, 1932,* p. 69.

14. Canada Airways Limited: *The Bulletin.*

15. *The Bulletin,* vii, 2.

16. *Canada Year Book, 1931, Canada Year Book, 1936.*

SUGGESTIONS FOR
FURTHER READING

The most recent and general economic history of Canada is W. T. EASTERBROOK and H. G. J. AITKEN, *Canadian Economic History* (Toronto, 1956). An older but still useful account is that by O. D. SKELTON, "General Economic History, 1867-1912," in *Canada and its Provinces* (Toronto, 1914), IX, pp. 95-274.

In addition to the works mentioned in the Preface to this edition, the following studies describe the history of railway transportation in Canada: O. D. SKELTON, *The Railway Builders*, vol. XXXII of the *Chronicles of Canada* (Toronto, 1916); S. J. MCLEAN, "National Highways Overland," in *Canada and its Provinces*, X, pp. 359-472; and NORMAN THOMPSON and J. H. EDGAR, *Canadian Railway Development from the Earliest Times* (Toronto, 1935). A brief account of the growth of water transportation in Canada is "Shipping and Canals" by M. J. PATTON in *Canada and its Provinces*, X, pp. 475-624.

Reference should also be made, for books and articles about the history of Canadian transportation, to the quarterly bibliography of historical literature published in the *Canadian Historical Review*. The successive numbers of the *Canada Year Book*, besides giving the latest statistical information on the progress of Canadian transportation, also provides special articles from time to time on subjects in this field. An example is the article on the St. Lawrence Seaway in the 1956 issue, pp. 821-29.

over Pacific railway, ii, 64

Duluth, South Shore and Atlantic Railway, Canadian Pacific buys control, ii, 111; competition with United States lines, 148

Duncan, Sir Andrew, chairman of royal commission, ii, 197-198

Dundas Street, planned and begun by Simcoe, i, 128; condition, 130, 138; stage-coaches, 135

Durham boat, description, i, 63-64; use, 64, 71, 90

Durham, Earl of, urges necessity of canals, i, 88-89

Edgar, J. D., sent to British Columbia to discuss Pacific Railway, ii, 62-63

Edmonton, Dunvegan and British Columbia Railway, route, ii, 187

Elgin, Earl of, abolition of corn laws, i, 91; opposed to navigation acts, 92

Ellice, Edward, offers to buy Hudson's Bay Co., i, 52-53; negotiations with Hudson's Bay Co., 55; sale of Hudson's Bay Co., ii, 41

Emmerson and North-Western Railway, chartered by Manitoba, ii, 112

Erie Canal, competition with St. Lawrence, i, 74, 86-93, ii, 221, 222, 229; connection with Chambly Canal, i, 85; improvement, ii, 235

Erie and Ontario Railway, built, i, 164

European and North American Railway, plans, i, 149-151; construction, 151; absorbed by Intercolonial, ii, 22

Fairweather, S. W., evidence before royal commission of 1931, ii, 204

Flavelle, Sir Joseph, chairman of board of Grand Trunk, ii, 175; member of royal commission of 1931, 201

Fleming, Sir Sandford, surveyor for Intercolonial, ii, 13-14, 17; chief engineer of Intercolonial, 18-19; plans for through traffic, 24; trip to Pacific coast, 33-34; named in Canadian Pacific charter of 1873, 53; tenders for Pacific railway, 60; appointed engineer-in-chief of Canadian Pacific, 65; conducts surveys, 65-69; removed from office, 72; estimate of cost of construction of Canadian Pacific, 86; survey used by Canadian Northern, 144

Freight rates, Intercolonial, ii, 24; Canadian Pacific in the west, 112-116; reduced by Canadian Northern and G.T.P.R. in west, 142; lower rates wanted for Peace River district, 187-188; recent questions, 197-199; lake carriers, 232-233

Fullerton, C. P., chairman of directors of Canadian National, ii, 209; argument against amalgamation of railways, 216-217

Fur trade, in French régime, i, 10-23; routes, 12-14, 26-33; competition between French traders and Hudson's Bay Co., 19-23; in period 1760-1821, 24-58; lost to Canada, 59; Red River settlement, ii, 35

Galt, A. T., seeks capital for St. Lawrence and Atlantic Railway, i, 155; president of St. Lawrence and Atlantic, 156; vice-president of Montreal and Kingston Railroad, 160; appointed Director of

G. P. deT. GLAZEBROOK

A distinguished historian and public servant, G. P. deT. Glazebrook was born in London, Ontario, in 1899. Educated at the University of Toronto and at Oxford, he joined the Department of History at the University of Toronto in 1924. During the Second World War he served as a Special Assistant in the Department of External Affairs, rejoining the University of Toronto faculty in 1946. After three years' service at the University he returned to Ottawa to re-enter the Department of External Affairs. From 1953 to 1956 he was Minister in the Canadian Embassy at Washington and later became an Assistant Under-Secretary of State for External Affairs. He retired from the Department in 1963, to resume lecturing and writing at the University of Toronto.

Mr. Glazebrook has written many books on Canadian political and economic history. They include *Sir Charles Bagot in Canada* (1929); *A History of Transportation in Canada* (1938); *A History of Canadian External Relations* (1950); *A Short History of Canada* (1950).

THE CARLETON LIBRARY